Winning With the King's Gambit

Joe Gallagher

An Owl Book
Henry Holt and Company
New York

Henry Holt and Company, Inc.
Publishers since 1866
115 West 18th Street
New York, New York 10011

Henry Holt® is a registered trademark
of Henry Holt and Company, Inc.

First published in the United States in 1993 by
Henry Holt and Company, Inc.
Originally published in Great Britain in 1992 by
B. T. Batsford Ltd.

Library of Congress Catalog Card Number: 92-56734

ISBN 0-8050-2631-2 (An Owl Book: pbk.)

First American Edition—1993

Printed in the United Kingdom
All first editions are printed on acid-free paper. ∞

10   9   8   7   6   5   4   3   2   1

Adviser: R. D. Keene, GM, OBE
Technical Editor: Andrew Kinsman

Contents

Symbols

+	Check
++	Double check
!	Good move
!!	Excellent move
?	Bad move
??	Blunder
!?	Interesting move
?!	Dubious move
1-0	White wins
0-1	Black wins
½-½	Draw
Ch	Championship
ol	Olympiad
Corr.	Correspondence

Introduction

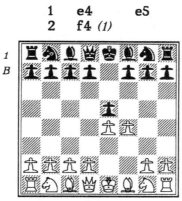

1   e4   e5
2   f4 *(1)*

1
B

The King's Gambit is, of course, an opening with a great history, but for the larger part of this century it has been lying dormant, a rare visitor to tournament practice. However, I am inclined to take the optimistic view and regard its demise as purely a matter of fashion.

The Spanish Game (or Ruy Lopez, who incidentally was the first person to publish King's Gambit analysis) has now ruled the open game for countless years, but there is evidence that its reign could be drawing to a close. The last few years have witnessed an upsurge in the popularity of Scotch's, Vienna's and Four Knights', including at the highest level – Kasparov used the Scotch with success in his latest match with Karpov, and Short employed various antiquated systems in his most recent Candidates' tussle with Speelman, even a couple of King's Gambit Declineds by transposition. I believe it can only be a matter of time before the King's Gambit (proper) joins in this revolution. I know that many players have been toying with the idea of introducing the King's Gambit into their repertoire, but have not yet found the courage to push that f-pawn two squares on their second move. My hope is that this book will help to allay many of their fears.

Winning With the King's Gambit, as the title should inform you, is a look at this opening from the White point of view. Whilst I have endeavoured to remain as objective as possible in my assessments of positions, much more time has been devoted to finding new ideas for White, rather than attempting to refute existing theory where White already stands well. I see this as a task for our future opponents.

The theoretical revival of the King's Gambit is really not that surprising, as it has always been based on sound positional principles. If Black accepts the gambit, then White is normally able to build a strong centre and if Black gives (or loses) the pawn back, White will also achieve a space advantage on the kingside. When Black plays to keep the material with ... g5, then White usually does best to undermine the pawn chain as quickly as possible by playing h4 (see the chapters on Fischer or Kieseritzky, for example), forcing Black to advance ... g4, which can often lead to a wrecked kingside.

The format of this book is one which is becoming increasingly popular and involves studying the opening through a series of annotated games. This is extremely important, as it enables the reader to familiarise himself (or herself) with the middlegame positions (and occasionally endgames) which arise from the King's Gambit.

This is a book for the practical player (but also one who will appreciate the special buzz around this opening), and for that reason not all variations of the King's Gambit are included, but only those which offer White good chances of obtaining the advantage. However, the chosen variations have been analysed in depth, as often it can be just as important to know which variations are bad (and why) as to which are good. The repertoire is based on the King's Knight Gambit, so my apologies to those fans of the Bishop's, and various other third move gambits, but my advice to you is to start playing 3 ♘f3.

1) Fischer Defence

1	e4	e5
2	f4	ef
3	♘f3	d6 *(2)*

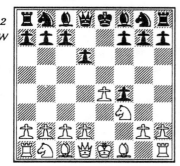

Over the last few years this variation has developed into the most popular way of accepting the gambit. Personally, I feel quite happy about this as Black seems to be struggling in most of the lines. I only hope that this chapter won't frighten off any potential opponents!

After his famous defeat against Spassky at Mar del Plata 1960, the great Bobby decided to refute the King's Gambit. In the summer of 1961, the *American Chess Quarterly* published his analysis. "A high-class wait-ing move", was how he described 3 ... d6.

The main point of the variation is demonstrated after the moves 4 d4 g5 5 h4 g4. White does not have the possibility of 6 ♘e5, as in the Kieseritzky Gambit. Therefore he has to go 'all in' with 6 ♘g5 (not to be recommended, I'm afraid) or return to base with the rather sad-looking 6 ♘g1 *(3)*, when quite a comical position has arisen on the board - after six moves neither side has managed to get a piece off the back rank!

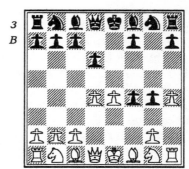

At the moment, Black is a pawn up but f4 is serious-ly weak and, if White manages to restore material equality without any side-effects, Black's punctured kingside will not allow him an easy game. Let's have a look at some games to see how Black attempts to solve his problems.

Game 1
Gallagher – Conquest
British Championship,
Blackpool 1988

1	e4	e5
2	f4	ef
3	♘f3	d6
4	d4	

White does have other possibilities, but 4 d4 is clearly the most critical. However, the plan of ♗c4 followed by d3 is also interesting and can be seen later in games 9 and 10.

| 4 | ... | g5 |

Other moves have been tried from time to time without much success, for example: 4 ... ♘f6 5 ♘c3 ♘h5 6 ♗e2 (maybe 6 ♕d3, ♗d2 and 0-0-0) 6 ... ♗g4 7 0-0 c6 (7 ... g6 8 ♘d5) 8 ♘e1! ♗xe2 9 ♕xe2 g6 10 ♘d3 leaves White with a clear advantage.

| 5 | h4 | |

5 ♗c4 is illogical: if White wants to play this he should play it on the fourth move, as then Black is forced play ... h6. The

Dutch player Bosboom has experimented with 5 ♘c3, his idea being 5 ... g4 6 ♗xf4 and on with the game. His game with Ermenkov, Amsterdam 1985, continued instead: 5 ... ♗g7 6 h4 g4 (6 ... h6 should be considered) 7 ♘g1 ♘c6 8 ♗b5 ♗d7 9 ♗xc6 bc 10 ♗xf4 ♘e7 11 h5 with advantage to White. Further tests awaited!

| 5 | ... | g4 |
| 6 | ♘g1 | |

As already mentioned, 6 ♘g5 runs into trouble. Not because of 6 ... h6 though, as after 7 ♘xf7 White has a decent version of the All-gaier Gambit (if there is such a thing), but 6 ... f6! and after 7 ♘h3 gh 8 ♕h5+ ♔d7 9 ♗xf4 ♕e8! 10 ♕f3 ♔d8 White doesn't have enough for the piece (Fischer).

| 6 | ... | f3!? *(4)* |

Black decides to give back his pawn in order to disrupt the white kingside. The other possibilities: 6 ...

♘f6, 6 ... ♗h6 and 6 ... ♕f6, will be considered in games 4 to 8.

7 gf

7 ♗g5 can be seen in games 2 and 3, whilst 7 ♗e3 occurred in the game Popovic – Spassky, New York 1986. However, after 7 ... ♗e7 8 ♗f2 ♘f6 9 gf ♖g8 10 ♗g2 ♘c6 11 ♘c3 gf 12 ♗xf3 ♘g4, Black had the initiative

7 ... ♗e7

8 ♗e3

This sensible developing move minimises the disruptive value of the check on h4. During the game I was sorely tempted to play 8 h5 but couldn't quite summon up the courage to do so. Only Mark Hebden has, in his game with R. Alvares, Costa del Sol 1987, which continued: 8 ... ♗h4+ 9 ♔e2 (Not such a pretty place for the king, but we still have our h-pawn) 9 ... gf+ 10 ♘xf3 ♗g4 11 ♔d3 ♘c6 12 c3 ♘e5+?! (I have a vague memory of looking at 12 ... f5 with Mark and after 13 ♗h3 fe+ 14 ♔xe4 ♘f6+ 15 ♔d3 coming to the conclusion that Black's king was in more trouble than White's. Maybe we were drunk!) 13 de de+ 14 ♔e3! ♕xd1 15 ♗b5+ c6 16 ♖xd1 cb 17 ♖d5 and White had the better endgame.

8 ... ♗xh4+

9 ♔d2 c5! *(5)*

This new idea of Conquest's certainly seems to be Black's best try. After 9 ... ♘c6 10 ♘c3 ♗f6 (or 10 ... ♗g5 11 f4 ♗f6 and White's centre is stronger than Black's passed pawns) 11 ♗b5 ♗d7 12 ♗xc6 bc 13 fg White held the advantage in Gallagher – Konrad, Lloyds Bank 1985.

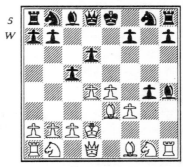

10 ♔c1!?

10 c3 also deserves consideration, but at the time I was afraid that I wouldn't be able to support my centre, as it would come under heavy pressure from moves such as ... ♘c6, ... ♗f6, ... ♕b6 etc.

10 ... cd

11 ♕xd4 ♗f6

12 ♕d2 ♘c6

13 ♘c3 ♗e6

14 ♘d5 ♗xd5?!

After this, White has very good play for the pawn; 14 ... ♗g7 looks better. I'm sure White has some compensation, but the position is such a mess it is hard to define exactly what. Maybe it's his safer king!

15	ed	♘e5
16	f4	♘d7
17	♖h5!	

Black is prevented from connecting his passed pawns.

17	...	♘e7
18	♗e2	g3
19	a4!	

White continues developing in beginner's fashion with his second rook about to enter the fray along the file.

19	...	a6

Black doesn't want to have to concern himself with any ♗b5+'s.

20	♖a3	♖c8
21	♗d4	♖g8
22	♖xh7?	

I set off on a false trail. With 22 ♖e3! White has the better chances.

22	...	♘f5
23	♗h5	♗xd4!

Not 23 ... ♘xd4? 24 ♖e3+.

24	♖xf7	♛b6!

Black is not afraid.

25	♖g7+ *(6)*	
25	...	♚d8!!

Black is willing to invest an enormous amount of material to keep the game going.

26	♖xg8+	♚e7!
27	♛e2+	♘e5!

28	♖xc8	

Both sides now had very little time remaining until move 40, which made the game even more random. White's great material advantage is offset by the amazing lack of co-ordination between his pieces.

28	...	♗xb2+
29	♚d2	♛xg1!
30	fe	

Loses, but what else?

30	...	♗c1+
31	♚c3	♛d4+
32	♚b3	♛b2+
33	♚c4	b5+
34	ab	ab+
35	♚d3	♛d4 **mate**

One of the advantages of the King's Gambit over other, more mundane, openings, is that even when you lose it can occasionally be enjoyable.

Game 2
Gallagher – Bode
Bad Wörishofen 1991

1	e4	e5

2	f4	ef
3	♘f3	d6
4	d4	g5
5	h4	g4
6	♘g1	f3
7	♗g5	

To my knowledge, this is the first time 7 ♗g5 had been played in a serious game.

| 7 | ... | ♗e7 |
| 8 | ♕d2 | f6 |

This can't be good, but the alternatives don't look rosy either.

(a) 8 ... ♗xg5 9 hg and the black squares on the kingside are already terminally ill.

(b) 8 ... f2+ 9 ♔xf2 (9 ♕xf2!?) 9 ... ♘f6 10 ♗d3! (This vacates the f1-square for the king) 10 ... g3+ 11 ♔xg3 ♖g8 12 ♔f2 ♘g4+ 13 ♔f1 and White stands clearly better, for example: 13 ... ♗xg5 14 hg ♕xg5 15 ♕xg5 ♖xg5 16 ♖xh7 ♘e3+ 17 ♔f2 ♖xg2+ 18 ♔xe3 ♖xg1 19 ♖h8+ ♔d7. A very curious position has arisen with both sides having terrible problems completing their development. However, the weakness of the black f-pawn enables White to gain a decisive advantage with 20 ♖f8!

(c) 8 ... h6 is examined in game 3.

9 ♗h6! *(7)*

Black had banked on something like 9 ♗e3 f5 with a good game. Now 9 ♗h6 f5 10 ♗g7! ♗xh4+ 11 ♔d1 and any compensation Black appears to have is just illusory. For example: 11 ... fe 12 ♗xh8 ♗g5 13 ♕e1! By skilfully manoeuvring his king and queen, White has achieved a won position. If now 13 ... d5, then 14 gf gf 15 ♘xf3 ♗g4 16 ♗e2!; or 11 ... ♗f6 12 ♗xh8 ♗xh8 13 ♖xh7 (or 13 gf) wins for White.

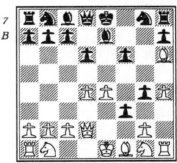

| 9 | ... | ♘xh6 |
| 10 | ♕xh6 | ♗e6 |

10 ... f2+ is possible, but it is not clear if it helps Black at all.

11 gf

11 ♕h5+ ♗f7 12 ♕xg4 is an alternative, but I didn't want to let the initiative slip away.

| 11 | ... | gf |

After 11 ... d5, I intended 12 ♘c3 de 13 0-0-0 ef and then deciding between 14 ♕h5+ ♗f7 15 ♕xg4 or 14 ♖e1. Both seem to be good for White.

12 ♘xf3 c6

Black has to work hard to try and develop.

13 ♘c3 ♕a5?

It was essential to play 13 ... ♗f8! 14 ♕d2 h5 to prevent White from castling. Even then, after 15 ♕f2! ♗h6 16 ♘d2, White's superiority is evident.

14 ♘g5! fg
15 ♕xe6 ♘d7
16 ♗c4!

Stronger than 16 ♗h3 ♘f8.

16 ... ♖f8?!

A better chance was 16 ... gh as now 17 0-0-0? ♕g5+ 18 ♔b1 0-0-0. White should instead play 17 e5! and if 17 ... d5 18 ♗e2 or 17 ... de 18 0-0-0 and Black is unlikely to survive for very long, e.g. 18 ... ed 19 ♖xd4 ♕g5+ 20 ♔b1 0-0-0 21 ♖hd1 and wins.

17 0-0-0 gh

Black is dreaming of escaping by ... ♕g5+ and ... 0-0-0. However,

18 e5!

This cuts all communications.

18 ... d5 *(8)*
19 ♗xd5! 1-0

19 ... cd 20 ♘xd5 ♕d8 21 ♖hf1 and Black is totally paralysed; or alternatively 19 ... 0-0-0 20 ♕xe7 cd 21 ♖xh4 and White will soon be two pawns ahead with a good position.

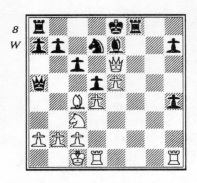

8
W

Game 3
Gallagher – Ziatdinov
Lenk 1991

1	e4	e5
2	f4	ef
3	♘f3	d6
4	d4	g5
5	h4	g4
6	♘g1	f3
7	♗g5	♗e7
8	♕d2	h6
9	♗xe7	fg

This is better than 9 ... ♘xe7 10 gf ♘g6 11 h5 with advantage to White; or 9 ... ♕xe7 10 ♘c3 and again Black has an unenviable position (10 ... d5 doesn't help: 11 0-0-0 de 12 ♘xe4!).

10	♗xg2	♘xe7 *(9)*
11	♘c3	

For the pawn, White has a lead in development and a strong centre; when you add this to Black's weakened kingside, you can already see the writing on the wall.

11	...	♘g6
12	♕f2	♘d7

This is a very strange move. My opponent said he didn't like his position after 12 ... h5, but this is no excuse for allowing yourself to be pushed around.

13 h5 ♘gf8
14 ♘ge2

White keeps open the option of castling short. Even though his king will feel less secure on the kingside, the swift placing of the rooks on the e- and f-files would be telling.

14 ... ♕f6
15 ♕g3 ♘e6

After 15 ... ♕g5 16 0-0 it is dangerous to take the h-pawn, e.g. 16 ... ♕xh5 17 ♘f4 ♕a5 18 ♘fd5! (threatening b4) 18 ... c6 19 ♕xd6 cd 20 ♘xd5! ♘g6 21 b4! winning. If Black had tried 17 ... ♕g5, then 18 ♘fd5 ♘e6 19 ♖f5 with an enormous attack.

16 0-0-0 ♕g5+
17 ♔b1 ♘f6?!

Black gets greedy, but good moves are hard to come by.

18 e5!

Of course.

18 ... de

18 ... ♘xh5 19 ♕h2 ♘hf4 20 ♘e4 g3 21 ♘2xg3 with a winning attack.

19 de ♘d7

Now if 19 ... ♘xh5 20 ♕h2 (20 ♖xh5 followed by ♘e4 also looks good) 20 ... ♘hf4 21 ♘e4 ♕xe5 *(10)*

22 ♖d5!! There's no answer to a move like this.

20 ♖d5!

I thought an awful long time as there were a number of tempting alternatives:

(a) 20 ♘e4 ♕xe5 21 ♖xd7 ♕xg3 22 ♘f6+ ♔f8 23 ♘xg3 ♗xd7 24 ♘xd7+ ♔e7 25 ♘e5 with a clear advantage for White. But I wanted more than this.

(b) 20 ♖xd7!? ♗xd7 21 ♘e4 ♕e7 22 ♘f6+ with a very dangerous attack. but then I thought "why sacrifice at all?". After 20 ♖d5, White has an attack of similar strength, but is only a pawn down.

20	...	c6
21	♘e4	♛e7

21 ... ♛g7 is no better. At the board I was considering the exchange sacrifice 22 ♖xd7 as 22 ... ♗xd7 loses to 23 ♘f6+ ♚e7 24 ♛d3!; but 22 ... ♚xd7 is a much tougher nut to crack: 23 ♛d3+ ♚c7 24 ♛d6+ ♚b6 25 ♘2c3 a5! and I can't see any forced win for White. Therefore it's better not to 'sac' the exchange and play instead 22 ♘d6+ ♚f8 23 ♛a3! Black is forced to play 23 ... c5, as 23 ... ♚g8 loses to 24 ♘xc8 cd 25 ♘e7+ ♚h7 26 ♛d3+.

22	♖d2	♘g5
23	♘d6+	♚f8
24	♘f5!	♛e6
25	♖f1	♚g8 (11)

This allows White to win a piece, but there was nothing better.

11
W

26	♖d6!	♛xe5

Otherwise Black will quickly get mated.

27	♖xd7!	♛xg3

27 ... ♛xe2 28 ♖d8+ ♚h7 29 ♖xh8+ ♚xh8 30 ♛c3+! is the main point.

28	♖d8+	♚h7
29	♖xh8+	♚xh8
30	♘fxg3!	

This removes Black's last hope of counterplay.

30	...	♗e6
31	♚c1	♖e8
32	♖f4	♗c8
33	♚d2	♖e5
34	♘d4	♚h7
35	♗f1!	c5
36	♗xd3+	♚h8
37	♘df5	♗e6
38	♘xh6	♘f3+
39	♚c3	b5

Threatening mate!

40	b3	c4

Black continues till the bitter end. The remaining moves were: 41 bc bc 42 ♗xc4 ♖e3+ 43 ♚b2 ♗xc4 44 ♖xc4 ♘e5 45 ♖c8+ ♚h7 46 ♘hf5 ♖f3 47 ♖c7 a6 48 a3 ♖f4 49 ♖e7 ♘c4+ 50 ♚c3 ♘xa3 51 ♖xf7+ ♚h8 52 ♖e7 ♘b5+ 53 ♚d3 a5 54 ♘h4 ♚g8 55 h6 ♖f7 56 ♖e4 ♚h7 57 ♘hf5 ♖a7 58 ♖xg4 a4 59 ♘e4 ♖a6 60 ♖g7+ ♚h8 61 ♘g5 ♘d6 62 ♘e7 1-0.

Game 4
Hebden – Borm
Orange 1987

1	e4	e5
2	f4	ef
3	♘f3	d6

4	d4	g5
5	h4	g4
6	♘g1	♘f6 *(12)*

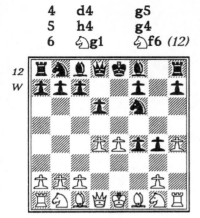

Black launches a counter-attack against the white e-pawn and hopes that this will give him time to defend with ♘h5.

7 ♗xf4!?

It looks strange to give up a central pawn for the one on f4, which might drop off anyway, but as always in this type of position Black's extra pawn is virtually useless.

White's main alternative is 7 ♕d3, after which Black should play 7 ... d5 (of course 7 ... ♘h5 loses to 8 ♕b5+) 8 e5 ♘h5 (8 ... ♘e4 occurred in Gallagher – Westerinen, Metz 1987, and after 9 ♗xf4 c5 10 ♘d2 ♘c6 11 ♘xe4 de 12 ♕xe4 ♕xd4 13 ♕xd4 ♘xd4 14 0-0-0, the game was roughly level) 9 ♘e2 ♗h6! (9 ... ♗e7 10 ♗xf4 c5 11 dc ♘c6 12 ♘bc3 ♘xf4 13 ♘xf4 ♘xe5 14 ♕e3 ♗f6 15 ♘cxd5 0-0 16 0-0-0 ♗g7 17

♘h5 ♘d7 18 ♘e7+ ♔h8 19 ♘xg7 ♔xg7 20 ♖xd7 1-0 Gallagher – Sanz, Gijon 1988) 10 g3 and now Bangiev gives 10 ... ♘c6! with a fully satisfactory game for Black. For example: 11 ♘xf4 (11 ♗g2 ♘e7 with the idea of ... ♗f5) 11 ... ♘xf4 12 ♗xf4 ♗xf4 13 gf ♘e7 with a good blockade on the light squares.

7	...	♘xe4
8	♗d3!	

An improvement on the previously played 8 ♘c3, which leads to unclear play after 8 ... ♘xc3 9 bc ♘c6 10 ♗d3 ♗e6!

8	...	♕e7

Hebden – Psakhis, Moscow 1986, continued 8 ... f5 9 ♘e2 ♗g7 10 ♗xe4 fe 11 ♗g5 ♗f6 12 ♘bc3 ♗xg5 13 hg ♕xg5 14 ♘xe4 ♕e3 15 ♘f6+ ♔d8 16 ♕d2! ♕xd2+ 17 ♔xd2 ♘c6 18 ♖af1 and White eventually picked up the two kingside pawns and won a long ending.

9	♘e2	♗g7
10	0-0	0-0 *(13)*

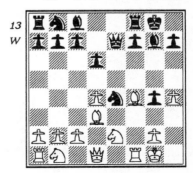

11 ♗xe4!

After this White's lead in development begins to take serious proportions.

11	...	♕xe4
12	♘bc3	♕c6
13	♕d2	d5

Black has to stop 14 ♗h6.

| 14 | ♘g3 | ♕f6 |

This move demonstrates the dire situation that Black is already in. Unable to find a satisfactory way of getting his pieces out, he decides to indulge in a spot of pawn hunting instead.

15	♗e5	♕xh4
16	♗xg7	♔xg7
17	♘xd5!	f5

Of course the knight on g3 is untouchable because of mate in three moves.

18	♕f4	♘c6
19	♘xc7	♖b8
20	♖ae1	

It is only a matter of time now.

20	...	♔g8
21	d5	♘e7
22	♘h5!	♕xh5

Black has little choice because of the threat of 23 ♕h6.

23	♖xe7	b5
24	♖fe1	♖b6
25	d6	♕h4
26	g3	♕f6 *(14)*
27	♘e8!	

An elegant finale.

| 27 | ... | ♕xb2 |
| 28 | ♕g5+ | ♔h8 |

29	♖xh7+	♔xh7
30	♖e7+	♔h8
31	♕h5+	♔g8
32	♕h7	mate

Game 5
Gallagher – S. Jackson
British Championship,
Blackpool 1988

1	e4	e5
2	f4	ef
3	♘f3	d6
4	d4	g5
5	h4	g4
6	♘g1	♗h6 *(15)*

This time Black wants to hang on to that f-pawn.

| 7 | ♘c3 | |

White develops, keeping

his options open. Maybe he will play ♘ge2 or perhaps a plan with ♕d3, ♗d2 and 0-0-0. 7 ♘e2 is also quite playable and, after 7 ... ♕f6 8 ♘bc3 ♘e7, we transpose to game 8.

7 ... c6

Black secures his d5-square in order to be able to defend the f-pawn with his queen. 7 ... ♗e6 will be seen in game 6; 7 ... ♘c6 and 7 ... ♘f6 in game 7.

8 ♘ge2

There are a couple of interesting alternatives:

(a) 8 ♗c4. White understandably prefers to develop his bishop before playing ♘e2, but he does leave himself exposed to counterplay on the queenside: 8 ... ♘f6 9 g3!? ♕e7?! (I wonder what White intended after 9 ... b5!, as 10 ♗d3 ♘h5 11 ♘ge2 doesn't work in this position: 11 ... ♘xg3! 12 ♘xg3 fg 13 ♗xh6 g2 14 ♖g1 ♕xh4+) 10 ♘ge2 b5 11 e5! de 12 de ♕xe5 13 ♗xf4 ♗xf4 14 gf ♕e7 15 ♗d3 ♘bd7 16 ♕d2 with a good game for White, Sanchez Almeyra – Anic, Lyon 1990.

(b) 8 ♕d3 b6!?. White often has to worry about this move after an early ♕d3. The f- and the g-pawns take away a lot of squares on the third rank (8 ... ♕f6 is less good, as

Black is just asking for e5). 9 ♘d1!? (Recommended by Bangiev) 9 ... ♗a6 10 c4 d5 11 ed cd 12 ♕e2+ ♕e7 13 ♘f2!? ♘f6 14 ♕xe7+ ♔xe7 15 ♘e2 ♗xc4 16 ♘xf4 and White has just enough compensation for the pawn

8 ... ♕f6 (16)

8 ... f3 9 ♘g3 (9 ♘f4 is also possible) 9 ... ♕f6 10 ♗xh6 f2+ (10 ... ♘xh6 11 ♕d2 is also pleasant for White) 11 ♔e2 ♘xh6 12 ♕d2 and White wins back the pawn with advantage.

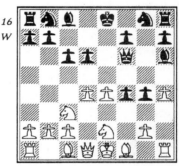

9 g3!

In this way, White takes control of all the dark squares. True, he allows Black a protected passed pawn on f3, but his central control is so great that this is hardly relevant.

9 ... f3

9 ... fg 10 ♘xg3 ♗xc1 11 ♖xc1 doesn't help Black. After 11 ... ♕f4 (otherwise White can develop harmoniously) 12 ♘ce2 ♕e3 13 ♕d2, White achieved a better

ending in Christiansen – Lobo, San Jose 1980, but 13 c4 followed by ♖c3 to expel the lone intruder looks even stronger to me.

10 ♘f4   ♛e7

Black has to play with extreme care. The slightest slip and it will all be over. For example: 10 ... ♘e7? 11 e5! de 12 ♘e4 ♛g7 13 ♘h5 ♛g6 14 ♘hf6+ ♔f8 15 h5 ♛g7 16 de ♘d7 17 ♛d6 1-0 Craig – Dempster, Corr. 1985; or 10 ... ♗xf4?! 11 ♗xf4 b5? (What is Black doing?) 12 ♛d2 ♛e7 13 0-0-0 ♘d7 14 ♗xb5! ♗b7 15 ♗c4 a5 16 ♖he1 ♘b6 17 ♗d3 ♘d7? 18 ♘d5 1-0 Hebden – Cantero, Spain 1986. That was certainly a bad day at the office for Senor Cantero. Basically, whatever Black does, White is going to complete his development and then try to smash open the centre.

11 ♗d3

11 ♔f2 also looks good, but I preferred to tuck my king away on the queenside.

11	...	♗g7
12	♗e3	h5
13	♛d2	♘d7
14	0-0-0	♘f8
15	♖he1	

White's preparations are complete and unfortunately for Black her king is still in the centre.

15 ...   ♗d7?! *(17)*

15 ... ♘e6 is somewhat

better, but Black is going to suffer. 16 e5 and 16 d5 both look very dangerous, or White can even choose to play in a quiet fashion.

17
W

16 e5   de

That Black has little choice apart from opening the centre is confirmed by the following variations:

(a) 16 ... d5 17 ♘cxd5! cd 18 ♘xd5 ♛d8 19 ♗g5! ♛c8 (19 ... ♗h6 20 ♘f6+ ♗xf6 21 ef+ is very good for White) 20 ♘f6+ ♗xf6 21 ef+ ♔d8 22 ♖e7! (Now Black has to take the rook otherwise White will simply munch his way through the seventh rank) 22 ... ♘xe7 23 fe+ ♔e8 24 ♗f6! ♖g8 25 ef=♛+ ♖xf8 (The point of 24 ♗f6 is revealed in the variation 25 ... ♔xf8 26 ♛b4+) 26 ♛b4 and wins

(b) 16 ... 0-0-0 17 ♘cd5! (White will pursue the black king wherever it runs) 17 ... cd 18 ♘xd5 ♛e8 (18 ... ♛e6 then 19 ♛a5 b6 20 ♛xa7) 19 ♛a5 ♔b8 20 ♛c7+

♚a8 21 ♗e4! ♗c8 (21 ... ♗c6 22 ♘b6+ ab 23 ♖d3 or 21 ... ♖b8 22 ♖d3 with the wonderful threat of 23 ♕xd7!!) 22 ♖d3 with a crushing attack.

17   de   ♘e6
18   ♘e4   ♗xe5
Again Black is forced to open further lines.

19   ♘xe6   ♗xe6
If 19 ... ♕xe6 20 ♗c4 is very strong.

20   ♗c5   ♕c7 *(18)*
20 ... ♕d7 21 ♘g5 and wins, for example: 21 ... ♕d5 22 ♘xe6 ♕xe6 23 ♗f5! ♕xf5 24 ♖xe5+ ♕xe5 25 ♕d7 mate.

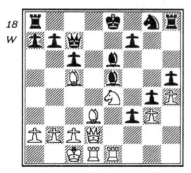

21   ♘d6+!!   ♗xd6
22   ♖xe6+
I was rather enjoying myself here.

22   ...   ♗e7!
The only chance as 22 ... fe 23 ♗g6+ ♔d7 24 ♗xd6 wins.

23   ♗d6!
The pressure just keeps on increasing.

23   ...   ♕xd6

I remember feeling quite disappointed after this as I was itching to play 23 ... ♕d7 24 ♗f5! as now 24 ... fe 25 ♗g6+ ♔f8 26 ♕f4+ ♔g7 27 ♕f7+ ♔h6 28 ♗f4+ is the end. Black is therefore forced to take on e6 with his queen: 24 ... ♕xe6 25 ♗xe6 fe. Now White has the very strong move 26 ♕e3! forcing 26 ... ♖h6 (26 ... ♔f7 27 ♗xe7 ♘xe7 28 ♖e1) 27 ♗xe7 ♔xe7 28 ♕c5+! ♔e8 29 ♕g5! and wins.

24   ♖xd6   ♗xd6 *(19)*

25   ♗a6!
It's amazing! This game just seems to stumble from tactic to tactic.

25   ...   0-0-0
25 ... ♗xg3 was a slightly better chance.

26   ♕c3!   ♘e7
27   ♖xd6   ba
28   ♖f6   ♖hf8
29   ♕c5   ♖d7
Of course this game is not going to finish in the normal way. White now removes the black pawns in

artistic fashion.

30	♕xh5	♖fd8

Threatening mate ...

31	♕xg4	

Pinning ...

31	...	♔b7
32	♕xf3	

And defending.

32	...	♘d5
33	♖xf7	♘b6
34	b3	a5
35	h5	a4
36	♔b2	ab
37	ab	a5
38	h6	a4
39	h7	ab
40	cb	♔a6
41	♖xd7	

The time control has been negotiated, so Black resigned.

This was awarded the best game prize and certainly made up for a miserable tournament.

Game 6
Gallagher – Hübner
Biel 1991

1	e4	e5
2	f4	ef
3	♘f3	d6
4	d4	g5
5	h4	g4
6	♘g1	♗h6
7	♘c3	♗e6 *(20)*

Black finds a novel way of protecting his d5-square (in order to play ... ♕f6 if necessary). The text has one important advantage over 7 ... c6: the d6-square is not weakened, which means that the dangerous attacking plan of e5 and ♘e4 will lose a lot of its potency.

White can, of course, gain time by attacking the bishop with d5 but this is extremely anti-positional and should only be played if there is a very strong follow up.

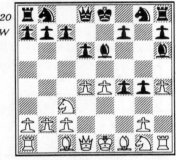

8	♕d3

I decided to play a plan with ♕d3, ♗d2 and 0-0-0 as Black can no longer harass the queen with ... b6 and ... ♗a6. However, if I get this position again I think I would prefer 8 ♘ge2, immediately fighting for some space on the kingside. Play could continue: 8 ... ♕f6 9 g3 (9 ♕d2!? f3 10 ♘f4 ♗xf4 {or 10 ... fg 11 ♗xg2 ♗xf4 12 ♕xf4 ♕xd4 13 e5! with good play for White} 11 ♕xf4 ♕xd4 12 gf with play for the pawn) 9 ... fg (9 ... f3 10 ♘f4 is pleasant for White)

10 ♘xg3 ♗xc1 11 ♖xc1 and, in spite of his material deficit, White has the better chances (The position is very similar to the note to Black's ninth move in Gallagher – Jackson).

8 ... a6!

This looks like a loss of time, but it turns out that without a possible ♕b5 White's options are severely limited. If instead 8 ... ♘c6 then 9 ♘ge2 ♕f6 10 ♕b5! is difficult to meet.

9 ♗d2 ♘c6

9 ... ♕f6 is also possible. If then 10 0-0-0 ♘c6 play transposes to a position I didn't feel like playing during the game. It is probably best for White to play 10 ♘d5 ♗xd5 11 ed, whilst 10 d5 ♗c8 11 ♘b5 also deserves attention.

10 ♘d5

As already mentioned 10 0-0-0 ♕f6 didn't appeal to me as 11 e5 de 12 d5 ♗f5 13 ♘e4 ♗xe4 14 ♕xe4 ♘d4 is good for Black (15 c3 ♕f5). 11 ♘d5 might be playable but if I'm going to do this I prefer the black queen on d8 whilst 11 ♘ce2 leaves White extremely cramped.

10 ... ♗xd5
11 ed ♘ce7
12 ♘e2!?

12 c4 seems more logical, but after 12 ... ♘f6 13 ♘e2 ♘h5 14 g3 ♕d7 15 ♘xf4

♘xf4 16 gf, I hadn't liked the kingside pawn structure.

12 ... ♘xd5
13 ♕e4+?!

White's idea is very risky. More prudent was 13 c4 ♘e3 14 ♘xf4 ♗xf4 15 ♗xe3 ♕e7 16 ♔d2 ♕xe3+ 17 ♕xe3 ♗xe3+ 18 ♔xe3 when the active king combined with Black's dubious pawn structure should enable White to hold the balance. If my c-pawn had been one square further back, I wouldn't have thought twice about entering this ending.

13 ... ♘ge7
14 c4

Not 14 ♘xf4 f5!

14 ... ♘f6

If 14 ... ♘e3 15 ♘xf4.

15 ♕xb7 *(21)*

At this stage, I was not altogether delighted with my position, but by now it was too late to change track.

21
B

15 ... ♕b8?

Black assumed that the ensuing endgame was very favourable for him and didn't seriously examine 15 ... ♖b8!. This seems to give him a winning attack after ♕xa6 ♖xb2 and now:

(a) 17 ♗c3 ♖b6 18 ♕a4+ ♔f8 19 d5 ♘f5! and White's days are numbered.

(b) 17 ♗xf4 ♖xe2+ 18 ♗xe2 ♕xf4 19 ♖f1 ♗g3+ 20 ♔d1 ♘e4 21 ♕b5+ c6 22 ♕h5 ♘f2+ 23 ♔c2 ♘g6 24 ♗xg4 0-0 when Black has a dangerous attack in addition to his material advantage.

(c) 17 0-0-0 ♖xd2 18 ♖xd2 f3 with a very strong attack.

(d) 17 ♗c1. This is the critical line, as if the rook retreats White will have no problems, e.g. 17 ... ♖b6 18 ♕a4+ ♔f8 19 ♘xf4 with the idea of ♘e6+. However, Black has a very strong reply, 17 ... ♕b8!!, after which White seems defenceless:

(d1) 18 ♗xb2 ♕xb2 19 ♕b5+ ♕xb5 20 cb ♘ed5. Despite being the exchange ahead White is completely lost. It is impossible for him to untangle his pieces and he is also in grave danger of getting mated. His only trump is the passed a-pawn, but this is not far enough advanced to cause any problems, e.g. 21 a4

♘e4 22 a5 f3!, with the threat of 23 ... ♗d2+ 24 ♔d1 ♘e3 mate.

(d2) 18 ♕a4+ ♔f8 19 ♘xf4 ♖b1 20 ♖xb1 ♕xb1 winning, as 21 ♕d1 loses to ... ♗xf4 and ... ♕e4+.

(d3) 18 ♕a3 ♖b1 19 ♖xb1 ♕xb1 20 ♕a8+ ♔d7 21 ♕xh8 (22).

22
B

White has won a rook, but his forces are totally disjointed and Black's next move is the nail in the coffin: 21 ... ♘eg8! (21 ... ♘e4 22 ♕xh7 and it is unclear if Black has anything better than perpetual check with 22 ... ♕b4+ and 23 ... ♕a4+; 22 ... f3 is dangerous, but White should escape with 23 ♕xh6 f2+ 24 ♔d1 ♕d3+ 25 ♗d2 ♘f5 26 ♕f4 ♘xd4 27 ♕xe4! ♕xe4 28 ♘xd4 ♕xd4 29 h5). After 21 ... ♘eg8 White's queen will take no further part in the game, e.g.

(d31) 22 ♔f2 g3+ 23 ♔g1 ♕g6 24 ♘xf4 (24 h5 ♕g4 is no better) 24 ... ♕c2! 25 ♘e2

♕xc1!! 26 ♘xg3 ♕e3+ 27 ♔h2 ♗f4 28 ♕g7 ♘h5 29 ♕xf7+ ♘e7 and mate follows.

(d32) 22 h5 with the idea of preventing ... ♕g6 meets with a brilliant refutation: 22 ... ♔e7!! and White is powerless to prevent ... ♔f8 and ... ♗g7.

| 16 | ♕xb8+ | ♖xb8 |
| 17 | ♗xf4! | |

White must liberate his position immediately, not spending any time counting pawns. 17 0-0-0 loses to 17 ... ♘e4 18 ♗xf4 ♗xf4 19 ♘xf4 ♘f2 20 ♖e1 ♘xh1 21 ♘d5 ♔f8!

| 17 | ... | ♗xf4 |
| 18 | ♘xf4 | (23) |

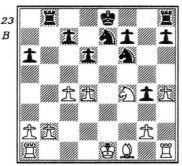

| 18 | ... | ♘e4?! |

It seems very strange not to take on b2 but in fact after 18 ... ♖xb2 19 ♗d3 ♘c6 20 0-0 ♘xd4 21 ♖ae1+ ♔f8 22 h5!? White has ample compensation for the pawns.

Black should instead play 18 ... ♘g6 immediately and then if 19 ♘xg6 hg 20 0-0-0

Black has a slightly better ending. Better is 19 ♘d3! with a roughly level game, e.g. 19 ... h5 20 0-0-0 0-0 21 ♘f2! ♖fe8 22 g3!? ♖e3 23 ♖d3 ♖be8 24 ♘d1.

| 19 | b3 | ♘g6? |

Black completely overlooked White's reply. Better is 19 ... ♘g3 or 19 ... ♘f5, but White is already over the worst.

| 20 | ♘h5! | g3 |

Otherwise ♗d3 will give White a clear advantage.

| 21 | ♗e2 | 0-0 |

If 21 ... ♘f2 22 0-0!

| 22 | 0-0 | ½-½ |

Here the peculiarities of club chess took over as I was informed by my captain that it was in our team's interest for me to offer a draw. White, of course, has the better chances now, e.g. 22 ... f5 23 ♗f3 ♘xh4 24 ♗xe4 fe 25 ♘f6+ (25 ♘xg3!?) 25 ... ♔g7 26 ♘xe4 ♘f5 27 d5. Black has a large number of weaknesses.

Game 7
Bangiev – Pashaian
Corr. 1987

1	e4	e5
2	f4	ef
3	♘f3	d6
4	d4	g5
5	h4	g4
6	♘g1	♗h6
7	♘c3	♘c6 (24)

Black has one other alt-
ernative, namely 7 ... ♘f6.
A complicated game arises
from 8 ♘ge2 d5 (After the
immediate 8 ... ♘h5, 9 g3
promises White a good
game) 9 ♗xf4!? (9 e5 ♘h5 10
g3 leads to a position
where the inclusion of d5
and e5 is not unfavourable
for Black) 9 ... ♗xf4 10
♘xf4 de 11 ♗c4! (This
seems more logical to me
than Makarichev's suggestion in *New in Chess* of ♕d2
followed by 0-0-0. Black is
weak on the f-file so the
good old-fashioned recipe
is called for: bishop on c4,
rook on f1. An eventual ♘d5
may also cause problems).
Black can try:

(a) 11 ... ♘c6 12 0-0 ♕xd4+
13 ♕xd4 ♘xd4 14 ♘fd5
♘xd5 15 ♘xd5 ♘e6 16 ♘f6+
♔e7 17 ♖ae1 and White has
more than enough compen-
sation.

(b) 11 ... ♘bd7 12 0-0 ♘b6
is too slow: 13 ♗xf7+ ♔xf7
14 ♘h5 ♘d7 15 ♘xe4 and

White's winning.

8 ♗b5!?

White has a major alter-
native in 8 ♘ge2 after
which Black is forced to
advance: 8 ... f3 9 ♘f4 (9
♘g3!? f2+ 10 ♔e2! {10 ♔xf2
♕f6+} also deserves attention) 9 ... f2+!? (If 9 ... ♕f6,
then 10 ♘cd5 ♕xd4 11 ♕xd4
♘xd4 12 ♘xc7+ ♔d8 13 ♘xa8
♘xc2+ 14 ♔d1 ♘xa1 15 ♘d5
and White's knight on a8
will now escape, whilst it
will take a miracle for
B!ack's to perform a similar
feat) 10 ♔xf2 g3+ 11 ♔xg3
♘f6 12 ♗e2 (12 ♔f2!? ♖g8 13
g3 ♗g4 14 ♕d3 ♕d7 15 ♘cd5
♗g7 16 ♘xf6+ ♗xf6 17 c3
0-0-0 18 ♘d5 ♗g7 19 ♗f4 f5
20 ♗g2 ♕f7?! 21 ef ♗xf5 22
♕xf5+ ♕xf5 23 ♘h3 with a
clear advantage to White,
Naftalin – Selke, Corr. 1988)
12 ... ♖g8+ 13 ♔f2 ♘g4+ 14
♗xg4 ♗xg4 15 ♕d3 ♗g7 16
♗e3 ♕d7 *(25)*

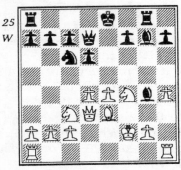

17 ♘cd5! (After 17 ♘ce2?!
0-0-0 18 ♘g3 f5! Black had
a strong attack in Planinc –

Gligoric, Ljubljana/Portoroz 1977). The German correspondence player Niemtz has been responsible for rehabilitating this line. Here are some examples after 17 ♘cd5! 0-0-0 18 b4:

(a) 18 ... f5 19 b5. White's attack now arrives in time: 19 ... ♘e7 20 ♕a3 ♔b8 21 ♘xe7 ♕xe7 22 e5 with a slight advantage for White, Niemtz - Bodkov, Corr. 1983/84.

(b) In the game Niemtz - Skorpik, Corr. 1983/84 rather than 18 ... f5, there occurred 18 ... ♘e7 19 ♘xe7+ ♕xe7 20 ♘d5 ♕e6 21 ♖ae1 ♖de8 22 ♕c4 ♕d7 23 b5 ♔b8 24 ♗f4 with a better game for White.

(c) 18 ... ♖de8! 19 b5 ♘d8 20 c4 (20 a4!?) 20 ... ♘e6 21 c5! (21 ♖ae1 f5, Dufraisse - Roos, Corr. 1987) 21 ... dc 22 dc ♗xa1 23 ♖xa1 ♘xf4 24 ♗xf4 with compensation.

8 ... a6

8 ... ♗d7 is too passive as Black no longer has the possibility of ... a5 and ... ♗a6.

9 ♗xc6+ bc
10 ♕d3

The usual plan of castling long and then having a look to see what's going on.

10 ... ♕f6

10 ... ♘e7 leaves the f-pawn devoid of protection,

e.g. 11 ♘ge2 ♘g6 12 g3! ♕f6 13 h5!

11 ♗d2 ♘e7
12 0-0-0 (26)

12 ... d5

(a) 12 ... a5!? 13 e5 de 14 ♘e4 gives good attacking chances.

(b) 12 ... 0-0 13 ♘ge2 a5!? 14 e5 de 15 ♘e4 ♕g7 16 de ♗a6 17 ♘f6+ ♕xf6 18 ef ♗xd3 19 fe ♗xe2 20 ef=♕+ ♗xf8!? 21 ♖de1 f3 22 gf gf 23 ♖hg1+ ♗g7 24 ♗c3 f2 25 ♖xg7+ ♔f8 26 ♖xh7 fe=♕+ 27 ♗xe1 with better chances for White in the endgame (Bangiev).

13 ♘ge2

As usual, White will not want to advance his e-pawn as this would give Black a fine square on f5.

13 ... f3
14 gf gf
15 ♖df1 ♗xd2+
16 ♕xd2 h5!

Black might want to exchange queens with ... ♕h6 at an appropriate moment.

17 ♘g1!? ♗g4
18 ♕e3 ♕h6

19	♕xh6	♖xh6
20	♘xf3	f6
21	e5?!	

It would have been better to play 21 ♘d2!. This both creates pressure on the f-file and sends the knight off on a pleasant journey towards c5. In that case, White would have had the better chances.

The rest of the game is given in brief: 21 ... ♘f5 22 ♘e2 0-0-0 23 ♔d2 ♖e8 24 ♖f2 fe 25 ♘xe5 ♘d6 26 ♘c3 c5?! 27 ♘xg4 ♘c4+ 28 ♔c1 hg 29 dc ♖e3!? 30 ♘xd5 ♖xh4 31 ♖d1 ♖eh3 32 c6 ♖h8 33 ♖f4 ♘e5 34 ♘e7+ ♔b8 35 ♖b4+ ♔a8 36 ♘d5 ♖3h7 37 ♖e4 ♘xc6 38 ♖xg4 ♔b7 39 ♘c3 ♖h1 40 ♖e4 ♖xd1+ 41 ♔xd1 ♖d8+ 42 ♔c1 ♖d6 43 b3 ♘b8 44 ♔b2 ♘d7 45 ♖h4 ♔c6 46 b4 ♔b7 47 ♖h5 ♔c6 48 ♔b3 ♔b7 49 ♘a4 ♔c6 50 ♘b2 ♘b6 51 a4 ♖f6 52 ♘d3 ♘d7 53 a5 ♖d6 54 ♖h8 ♖f6 55 ♖a8 ♔b7 56 ♖d8 ♔c6 57 b5+ 1-0 (if 57 ... ab 58 a6 ♖f8 59 ♘b4+ is winning).

Game 8
Bangiev – Figer
Corr. 1987

1	e4	e5
2	f4	ef
3	♘f3	d6
4	d4	g5
5	h4	g4
6	♘g1	♕f6 (27)

As we have already seen, Black has to take special care when he develops his queen to f6, as the advance e5 is always in the offing.

7	♘c3	♘e7

7 ... c6 is also playable and now everybody has recommended 8 e5 de 9 ♘e4 ♕e7 10 de ♕xe5 11 ♕e2 with a dangerous attack, e.g. 11 ... ♗g7 12 ♘d6+ ♔f8 13 ♗xf4 or 11 ... ♘d7 12 ♗d2 or 11 ... ♗e6 12 ♗d2 and Black has problems on the long diagonal.

But what about 11 ... ♗e7 12 ♗d2 ♘f6!. I now can't find any position that I would feel like playing for White, e.g.

(a) 13 ♘xf6+ ♗xf6 14 ♗xf4 ♕xe2+ 15 ♗xe2 ♗xb2. White has probably a good pawn's worth of compensation, but unfortunately he is two down.

(b) 13 ♗c3 ♕xe4 14 ♕xe4 ♘xe4 15 ♗xh8 ♘g3 16 ♖h2, (For the exchange Black has two pawns and everything will now hinge on whether the f- and g-pawns are strong or weak). 16 ... ♗e6 looks like Black's best (If 16 ... ♘f5 17 0-0-0 ♗xh4? 18 ♖xh4 ♘xh4 19 ♗f6; Black could also try to lock the bishop out of the game with 16 ... f6, but he would then run into trouble along the a2-g8 diagonal and on the e-file. However, 16 ... ♗d6 17 0-0-0 ♗c7 is unclear) 17 ♗e5 (After other moves Black has good compensation, e.g. 17 ♘e2 ♗xf1 18 ♔xf1 ♗d6; or 17 0-0-0 ♘d7) 17 ... ♘xf1! 18 ♔xf1 ♗c4+ 19 ♔e1 ♗c5! (Black is hanging onto his pawn by tactical resouces) 20 ♘e2 (20 0-0-0 ♗e3+ 21 ♔b1 ♘d7 or 20 ♖h1 ♗e3 are good for Black) 20 ... g3! (20 ... f3 is not so good after 21 gf gf 22 ♘d4 ♘d7 23 ♘xf3! ♘xe5 24 ♘xe5 ♗d6 25 ♖g2!) 21 ♖h3 (21 ♖h1 f3! 22 gf g2 with advantage to Black) 21 ... ♗f2+ 22 ♔f1 (22 ♔d1 f3 is strong) 22 ... ♗e3 23 ♔e1 and Black has the pleasant choice between 23 ... ♗xe2 or 23 ... ♗e6.

So, instead of 8 e5?!, 8 ♘ge2. Now Black can play 8 ... ♗h6, transposing to Gallagher - Jackson (and we don't mind that!), or push with 8 ... f3 9 ♘g3 f2+ 10 ♔e2 (OK, we've had to move our king, but take a

look at Black's position. What a mess!) 10 ... b6 doesn't help: 11 ♗g5 ♗a6+ 12 ♔e3 ♗h6 13 ♕xg4.

8 ♘ge2 ♗h6

8 ... f3, as usual, doesn't solve Black's problems: 9 ♘f4 (9 ♘g3 also looks good) 9 ... fg (Black should have tried 9 ... f2+ 10 ♔xf2 g3+, regardless of whether it's good or not) 10 ♗xg2 c6 11 e5! with a crushing attack in Bangiev - Mayr, Corr. 1986.

9 ♕d2

This strange move is seen from time to time in the King's Gambit, normally when White is in a hurry to retrieve the gambit pawn. However, in this position it doesn't seem to work too well. Bangiev also considers 9 g3!? fg! 10 ♗xh6 ♕xh6 (10 ... ♕f2+ 11 ♔d2 g2 12 ♗xg2 ♕xg2 13 ♗g5 with active play for the pawn) 11 ♕d2 ♕xd2+ 12 ♔xd2 ♘bc6 13 ♗g2 ♗d7 14 ♖af1 with a distinct initiative compensating for the lost material.

I think White would do best here to play 9 ♕d3 with the usual idea of ♗d2 and 0-0-0.

9 ... ♘bc6!

Black puts d4 under immediate pressure. 9 ... ♗d7 is rather passive; Planinc - Portisch, Ljubljana 1973 continued: 10 g3 ♘bc6

(10 ... fg? 11 ♕xh6 is good for White) 11 gf 0-0-0 12 ♗g2 ♕g7 13 d5 ♘e5 14 ♕e3 ♔b8 15 ♕f2 with the better game for White.

10   g3?! *(28)*

This recommendation of *ECO* is not good. Instead, White should take advantage of the one drawback created by Black's ninth move (i.e. the inability to defend c7 sensibly) and play 10 ♘b5. After 10 ... ♔d8 11 d5 (Bangiev considers the complications after 11 e5 ♕f5 12 ed ♘d5 13 dc+ ♔d7 to be in White's favour, but he didn't suggest a way to beat off the black attack. I certainly can't see anything resembling a White advantage) 11 ... ♘e5 12 ♘xf4 a6! 13 ♘d4 g3 with an unclear position. The game Gallagher – G. Flear, Lenk 1992 continued 14 ♘de2 ♖g8 15 ♕d4 ♗g4 16 ♗e3 ♗xe2 17 ♘xe2 ♘f3+!? 18 gf ♕xf3 19 ♗xh6 ♕xh1 20 ♗g5! g2 21 ♔f2! ♖xg5! 22 hg

gf=♕+ 23 ♖xf1 ♕h4+ 25 ♘g3 ♔d7 26 ♕f6 ♖g8 27 ♖h1 ♕xg5 28 ♕xg5 ♖xg5 29 ♖xh7 ♔e8 ½-½.

10   ...   ♗g7

The bishop switches diagonals in order to assist the attack on d4, whilst at the same time unpinning itself. To avoid losing a pawn, White is forced into the extremely ugly ...

11   d5?!   fg!

Well, it turns out he loses one anyway as 12 dc ♕f2+ followed by ... g2 is disastrous.

12   ♘xg3   ♘d4
13   ♗g2   ♘f3+!
14   ♗xf3   ♕xf3
15   ♘ce2   ♗e5

The full effects of 11 d5 are shown as Black completely dominates the centre.

16   ♖g1

16 ♕d3 is probably a slight improvement although after 16 ... f5! 17 ♖f1 fe 18 ♖xf3 (or 18 ♘xe4 ♕xd3) 18 ... ed 19 ♖xd3 ♘f5, Black stands clearly better.

16   ...   f5
17   ♕h6

The only way to try to develop.

17   ...   ♖f8
18   ♗g5   f4!
19   ♖f1   fg

Not really a queen sacrifice but elegant nevertheless.

20	♖xf3	gf
21	♗xe7	f2+
22	♔d2	♔xe7
	0-1	

For those of you who like to stray from the beaten path, games 9 and 10 offer an alternative way of treating the Fischer Defence.

Game 9
Gallagher – Lane
Hastings Masters 1990

1	e4	e5
2	f4	ef
3	♘f3	d6
4	♗c4	(29)

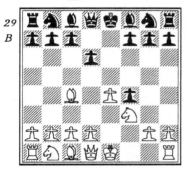

| 4 | ... | h6 |

4 ... g5 is inadvisable and the last outing that I know of was 143 years ago: 5 h4 g4 6 ♘g5 ♘h6 7 d4 f6 8 ♗xf4 fg 9 ♗xg5 (9 hg also looks good) and White had a very strong attack, Morphy – Tilghman, Philadelphia 1859.

| 5 | d3! |

5 d4 is more common,

but the text has certain advantages:

(a) The knight has the extra option of hopping into d4 in case of being hassled by the g-pawn.

(b) 5 d3 offers some solidity to the white centre, which can be quite useful if you're going to play on the wing.

| 5 | ... | g5 |
| 6 | g3! |

The undermining process begins straight away.

| 6 | ... | ♗h3!? |

Black has a number of alternatives:

(a) 6 ... fg 7 hg. This gives White excellent attacking chances, e.g. 7 ... ♗g4 8 ♗xg5! hg 9 ♖xh8 ♘h6 10 ♘c3 ♕f6 11 ♖xf8+ ♔xf8 12 ♘d5!, Bhend – Issler, Corr. 1970; or 7 ... ♗g7 8 ♘xg5 hg 9 ♖xh8 ♗xh8 10 ♕h5 ♕f6 11 ♘c3 c6 12 ♗xg5 ♕g7 13 0-0-0 with a strong attack.

(b) 6 ... ♘c6 7 gf g4 (Bhend gives 7 ... ♗g4 as leading to rough equality after 8 0-0 ♘d4 9 ♘bd2 gf 10 c3 ♘e6! although this is very hard to assess without any practical experience. Maybe 8 c3 is an improvement as 8 ... gf 9 ♗xf4 ♘e5? 10 ♗xe5 and 11 ♗xf7+ wins for White) 8 ♘g1 ♕h4+ 9 ♔f1 ♘f6 10 ♔g2 ♘h5 11 ♘c3 g3 12 ♕e1! ♖g8 13 h3 with advantage to White, as his king is perfectly safe.

(c) 6 ... g4, see game 10.

7 ♘d4?!

After half an hour's reflection, I still managed to overlook my opponent's reply. At first, 7 gf appealed to me because of the variation 7 ... g4 8 ♘d4 ♗g2? 9 ♕xg4 ♗xh1 10 ♗xf7+ ♔xf7 11 ♕e6+ ♔g7 12 ♘f5+ ♔h7 13 ♕f7+ and mate. But, of course, 8 ... ♕h4+ is better when I was unable to assess the position after 9 ♔e2 ♗g2 10 ♕e1! ♕h3 11 ♖g1. After the game Gary Lane said he had been most worried about 7 ♕d2!?. This prevents ... ♗g2 and takes the sting out of ... ♕h4+, thereby threatening to capture on f4. 7 ♕e2 also deserves attention, as 7 ... g4 8 ♘h4 f3 9 ♕f2 doesn't really help Black.

7 ...   d5!

The only move, but a good one.

8 ed

Unfortunately, 8 ♗xd5 c6 9 ♕h5 cd 10 ♕xh3 de 11 c3 looks good for Black. After 8 ed Black has succeeded in closing the a2 - g8 diagonal, which gives him time to complete his development and remove his king to a safe haven.

8 ...   ♗g7

9 c3

9 ♘f3!?

9 ...   ♗xd4

10 cd   ♗g2

11 ♖g1

I wasn't too attracted by the endgame after 11 ♕e2+.

11 ...   f3!? (30)

A truly amazing position has arisen on the board. Will White's powerful pawn centre prove triumphant, or will Black's bishop on g2 have the last word?

11 ... ♗xd5 also came into consideration, but after 12 ♘c3, Black will have to straighten out White's remaining d-pawns: 12 ... ♗xc4 13 dc fg 14 hg. White has sufficient play for the pawn because of Black's weak kingside, e.g. 14 ... ♘f6 (14 ... ♕e7+ 15 ♔f2) 15 ♕f3! 0-0 16 ♗e3.

12 ♗e3

12 ♘d2? ♕f6 is very menacing. White's main priority is to get his king out of the centre. In similar positions where Black has a pawn on f3, there is normally a cosy square for the white king

on f2. Here, however, with the black pawn back on g5 (instead of g4) a knight check on g4 could prove extremely embarrassing.

| 12 | ... | ♘f6 |
| 13 | ♘c3 | 0-0 |

If 13 ... ♘g4 14 ♕d2 ♕e7 15 0-0-0 and Black can't win a piece because of the pin on the e-file.

14	♕d2	♖e8
15	0-0-0	♘g4
16	♖ge1	

16 ♖de1 loses to 16 ... ♖xe3. For a while I was tempted by a dubious queen sacrifice: 17 ♖xe3 f2 18 ♖xg2 *(31)* f1=♕+ 19 ♖e1 ♕f5 20 h3 ♘f6 21 ♖f2 with some vague attacking chances.

Apart from 18 ... f1=♕+, Black has another possibility 18 ... f1=♘!!?. After the dust settles Black will be a piece up: 3 knights (!) against knight and bishop.

16	...	♘d7
17	♗g1	♘df6
18	h4!	

White has to quickly break up the black kingside.

18	...	♖xe1
19	♖xe1	♘h5
20	♘e4	gh
21	gh	♕xh4 *(32)*

22 d6!

At long last, the bishop comes into play and the f7-square begins to look vulnerable.

| 22 | ... | cd |
| 23 | ♘xd6 | f2? |

23 ... ♖f8 was necessary, when the game is rather unclear, e.g.

(a) 24 ♘xf7 (This seems insufficient) 24 ... ♖xf7 25 ♗xf7+ ♔xf7 26 ♕f4+ ♘hf6 27 ♕c7+ ♔g6 28 ♖e7 ♕g5+ 29 ♗e3 (29 ♔c2 ♔h5) 29 ... ♕xe3+! 30 ♖xe3 ♘xe3 and Black's f-pawn should do the rest.

(b) 24 ♖e4 ♘hf6 25 ♖f4 ♕g5 26 ♘e4 ♘xe4 27 de f2! 28 ♗xf2 ♘xf2 29 ♕xf2 ♖c8 is good for Black.

(c) 24 ♘e4. This solid move is probably the best; the position remains a mess.

24 ♗xf2 ♛xf2

If 24 ... ♘xf2 25 ♗xf7+ ♔h7 (Otherwise 26 ♛xh6+) 26 ♗xh5 and wins quickly as 26 ... ♘xd3+ 27 ♛xd3 is check.

25 ♗xf7+ ♔f8
26 ♗xh5

And not 26 ♛b4 a5!

26 ... ♛xd2+
27 ♔xd2 ♘f6
28 ♗d1!

White is a pawn up, but more importantly the exposed position of the black king will be relevant right into the endgame.

28 ... h5
29 ♖e6 ♘g4
30 ♗b3 ♖d8
31 ♖g6 ♔e7

The king heads for the hills. What followed can no doubt be improved upon, but both players were in desperate time trouble.

32 ♘f5+ ♔d7
33 ♖g7+ ♔c8
34 ♖h7 ♘f6
35 ♖h6 ♖f8
36 ♘g7 ♘d5
37 ♗xd5! ♗xd5
38 ♖xh5 ♗xa2
39 ♖a5 ♗g8
40 ♖xa7 ♔c7
41 ♖a5

The time control has been reached and White is two pawns up. Although they are doubled, the outcome is not in doubt:

41	...	**♖d8**
42	♔c3	♔b6
43	♖c5	♗d5
44	♘f5	♗e6
45	♘e3	♗f7
46	♖f5	♗g8
47	♖c5	♗f7
48	♘c4+	♔a7
49	b4!	♗g8
50	b5	♗d5
51	b6+	♔b8
52	♖c7	♗g2
53	♘e5	♗h1?

53 ... ♗h3 would enable Black to last a little longer. Now he is going to get mated.

54 ♘d7+ ♔a8
55 ♖c5! 1-0

Game 10
Gallagher – G. Flear
Paris 1990

1	e4	e5
2	f4	ef
3	♘f3	d6
4	♗c4	h6
5	d3	g5
6	g3	g4 *(33)*

33
W

7 ♘d4

A rather strange move to play in the King's Gambit, but I felt pleased to justify moving the d-pawn only one square.

7 ... ♗g7

It is not clear whether this or the immediate 7 ... f3 is stronger. In the latter case, White could play something like 8 ♗e3, ♘c3, ♕d2 and 0-0-0.

8 c3 f3
9 ♕b3 ♕d7

This clumsy-looking move is necessary, as after 9 ... ♕e7 10 ♘f5! ♗xf5 11 ♕xb7 ♘f6 12 ♗b5+! wins.

10 ♗f4

10 ♘f5 is interesting, but I didn't want to expose myself to a d5-break, e.g.10 ... ♗f8 11 ♗f4?! d5! 12 ♗xd5 c6 13 ♗c4 b5 and White probably won't have quite enough for the sacrificed material.

10 ... ♘c6

Now the attempt to win material with 10 ... d5 is not so good: 11 ♗xd5 ♗xd4 (11 ... c6 12 ♗xb8 cd {12 ... ♖xb8 13 ♗xc6} 13 ♘f5 with a strong attack) 12 cd c6 13 ♘c3! cd 14 ♘xd5 ♘a6 15 ♖c1 and Black is struggling to find a legal move.

11 ♘f5 ♗e5
12 ♘d2 ♘a5
13 ♕b4 ♘xc4
14 ♘xc4 ♗xf4
15 gf ♘e7

16 ♘ce3 ♘xf5
17 ♘xf5 (34)

After this logical series of moves, we arrive in a position where White has excellent play for the pawn. The white knight is superior to the black bishop and, as well as lagging behind in development, Black has chronic dark-square weaknesses.

17 ... c5!

Black has to prevent ♕d4 at all costs.

18 ♕b5! ♔d8!

The only way to save the d6-pawn. After 18 ... ♕xb5 19 ♘xd6+ ♔e7 20 ♘xb5, White's strong centre is the dominant factor in the position.

19 ♕xd7+

19 ♕b3 is also playable.

19 ... ♔xd7
20 h3!

Black's pawn chain begins to crumble. Of course, 20 ... h5 is refuted by 21 hg.

20 ... gh
21 ♔f2 ♔c7

22 ♘e3   f5

If White was allowed to play 23 f5, he would have been able to deal with the black kingside at his convenience.

23 ♔xf3?!

This seems premature. By 23 ♘d5+ ♔c6 24 ♘e7+ ♔c7 25 ♘xc8 ♖axc8 26 ♔xf3 White gets a better ending. 23 ♖ag1 also looks good.

| 23 | ... | ♗d7 |
| 24 | ♘d5+ | ♔c6 |

25 ♖ag1

After the game I'd felt that I'd missed my chance by not playing 25 c4 here. However, by 25 ... h5! Black gets a reasonable game.

25 ...   c4

White's centre begins to creek. It's time to bail out.

26	♖g7	cd
27	♘b4+	♔c7
28	♘d5+	♔c6
29	♘b4+	♔c7
30	♘d5+	½-½

2) Cunningham Defence

1	e4	e5
2	f4	ef
3	♘f3	♗e7 *(35)*

In practice, 3 ... ♗e7 is usually seen as one of the most solid ways of meeting the King's Gambit. Black calmly starts to develop his kingside whilst also giving himself the option of ... ♕h4+. It is especially popular amongst the well-schooled ex-Soviet players.

To check or not to check? That is a much posed question in this variation. The general opinion seems to be that if the white king has f1 at his disposal, Black's loss of time is a bigger problem than White's lost right to castle. On the other hand, if the monarch has to bravely advance to e2, Black usually can't resist the check.

White has two main choices on his fourth turn: 4 ♗c4 and 4 ♘c3. Even if you intend to play the 4 ♘c3 variation, you should still familiarise yourself with the lines arising from 4 ♗c4, as there are many transpositional possibilities.

Game 11
Gallagher – P. Wells
Islington 1990

1	e4	e5
2	f4	ef
3	♘f3	♗e7
4	♗c4	

One of my very first King's Gambits was against Maya Chiburdanidze in a London weekend tournament in 1985. 3 ... ♗e7 was the end of my theoretical knowledge but I had a recollection of the king coming to e2, so I played 4 d4, assuming it was the normal move. The game continued 4 ... ♗h4+ 5 ♔e2 d5 (This is why 4 ♘c3 is stronger; it covers the d5-square) 6 e5 ♗g4 7 ♗xf4 ♘e7 8 h3 ♘g6!? 9 hg!? ♘xf4+ 10 ♔e3! ♗g3 *(36)*

36
W

What a baptism. I remember now spending some time looking at 11 ♘g1!?, with the idea of winning the bishop with ♔f3 and ♔xg3 but I had the feeling Black might be able to get a strong attack, so I played 11 ♘c3 and after 11 ... f6 12 ♘e2 ♘xe2 13 ♕xe2 fe I had to go pawn grabbing with 14 ♕b5+. There followed: 14 ... ♘c6 15 ♕xb7 ♘xd4 16 ♗d3! ♖b8 17 ♕a6 e4 18 ♕g6+!! (This certainly startled my opponent) 18 ... hg 19 ♖xh8+ ♔d7 20 ♖xd8+ ♖xd8 21 ♔xd4 ed 22 ♔xd5! dc 23 ♖c1 with a small advantage for White, although the game was eventually drawn in a blitz finish. After this game my appe-tite for King's Gambits became insatiable.

4 ... ♘f6

4 ... ♗h4+ 5 ♔f1 (Cunningham used to play 5 g3 fg 6 0-0 gh+ 7 ♔h1. In previous centuries, many quick wins were scored with these visual sacrifices, but modern defensive technique has rendered 5 g3 harmless. These days, players don't take everything that's offered as a matter of honour, but return the material – or at least some of it – at an appropriate moment to nullify the attack. So, instead of 6 ... gh+, 6 ... d5 7 ♗xd5 ♘f6 8 ♗xf7+ {8 ♘xh4 ♘xd5 9 ed ♕xh4 10 ♕e2+ ♔d8 is good for Black} 8 ... ♔xf7 9 e5 {9 ♘xh4 ♕d4+} 9 ... ♗h3 10 ef ♗xf1 11 ♕xf1 gh+ 12 ♔h1 ♗xf6 with a clear advantage for Black in Krejcik – Schlechter, Vienna 1918) 5 ... d5 (This is the only way for Black to fight for the initiative) 6 ♗xd5 (6 ed is interesting and, in fact, transposes to the note to Black's fourth move in Spassky – Bronstein, game 24) 6 ... ♘f6 and now White has:

(a) 7 ♘xh4!? ♘xd5 8 ed ♕xh4 9 ♕e1+ (9 d4) with a favourable pawn structure in the ending.

(b) 7 ♘c3 0-0 8 d4!? (8 d3 is more solid) 8 ... ♘xd5 9

♘xd5 f5 10 ♘xh4 fe 11 ♕h5 ♗e6 12 ♘xf4 ♕xd4! with good attacking chances for Black.

(c) 7 ♗b3 ♗g4 8 d3 0-0 *(37)*.

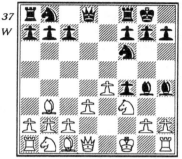

37
W

9 ♕d2!? (9 ♗xf4 allows 9 ... ♘xe4 and 9 ♘c3 ♘h5! 10 ♘d5 ♕d6 11 ♕d2 ♗xf3 12 gf c6 13 ♘c3 ♔h8 14 ♕g2 led to a slight advantage for Black in J. Wells – Corkett, Corr. 1989, although White should be able to improve on 10 ♘d5) 9 ... ♗xf3 10 gf ♘h5 11 ♕g2! ♘c6 12 ♕g4 ♕g5 13 ♖g1 ♕xg4 14 fg! with a good game for White.

5 e5

The only testing move:

(a) 5 d3 is passive: 5 ... d5 6 ed ♘xd5 7 ♗xd5 ♕xd5 8 ♗xf4 is about equal.

(b) 5 ♘c3 has a justifiably poor reputation: 5 ... ♘xe4 6 ♘e5 (6 ♗xf7+ ♔xf7 7 ♘e5+ ♔g8! 8 ♘xe4 d6! 9 ♘f3 d5 is bad) 6 ... ♘g5 7 d4 d6 8 ♘d3 f3! 9 gf 0-0 (9 ... ♘h3!?) 10 ♗e3 ♖e8 11 ♔d2 ♗f6 12 ♕f1 ♘c6 13 d5 ♖xe3

14 ♔xe3 ♘h3 and White was in bad shape, Zweigberk – Oechslein, Corr. 1962.

5 ... ♘g4

5 ... ♘h5 is rather dubious: 6 ♘c3 d6 7 ed ♕xd6 8 d4 ♘c6 9 0-0 0-0 10 ♗e2 ♗g4 11 ♘e4 followed by 12 ♘f2 with good attacking chances for White (Estrin and Glaskov).

6 d4!?

For 6 0-0 see game 12.

6 ♘c3 is the main alternative, with play often transposing to the text. It is difficult to say which is the more accurate move order: 6 ... d6 (6 ... d5?! 7 ♗xd5 ♗h4+ 8 ♔f1 ♘c6 9 ♗xc6+ bc 10 d3 0-0 11 ♗xf4 f6 12 e6 f5 13 ♘xh4 ♕xh4 14 ♕e1 is good for White {Keres}; or 6 ... ♗h4+?! 7 ♔f1 ♘f2? 8 ♕e1 winning) and now:

(a) 7 d4 de 8 de ♕xd1+ 9 ♘xd1 ♗e6! 10 ♗xe6 fe 11 h3 ♘h6 12 ♗xf4 and although White has slightly the better of it, Black should be able to defend.

(b) 7 ed ♕xd6 (7 ... ♗xd6 8 ♕e2+ is similar to the main game) 8 ♕e2 (8 d4 is the note to Black's seventh move) 8 ... 0-0 9 d4 ♘c6 10 ♘d5 (10 ♘b5 is interesting when Black should play 10 ... ♕h6! with an unclear game) 10 ... ♘e3! 11 ♗xe3 fe 12 ♕xe3 ♖e8 13

0-0= Gallagher – Vladimirov, Hastings 1990/91.

6 ... d5

6 ... ♗h4+ occurred in Gallagher – Hebden, Hastings 1989/90. After 7 ♔f1 ♘e3+ (not 7 ... ♘f2 8 ♕e1) 8 ♗xe3 fe 9 ♕d3 0-0 10 ♘c3 d6 11 ♕xe3 ♘c6 White could have obtained dangerous attacking chances by 12 ♕e4! ♗e7 13 h4.

7 ed!

Previous publications have usually condemned 6 d4, but for some reason they have only considered 7 ♗d3 here. That this is a mistake can be seen from the continuation of the game Lutikov – Estrin, Leningrad 1951: 7 ... ♗h4+! 8 ♔e2 ♘f2 9 ♕e1 ♘xd3 10 ♕xh4 ♘xc1+ 11 ♖xc1 ♕xh4 12 ♘xh4 ♘c6 13 c3 0-0 14 ♔f2 f6 with advantage to Black.

7 ... ♗xd6

As this seems to lead into a bad endgame, 7 ... ♕xd6 is more critical. The game Gallagher – Chiburdanidze, Biel 1990, worked out badly for me after 8 ♘c3 ♗e6 9 d5?! ♗d7 10 ♕e2 0-0 11 ♘e4 ♕b6 12 ♗xf4 ♗f5 13 ♘g3 ♗g6 14 h3 ♗d6 15 ♗xd6 ♕xd6 16 0-0-0 ♕f4+ 17 ♔b1 ♘e3 18 ♖d4 ♕xg3 19 ♕xe3 ♕xg2 20 ♖h2 ♕g3 21 ♖g4 ♕d6 and White was a pawn down with no attack.

However, 9 d5 doesn't really fit in with White's scheme of development. Instead, 9 ♗d3! would enable White to fight for the advantage; 9 ... ♘e3 can be answered by 10 ♕e2.

The game Hebden – Fassert, Guernsey 1988, followed a course more to White's liking: 7 ... ♕xd6 8 0-0 0-0 9 ♘c3 c6? (This is a serious mistake after which White's attack soon becomes irresistible) 10 h3 ♘e3 (10 ... ♘f6 11 ♘e5) 11 ♗xe3 fe 12 ♘e5 ♗h4 (This is rather optimistic, but 12 ... ♗e6 13 ♘e4 is pretty terrible) 13 ♖xf7 ♗e6 14 ♘e4 ♗f2+ 15 ♔h2 ♕xe5+ 16 de ♗xf7 17 e6 1-0.

8 ♕e2+!

A good moment to opt for an ending.

8 ... ♕e7

8 ... ♔f8 is not recommended.

9 ♕xe7+ ♔xe7
10 ♘c3 ♗e6

It's not easy for Black to find a path to equality. If the f-pawn is lost, then White's control in the centre should guarantee him at least a slight edge. 10 ... ♗f5 is an alternative, but after 11 ♗b3 (or 11 ♘d5+ ♔d8 12 c3 ♖e8+ 13 ♔f1 ♘e3+ 14 ♗xe3 fe 15 ♖e1 with a good game) 11 ... ♖e8 12 0-0, the threats of 13 ♘d5+, 13 ♘b5 and 13 ♘g5 promise White a good game.

11 ♗d3 ♖d8

An attempt to hang on to the f-pawn would prove unsuccessful, e.g. 11 ... h6 12 ♘e4 g5 13 h4!; 11 ... ♘e3 also leads to a good game for White after 12 ♗xe3 fe 13 0-0 f5 14 ♘g5 f4 15 ♘e2.

However, after 11 ... ♖d8 White can also steer the game into a favourable ending.

12 ♘e4 ♗d5
13 ♘xd6 ♖xd6
14 ♗xf4 ♖e6+
15 ♔d2 ♘f2

Black has to exchange the active white minor pieces as quickly as possible.

16 ♖he1 ♘xd3
17 ♔xd3 ♗xf3
18 gf ♘a6 *(38)*

There are several factors which, when put together, add up to a sizeable advantage for White:

(a) Extra central pawn on d4, typical of many King's Gambit endings.

(b) Good bishop against poorly placed black knight.

(c) An active king.

(d) The opportunity to use the semi-open g-file to cause Black some problems on the kingside.

When you bear in mind that, on top of all these pure chess reasons, Black was already desperately short of time (not uncommon in the King's Gambit), one begins to appreciate the full extent of his difficulties.

19 c4 ♔d7
20 ♖xe6 fe

Black wants to contain White's centre but in doing so further weakens his kingside.

21 ♗e5 g6
22 ♔e4 ♘b4
23 h4! ♘c6
24 h5 gh
25 ♖h1 ♖f8
26 ♖xh5 ♖f7
27 ♖h1!

White's rook is much more active on the first rank, as it can easily switch to the queenside where White is about to open up a second front.

27 ... ♘e7

Of course 27 ... ♘xe5 leads to a very depressing rook ending for Black.

28 b4 c6
29 a4 b5?

Black had to wait passively and hope that the reduced material would give him drawing chances. With the text, he gains a nice outpost for his knight, but the price paid is too high.

30	ab	cb
31	cb	♘d5
32	♖a1!	♘c3+
33	♔d3	♘xb5

33 ... ♖xf3+ 34 ♔c4 ♘d5 looks dangerous, but after 35 ♖xa7+ ♔c8 36 b6!, White's king is free to stroll into the Black position.

34	♔c4	♘d6+ *(39)*

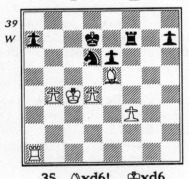

35	♗xd6!	♔xd6
36	♖a6+!	♔e7
37	♖xa7+	♔f6
38	♖xf7+	♔xf7
39	d5	h5
40	de+	♔xe6
41	♔d4!	1-0

Game 12
Illescas – Fernandez
Las Palmas 1987

1	e4	e5
2	f4	ef
3	♘f3	♗e7
4	♗c4	♘f6
5	e5	♘g4
6	0-0 *(40)*	

The young Spanish grandmaster Illescas is one of the very few strong players who employ the King's Gambit with any regularity.

6	...	♘c6

6 ... d5 is also possible and after 7 ed ♕xd6 8 d4 we reach similar positions to those in the note to 7 ... ♗xd6 in Gallagher - Wells.

7	d4	d5
8	ed	

8 ♗b3 would be an error as the blocked nature of the centre allows Black to play 8 ... g5!

8	...	♗xd6

Again 8 ... ♕xd6 should be considered.

9	♕e1+!	

This check gives Black three choices. He can (a) interpose his queen allowing; White a pleasant ending; (b) drop his knight back to e7 giving White time to start an attack; or (c) give up the right to castle and hope to hang on to his extra pawn.

9 ... ♔f8

(a) 9 ... ♕e7 10 ♕xe7+ ♔xe7 (10 ... ♘xe7 11 ♘g5) 11 ♘c3 ♗f5 12 ♘d5+ with a slight advantage to White.

(b) 9 ... ♘e7 10 h3 ♘h6 (or 10 ... ♘f6 11 ♘e5 ♗xe5 12 ♕xe5 0-0 13 ♕xf4 with a clear advantage to White) 11 ♘e5 g5 12 h4 f6 and now Estrin and Glaskov consider that White has the better chances after 13 hg fg 14 ♘f3.

10 ♘c3 *(41)*

10 ... ♗f5

Alternatively:

(a) 10 ... ♘xd4 11 ♘xd4 ♗c5 12 ♖xf4 ♗xd4+ 13 ♔h1 was good for White in Bhend - Muller, Basel 1963. Instead of 12 ... ♗xd4+, 12 ... ♕xd4+ looks like fun, but after 13 ♖xd4 ♗xd4+ 14 ♔f1 ♘xh2+ 15 ♔e2 ♗g4+ 16 ♔d3

♖d8 17 ♘d5 White is over the worst.

(b) 10 ... g5 11 h3. Bhend now gives 11 ... ♘h6 12 ♘e4 ♗e7 13 d5 as slightly better for White, whilst Estrin and Glaskov also consider 11 ... h5!? 12 ♘e4 ♗e7 13 ♕c3 ♖h7 14 ♘fxg5 ♗xg5 15 ♘xg5 ♕xg5 16 ♗xf4 ♕d8 17 d5! ♘e7 18 hg ♗xg4 19 ♗g5 ♘xd5 20 ♖xf7+ ♔xf7 21 ♗xd8 winning for White.

11 ♘h4 ♕g5

After this, White achieves a clearly better ending, but the complications don't look too good for Black. After 11 ... ♘xd4, Freeman - Borwell, Corr. 1970, continued 12 ♗xf4 ♘e6 13 ♗xe6 ♗xe6 14 ♗g3 ♗xg3 15 ♕xg3 ♘f6 16 ♘f5 with good play for the pawn. 14 ♖d1 looks even better, e.g. 14 ... ♗c5+ 15 ♔h1 ♕e7 16 ♘e4 ♗b6 17 h3 with a clear advantage to White.

12 ♘xf5 ♕xf5
13 ♕e4! ♕xe4
14 ♘xe4

The f-pawn is now lost and White's superiority is evident.

14 ... ♖d8

14 ... ♘xd4 15 ♘xd6 cd 16 ♗xf4 ♖d8 17 ♖ad1 leaves Black helpless.

15 c3 ♘a5
16 ♘xd6 ♖xd6
17 ♗e2 ♘e3

| 18 | ♖xf4 | ♖e6 |
| 19 | ♗f3 | c6 |

19 ... ♞c2 20 ♖b1 ♖e1+ 21 ♔f2 ♖h1 22 ♘d5! f6 23 ♖xf6+! wins.

20 b3!

Now White's queenside enters the game with devastating effect.

20	...	♞d5
21	♗a3+	♔g8
22	♗xd5	cd
23	♖f5	♖a6
24	♖xd5	g6
25	♖d7	♞c6
26	♗b2	1-0

Game 13
Spassky – Holmov
Leningrad 1963

1	e4	e5
2	f4	ef
3	♞f3	♗e7
4	♞c3	(42)

| 4 | ... | ♞f6 |

Of course the check on h4 is more critical and will be examined in games 14 and 15.

5 e5

White has a major alternative here in 5 d4 after which 5 ... d5 is Black's only sensible reply. And now:

(a) 6 ed ♞xd5 7 ♞xd5 ♕xd5 8 c4 ♕e4+ 9 ♔f2 ♗g4 10 ♗d3 ♗h4+ 11 g3 ♕xf3+ 12 ♕xf3 ♗xf3 13 ♖e1+ ♗e7 14 ♔xf3 fg 15 ♗f4 ♞c6 16 d5 ♞d4+ 17 ♔xg3 ♔d7 18 ♗e5! (The game Yuneev – Rosentalis, USSR Ch 1989, saw 18 ♗xc7? ♗h4+ with advantage to Black) 18 ... c5 (or 18 ... ♗f6 19 ♗xf6 gf 20 ♔f4) 19 dc+ (19 ♗xd4 cd 20 ♗f5+ is also possible) 19 ... ♞xc6 20 ♗f5+ ♔e8 21 ♞c3 with good play for the pawn.

(b) 6 ♗d3 and Black has several moves:

(b1) 6 ... c5 7 dc de 8 ♞xe4 ♞xe4 9 ♗xe4 ♕xd1+ 10 ♔xd1 led to an unclear ending in Udasina – Akhmilovskaya, Kishniev 1983, but 7 e5 certainly suggests itself.

(b2) 6 ... ♗b4 7 e5 ♞e4 8 0-0! ♞xc3 9 bc ♗xc3 10 ♖b1 ♞c6 11 ♗xf4 ♞xd4 12 ♞g5 ♞f5 13 ♞xf7 ♔xf7 14 g4 with advantage to White (Glaskov).

(b3) 6 ... de (The solid way is probably the best) 7 ♞xe4 ♞xe4 (7 ... ♞c6 8 ♗xf4 0-0 9 c3 ♞xe4 10 ♗xe4 ♗h4+ 11 ♔f1 ♗g4 12 ♕d3 is considered good for Black by Korchnoi and Zak and better for White by Estrin and Glaskov. My view leans towards the latter. Play could continue 12 ... ♔h8 13 ♘xh4 ♕xh4 14 ♕g3 ♕h5 15 ♔g1 with the idea of h3 and ♔h2 to connect the rooks) 8 ♗xe4 ♗d6 9 0-0 ♘d7 (9 ... 0-0 10 ♘e5 gives White an edge) 10 ♕d3 (The immediate 10 c4 occurred in Balashov - Rosentalis, Minsk 1983 and after 10 ... c6 {10 ... c5 is interesting} 11 ♗c2 0-0 12 ♘e1!? ♕h4 13 ♕f3 g5 14 ♕d3 ♘f6 15 ♘f3 ♕h5 16 ♗d2 ♗g4 17 ♖ae1 ♖ad8 18 ♗c3, White had reasonable compensation for the pawn) 10 ... h6 11 c4 c5 12 b4 cd 13 c5 ♗e7 14 ♗xf4 and White held the advantage in Spassky - Najdorf, Varna 1962.

>5 ... ♘g4
>6 d4!?

6 ♗c4 would take us back into familiar territory (see notes to White's sixth move from game 11).

>6 ... ♘e3

6 ... ♗h4+ looks stronger: 7 ♔e2 ♘e3 (7 ... d6 8 ♗xf4 ♘f2 9 ♕e1 ♗g4 10 ed! is good for White) 8 ♗xe3 (8 ♕d3 should be considered) 8 ... fe 9 ♔xe3 d6 10 ed and now by 10 ... 0-0 Black would get some attacking chances in return for the material. Instead, Bangiev - Egin, Simferopol 1985, con-

tinued 10 ... cd?! 11 ♘xh4 ♕xh4 12 ♕e1! ♕g5+ 13 ♔f2+ ♔d8 14 ♔g1 ♖e8 15 ♕f2 ♕e3 16 ♕xe3 ♖xe3 17 ♘d5 ♖e8 18 c3 with the better game for White.

>7 ♗xe3 fe
>8 ♘c4 d6
>9 0-0

9 ♕d3 first, with the option of castling long, looks more accurate.

>9 ... 0-0
>10 ♕d3 ♘c6
>11 ed cd

Better was 11 ... ♗xd6 but White retains an edge after 12 ♘e4 ♗e7 13 ♕xe3. His strong centre pawn and the half-open f-file more than compensate for the two bishops.

>12 ♖ae1 ♗g4
>13 ♖xe3

White's forces are harmoniously deployed.

>13 ... ♔h8
>14 ♘d5 ♗g5
>15 ♘xg5 ♕xg5
>16 ♖g3 ♕h5
>17 ♘e3! *(43)*

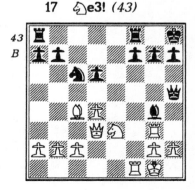

This effective repositioning of the knight will force Black to exchange his main defender of the kingside. He will then be at the mercy of White's rampant major pieces.

17 ...   ♗d7

And not 17 ... ♕e6 18 ♗xe6 fe 19 ♖xf8+ ♖xf8 20 ♖h3!

18 ♘f5   ♗xf5
19 ♖xf5   ♕h4
20 c3   ♕e7
21 ♖e3!

The queen is driven to an inferior square.

21 ...   ♕d7
22 ♖ef3   ♘d8

22 ... f6 would lead to disaster on the white squares. After 23 ♖h5 h6 24 ♕g6!, White threatens both 25 ♗d3 and 25 ♖fh3, whilst 24 ... ♘e7 and 24 ... ♕e8 both fail to 25 ♖xh6+.

23 ♕e4!

As well as preventing ♘e6, the queen now has access to the h-file.

23 ...   g6
24 ♕h4!   ♖g8

24 ... ♕xf5 25 ♖xf5 gf 26 ♕f6+ is obviously hopeless for Black.

25 ♖xf7   1-0

Game 14
Gallagher – Faure
Geneva 1989

1 e4   e5
2 f4   ef
3 ♘f3   ♗e7
4 ♘c3   ♗h4+
5 ♔e2 *(44)*

5 ...   c6

Black naturally wants to create some play in the centre whilst the white king has taken up residence there. The immediate 5 ... d5 is much sharper and is seen in game 15, but Black's other moves are not so critical:

(a) 5 ... ♗e7 (Black retreats his misplaced bishop, but two tempi is a heavy price to pay for White having to move his king) 6 d4 g5 (6 ... ♘f6 is probably best. After 7 ♗xf4 d5 8 ♘xd5 ♘xd5 9 ed ♕xd5 10 ♔f2 White had an edge in Balashov – Agzamov, USSR Ch 1983) 7 ♔f2 d6 8 ♗c4 ♘f6 (If 8 ... ♘h6 9 h4 g4 10 ♘g5 ♗xg5 11 hg ♕xg5 12 ♘d5) 9 h4 ♘xe4+ 10 ♘xe4 d5 11 hg dc 12 ♗xf4 with a very good game for White (Cheremisin).

(b) 5 ... ♗g5 6 d4 ♗h6 7

♔f2 ♘f6 8 ♗c4 ♘g4+ 9 ♔g1 0-0 10 h3 ♘e3 11 ♗xe3 fe 12 ♔h2 d6 13 ♖f1 and, according to Euwe, White has a clear advantage.

(c) 5 ... d6 6 d4 ♗g4 7 ♗xf4 ♗g5 (or 7 ... ♘c6 8 ♕d3 ♘ge7 9 ♔d2 ♗xf3 10 gf ♕d7 11 ♖d1 0-0-0 12 ♔c1 with a slightly better game for White in Planinc – Ivkov, Yugoslav Ch 1976) 8 ♗xg5!? (8 ♕d2) 8 ... ♕xg5 9 ♕d3 ♘c6 10 ♕e3 ♕h5 11 ♔d2 ♕h6?! 12 ♘d5 0-0-0 13 c3 with the better game for White in Ermenko – Kulmanovsky, Corr. 1982/83.

6   d4   d5
7   ♕d2!? *(45)*

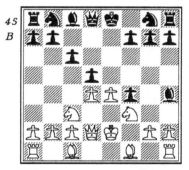

This strange move comes from the fertile mind of Mark Hebden. The white queen will be very active on f4 and should be able to control events in the centre. The alternatives are:

(a) 7 e5?! (As usual, it's rarely good to block the centre in this manner) 7 ... ♗g4 8 ♗xf4 f6 with good play for Black. The game Hebden – Flear, Lewisham 1982, continued: 9 h3 ♗xf3+ 10 ♔xf3 fe 11 ♗xe5 ♘e7 12 g3 0-0+ 13 ♔g2 ♘f5 14 ♔h2 ♘e3 with a clear advantage to Black.

(b) 7 ♗xf4 de (7 ... ♗g4 8 ♕d3 ♘e7 9 ♔d2! ♗xf3 10 ♕xf3 ♘g6 11 ♗e3 de 12 ♕xe4+ ♕e7 13 g3 ♕xe4 14 ♘xe4 ♗e7 15 ♖e1 ♘d7 16 h4 with a good game for White in Spassky – Meyer, Bundesliga 1984/85) 8 ♘xe4 ♕e7 9 ♕d3 (9 ♗e5!? could lead to a total mess after 9 ... f6 10 ♘d6+ ♔d8 11 ♘xh4 fe 12 ♘hf5 ♗xf5 13 ♘xf5 ♕e6 14 de+ ♔c8) 9 ... ♗f5 10 ♗e5 ♗xe4 11 ♕xe4 ♗f6 12 ♔d3!? ♘d7 13 ♗d6 ♕xe4+ 14 ♔xe4 and White has a slightly better endgame.

7   ...   de

7 ... g5? 8 ♔d1! led Black into real trouble in Gallagher – Jacobs, Portsmouth 1986. The game continued 8 ... ♘f6 9 ed ♗g4 10 ♗e2 ♗xf3 11 ♗xf3 cd 12 g3! fg 13 ♕e1+ ♘e4 14 ♘xe4 de 15 ♕xe4+ ♔f8 16 ♕xb7 ♕xd4+ 17 ♗d2 gh 18 ♕b4+ ♕xb4 19 ♗xb4+ ♔g7 20 ♗xa8 and White's extra rook dealt easily with the black pawns.

8   ♘xe4   ♘f6

8 ... ♗e7 9 ♕xf4 ♘f6 10 ♘xf6+ ♗xf6 11 ♔f2 0-0 12 ♗d3 is pleasant for White.

9   ♕xf4   ♘xe4

9 ... ♕e7 10 ♔d3.

10	♕xe4+	♕e7
11	♔d3!?	♕xe4+
12	♔xe4	(46)

Like in the good old days, the monarch leads his army in to battle. Although Black may be able to gain some time attacking the king it is, nevertheless, well centralised for the end-game.

12	...	♗f6
13	♗c4	0-0
14	♗g5	♘d7
15	♖ae1	h6
16	♗xf6	

White could also consider keeping the bishops on.

16	...	♘xf6+
17	♔f4!?	

This is rather provocative. 17 ♔d3 should guarantee White an edge, e.g. 17 ... ♗f5+ 18 ♔d2 ♘e4+ 19 ♔c1 ♘d6 20 ♗b3.

17	...	g5+!?
18	♔e3	

Going the other way looked distinctly dangerous.

18	...	♗f5
19	♘e5?!	

19 ♔d2 was better.

19	...	♘d5+?!

19 ... ♗xc2 seems perfectly safe for Black, e.g. 20 ♖hf1 ♔g7 (20 ... ♘d5+ 21 ♗xd5 cd 22 ♖c1 {or 22 ♖f6 ♔g7 23 ♖ef1 ♗g6 24 ♘xg6=} 22 ... ♖ac8 23 ♔d2 {23 ♖f2 ♗f5} 23 ... ♗e4 24 ♘d7 ♖xc1 25 ♖xc1 ♖d8 26 ♘f6+ ♔g7 27 ♘xe4 de 28 ♔e3 f5 29 ♖c7+ is a very unclear rook ending) 21 ♖f2 ♗g6 22 ♖ef1 ♘d5+ 23 ♗xd5 cd 24 ♖f6 and White threatens to exchange to a drawn king and pawn ending (If 24 ... ♖fe8 25 ♖xf7+!).

20	♔d2	♖ad8
21	♖hf1	

21 ♔c1 ♘b6 22 ♖hf1 (22 c3) 22 ... ♘xc4 23 ♖xf5 ♖xd4 24 ♘xc4 ♖xc4 25 ♖e7 and White's active rooks compensate for the pawn.

21	...	♗e6
22	♔c1	

If 22 c3 then 22 ... c5.

22	...	♘f4!

Suddenly, White's position feels rather loose and he is now forced to sacrifice a pawn.

23	g3!	

Not 23 ♗xe6 fe! with a good game for Black.

23	...	♖d4!
24	♗xe6!?	

24 gf ♗xc4 25 ♘xc4 ♖xc4

26 fg hg 27 ♖e7 and White should be able to hold the balance.

24	...	♘xe6
25	♖f6	♔g7
26	♖ef1	♘d8

This is passive, 26 ... ♘f4! 27 c3 ♖d5 (27 ... ♘d3+ 28 ♔c2) 28 ♘g4 ♘g6 leaves White with insufficient compensation.

27 h4!

White must try to prise open the kingside before Black can consolidate.

27 ... gh

If 27 ... ♖e8 28 ♘xf7! ♖f8 29 hg hg 30 ♘d6! ♖xf6 31 ♘e8+ with equality. Maybe Black can try 27 ... g4, but White remains with sufficient play for the pawn.

28 gh ♖e4? (47)

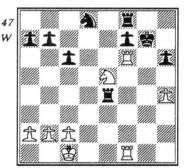

Better is 28 ... ♖d5 29 ♖6f5 f6 30 ♖g1+ ♔h7 31 ♘g6 ♖xf5 32 ♘xf8+ ♔h8 33 ♘g6+ with a draw by perpetual check.

28 ... ♖xh4 also seems to draw: 29 ♘g6 fg 30 ♖xf8 ♖d4 31 ♖e8 ♖d7 32 ♖fe1 ♔f7

33 ♖h8 ♔g7 34 ♖he8 ♔f7 with a repetition.

29 ♘d7! ♖fe8

29 ... ♖g8? 30 ♖g1+ ♔h7 31 ♖xf7+ ♘xf7 (31 ... ♔h8 32 ♖xg8+ and 33 ♖f8+) 32 ♘f6+ ♔h8 33 ♖xg8 mate, is rather pretty.

30	♖g1+	♔h7
31	♖ff1!	

White wins the exchange and the rest wasn't too difficult.

31	...	♖4e6
32	♘f6+	♖xf6
33	♖xf6	♖e7
34	♖d6	♘e6
35	♖gd1	♔g7
36	♖d7	♔f8
37	♖xe7	♔xe7
38	♖f1	f6
39	♖f3	♘g7
40	♔d2	f5
41	♖b3	b6
42	♖a3	a5
43	♖c3	♔d6
44	♖g3!	♘e6
45	♖g6	♔e5
46	♖xh6	f4
47	c3	1-0

Game 15
Arnason – Wedburg
Randers 1985

1	e4	e5
2	f4	ef
3	♘f3	♗e7
4	♘c3	♗h4+
5	♔e2	d5 (48)

Black returns the extra pawn in order to speed up

his development.

6 ♘xd5 ♘f6

In Gallagher - Jacobs, Calella 1985, Black tried a more direct approach: 6 ... ♗g4 7 d4 f5!? 8 ♕d3 ♘e7 9 ♘xf4 ♘bc6 10 c3 ♕d7 11 e5 g5 and I now blundered with 12 g3? gf 13 gh ♘xe5. Instead, the simple 12 ♘h3 would have given White a good game.

7 ♘xf6+ ♕xf6
8 d4

8 d3 deserves serious consideration. By keeping his centre more compact, White rules out any sacrifices from Black. Bangiev - Petrov, Simferopol 1985, continued: 8 ... ♗g4 9 ♕d2 ♕b6 10 ♔d1 ♗xf3+ 11 gf g5 and now 12 c3! would give White the better chances.

8 ... ♗g4
9 c3 c5!?

9 ... ♘c6 has occurred more frequently, but by 10 ♕d2! White obtains a promising position, e.g. 10 ... g5 11 ♔d1! (White's strong centre enables him to calmly improve the position of his king. Once the knight on f3 becomes unpinned, Black will face serious problems) 11 ... 0-0-0 12 ♔c2 ♕h6 (12 ... ♗xf3 13 gf is clearly better for White) 13 ♘xh4 (13 h3!? ♗g3 14 hg is an idea of Bucker's) 13 ... ♕xh4 and now 14 g3! gives White the advantage.

10 dc ♕e7
11 ♕d5!

Black has no time to profit from the exposed position of the queen, as after 11 ... ♘c6 12 ♗xf4 ♖d8, White has 13 ♗d6.

11 ... ♘d7
12 ♗xf4 ♘f6
13 ♕e5 ♘xe4
14 ♔e3! ♗xf3
15 ♗b5+ ♔f8
16 ♕xe7+ ♗xe7
17 ♔xf3 ♘xc5 (49)

The complications are over and White has emerged with a clear advantage due to his active bishops and better king position.

18	♖ad1	a6
19	♗c4	♖c8
20	♖he1	g5!?

The best chance to get his rook into the game, but of course the dark squares are now terribly weak.

21 ♗e5

It could well have been time to part with the two bishops. 21 ♗d6 looks good for White.

21	...	♖g8
22	g4	♖g6
23	b4	b5
24	♗d5	♘d7
25	♗d4	♗f6!

Now Black is able to exchange the bishops under more favourable circumstances. Although White still has an edge, his own weaknesses give Black just enough play to hold the draw.

26	♖e3	♗xd4
27	♖xd4	♖d6
28	♗b7	♖f6+
29	♔g3	♖c7
30	♗f3	♘b6
31	♖ed3	♘c4
32	♖d5	h6
33	h4	gh+
34	♔xh4	♖e7
35	g5	hg+
36	♖xg5	♖e1
37	♖d1	♖f4+
38	♖g4	♖xg4+
39	♗xg4	♖e4
40	♖d4	♖e3
41	♗c8	♖xc3
42	♗xa6	♘a3
43	♔g5	♖c2
44	♖d5	♖xa2
45	♗xb5	½–½

3) Kieseritzky Gambit

1	e4	e5
2	f4	ef
3	♘f3	g5
4	h4	g4
5	♘e5	

Before dealing with the Kieseritzky, I would just like to comment a little on the moves leading up to the Gambit, as these will not be examined elsewhere in this book.

3 ... g5 is, of course, one of the most important replies to the King's Gambit. Black isn't going to play half-heartedly; the soundness of the gambit is going to be tested. The two most common fourth moves for White are 4 ♗c4 and 4 h4. In this book, we shall be only examining the latter. Although 4 ♗c4 is undoubtedly of great interest, both historically and analytically (especially the famous Muzio or Polerio Gambit), I feel that the best White can hope for is an equal game. So, in a book titled *Winning With the King's Gambit*, we sometimes have to be a little ruthless.

4 h4 has the advantage of forcing 4 ... g4, thereby weakening Black's kingside pawns. Now, White has to consider 5 ♘g5. I have to admit that I have a certain weakness for the Allgaier Gambit, and it is with a heavy heart that I inform you that my attempts to rehabilitate the line have not been rewarded. However, the Hamppe-Allgaier Gambit can be seen in chapter five of this book.

5 ♘e5 is the Kieseritzky, a gambit which has been known for over four hundred years. Strangely enough, this is more than one can say for Mr Kieseritzky.

Black now has many ways to combat the gambit, which will be studied in the following games.

Game 16
Bronstein – Dubinin
Leningrad 1947

1	e4	e5

2	f4	ef
3	♘f3	g5
4	h4	g4
5	♘e5 (50)	

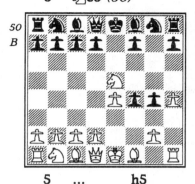

5	...	h5

The so-called "Long Whip" variation. The fact that it is not seen very often these days does not need much explanation. Black falls behind in development and soon becomes exposed to a strong attack.

There are many other possibilities, of which 5 ... d5, 5 ... d6, 5 ... ♗g7 and 5 ... ♘f6 will be seen in subsequent games. The other less common alternatives are dealt with below:

(a) 5 ... ♕e7 6 d4 and now:

(a1) 6 ... f5 is best met by 7 ♗c4 ♘h6 (7 ... ♘f6 8 ♘c3 d6 9 ♗f7+ ♔d8 10 ♗xf4 ♘bd7 11 ♗b3 ♔e8 12 ♘f7 ♖g8 13 ♘g5 ♖g7 14 ♘e6 winning is Cozio's analysis from 1766) 8 ♗xf4 ♕b4+ 9 ♘c3 d6 10 a3 ♕b6 11 ♘d5 ♕xb2 12 ♘xc7+ ♔d8 13 ♘b5

with a crushing attack for White in Szewczak – Donato, Golden Knights 1980.

(a2) 6 ... d6 7 ♘xg4 f5 (after 7 ... ♕xe4+ 8 ♕e2 d5 {8 ... ♗f5 9 ♗xf4 ♕xe2+ 10 ♗xe2 ♗xc2 11 ♘c3 ♗f5 12 ♘d5 is also good for White} 9 ♘f2 ♕xe2+ 10 ♗xe2 ♗d6 11 ♘d3 with advantage to White in Kieseritzky – Dumonch, Paris 1849) 8 ♘f2 ♘f6 9 ♗xf4 ♘xe4 (9 ... fe 10 d5!) 10 ♕h5+ ♔d8 11 ♗e2 ♘f6 12 ♕f3 ♘c6 13 c3 and White is clearly on top.

(b) 5 ... ♘c6 6 d4! ♘xe5 7 de d6 8 ♗xf4 ♕e7 (8 ... ♗g7 9 ♘c3 de 10 ♕xd8+ ♔xd8 11 0-0-0+ ♗d7 12 ♗e3 with a clear advantage to White) 9 ♗b5+ c6 10 ed ♕xe4+ 11 ♕e2 with a better game for White (Bhend).

(c) 5 ... ♗e7 6 ♗c4! ♗xh4+ 7 ♔f1 d5 8 ♗xd5 ♘h6 9 d4 ♗g5 10 ♘c3 c6 11 ♗b3 f6 12 ♘d3 ♕xd4 13 ♗xf4 ♗xf4 14 ♘xf4 ♕xd1+ 15 ♖xd1 with a clear advantage for White (Bilguer).

6	♗c4	♖h7

Black has fared no better with 6 ... ♘h6: 7 d4 ♕f6 (7 ... d6 8 ♘d3 f3 9 gf gf {9 ... ♗e7 10 ♗e3 ♗xh4+ 11 ♔d2 is good for White} 10 ♕xf3 ♗g4 11 ♕f2 ♕d7 12 ♘c3 c6 13 ♗g5 with an excellent position for White, Peev – Atansov, Bulgaria 1954) 8 0-0! ♕xh4 9 ♖xf4 ♗d6 10 ♘f3!

♕g3 11 e5 ♗e7 12 ♘h2 ♕h4
13 ♘c3 ♗d8 14 ♘e4 ♘c6 15
♘f3 with a winning position
for White in Hebden – J.
Benjamin, London 1987.

7 d4

The immediate sacrifice
on f7 is unnecessary.

7 ... ♗h6

After 7 ... d6 8 ♘xf7 ♖xf7
9 ♗xf7+ ♔xf7 10 ♗xf4 White
has a monstrous attack;
alternatively, 7 ... f3 8 gf d6
9 ♘d3! (Now that Black has
managed to keep the f-file
closed the sacrifice on f7 is
not so clear) 9 ... ♗e7 10
♗e3 ♗xh4+ 11 ♔d2. Positions
of this type arise quite frequently in the King's Gambit and are nearly always
favourable for White. This
one is no exception. The
game Kolisch – Anderssen,
Paris 1860, continued: 11 ...
♗g5 12 f4 ♗h6 13 ♘c3 ♗g7 14
f5 ♘c6 15 ♕g1 ♗d7 16 ♖e1
and White stood clearly
better.

8 ♘c3 ♘c6
9 ♘xf7! ♖xf7
10 ♗xf7+ ♔xf7
11 ♗xf4!

This neat tactical point
ensures that Black will be
defenceless against the
coming onslaught.

11 ... ♗xf4
12 0-0 ♕xh4

This is just a waste of
time.

13 ♖xf4+ ♔g7

14 ♕d2 d6

White's attack will be
finished long before Black
can get his queenside into
the game.

15 ♖af1 ♘d8
16 ♘d5 ♗d7 *(51)*

17 e5

Of course White is not
interested in taking the c-
pawn, and instead intro-
duces the e-pawn into the
attack.

17 ... de
18 de ♗c6
19 e6! ♗xd5
20 ♖f7+ ♘xf7
21 ♖xf7+ ♔h8
22 ♕c3+ ♘f6
23 ♖xf6

And instead of resigning,
Black staggered on a few
more moves.

Game 17
Teschner – Dahl
Berlin 1946

1	e4	e5
2	f4	ef
3	♘f3	g5

4	h4	g4
5	♘e5	d5 *(52)*

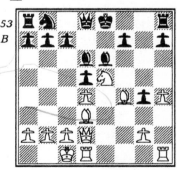

The Bretano variation.

6   d4!

This secures the knight on e5 and attacks the f-pawn. As usual in the King's Gambit, when this drops, Black's kingside resembles swiss cheese.

6	...	♘f6
7	♗xf4	♘xe4

Very similar positions were encountered in game 4.

8   ♘d2!

This is the key move, introduced into practice by Caro. Once Black's only active piece is exchanged, he will have grave difficulties in beating off the white attack.

8   ...   ♘xd2

Other moves don't help:

(a) 8 ... ♕f6 9 g3 ♗h6 10 ♘xe4 de 11 ♘xg4 ♗xg4 12 ♕xg4 ♗xf4 13 ♕xf4 ♕xf4 14 gf with a good ending for White.

(b) 8 ... ♗g7 9 ♘xe4 de 10 ♗c4 0-0 11 c3 ♘d7 12 ♘xf7! with a very strong attack in Lutikov - Shakh-Zade, Tashkent 1950.

9   ♕xd2   ♗g7

Alternatives are:

(a) 9 ... ♗e6 10 0-0-0 ♘d7 11 ♖e1 ♗g7 (11 ... ♗e7 12 ♕e2 ♖g8 13 ♘xf7! ♗xf7 14 ♗xc7! was rather attractive, Cleemskerk - Rhijn, Corr. 1896. Relatively best is 11 ... ♗d6 transposing to 'b') 12 ♘xg4 0-0 13 ♗g5 ♘f6 14 ♘xf6+ ♗xf6 15 ♗d3 with a winning position for White in Caro - Schiffers, 1897.

(b) 9 ... ♗d6 10 0-0-0 ♗e6 11 ♗d3 *(53)* and now:

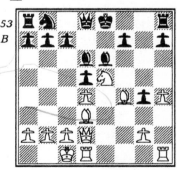

(b1) 11 ... f6 (This wins a piece but subjects Black to a fearsome attack) 12 ♖de1! fe (If 12 ... ♗xe5, 13 ♗xe5! ♔d7 14 ♗xf6! ♕xf6 15 ♖hf1 ♕g7 16 ♖xe6! ♔xe6 17 ♗f5+ ♔e7 18 ♕b4+ wins for White) 13 ♗xe5 ♔d7 14 ♕h6!. This is more efficient than taking the rook, and Black now has no defence, e.g. 14 ... ♗xe5 15 ♖xe5 ♖e8 16 ♖xe6

♖xe6 17 ♘f5; or 14 ... ♗f8 15
♘g7! ♕e7 16 ♘xf8 ♖xf8 17
♖xe6!; or 14 ... ♖e8 15 ♘xd6
♔xd6 (15 ... cd 16 ♖xe6) 16
♘f5 ♕d7 17 ♖e3! with the
simple threat of 18 ♖he1. 17
... ♘c6 (to defend with
... ♘d8) allows 18 ♕f4+.

(b2) 11 ... ♘d7!. With this,
Black should avoid getting
mated: 12 ♖de1 ♘xe5 13
♗xe5 ♗xe5 14 ♖xe5 ♕d7 15
♕g5! ♕e7 16 ♗f5 and, as
Keres points out, White
has a very good ending in
prospect.

10 ♗h6

White doesn't waste any
time in removing the de-
fender of the black squares.

10 ... ♗xh6?

Stronger is 10 ... 0-0 and
now 11 ♗d3!? f6?! 12 ♗xg7!
♔xg7 13 0-0-0! gives White
a strong attack. Also possible are 11 0-0-0 and 11 ♗e2.

11 ♕xh6 ♗e6
12 ♗d3 ♘d7
13 ♘xf7! ♗xf7

13 ... ♔xf7 loses to 14
0-0+ ♔e7 (If 14 ... ♘f6 15
♖f4 is simplest) 15 ♖ae1
♕g8 16 ♗f5 ♘f8 17 ♗xe6
♘xe6 18 ♖f6 and wins.

14 0-0 ♘e5
15 ♖ae1 1-0

Game 18
De La Villa - Fernandez
Barcelona 1990

1 e4 e5

2	f4	ef
3	♘f3	g5
4	h4	g4
5	♘e5	d6 (54)

54
W

This line doesn't have a
very good reputation but,
along with 5 ... ♘f6, it
seems to offer Black the
best chances of reaching
equality.

6 ♘xg4 ♘f6

Black has several alter-
natives:

(a) 6 ... f5? 7 ♘f2 ♘f6 8
d4 fe 9 ♗xf4 d5 10 g4 is
better for White.

(b) 6 ... h5 7 ♘f2 ♘f6 8 d4
♗h6 9 ♗e2. White has a
clear advantage because of
the weakened black king-
side. Keres gave the following line: 9 ... ♘c6 10 ♘c3
♘g4 11 ♘xg4 ♗xg4 (11 ... hg
12 ♘d5 ♗g5 13 g3!) 12 ♗xg4
(12 ♕d3 ♗xe2 13 ♘xe2 ♕f6
14 ♗d2 with a good game
for White - Glaskov) 12 ...
hg 13 ♘d5 f3 14 g3.

(c) 6 ... ♗e7 7 d3! (This
new idea seems to give
White clearly the better

game. Previous authors have only considered 7 d4, after which Black can achieve equality, e.g. 7 ... ♗xh4+ 8 ♘f2 ♕g5 9 ♕f3 ♘c6! 10 ♕xf4! ♗xf2+ 11 ♔xf2 ♕xf4+ 12 ♗xf4 ♘xd4 13 ♘c3! ♗e6! 14 ♘b5 ♘xb5 15 ♗xb5+ ♗d7. White has enough for the pawn, but no more. A correspondence game, Ressegnier – Letz, 1912, continued 16 ♗e2 ♘f6 17 e5 ♘e4+ 18 ♔e3 d5 19 c4 c6 20 ♖ad1 ♗e6 21 ♗f3 f5! 22 ef ♘xf6 23 ♗e5! and a draw was soon agreed) 7 ... ♗xh4+ 8 ♘f2 ♕g5 9 ♕d2! (Now the queen is better off here, as on f3 there would be some risk of getting trapped) 9 ... ♗g3 (The main advantage of 7 d3! is that Black is unable to counter-attack against the centre. Instead, he has to try to hang on to his f-pawn) 10 ♘c3 ♘f6 (if 10 ... ♘c6 11 ♘d5 is strong) 11 ♘e2! (It turns out that the f-pawn cannot be held and 11 ... ♘g4 fails to 12 ♘xg3) 11 ... ♗xf2+ 12 ♔xf2 ♘g4+ 13 ♔g1 ♘e3 14 ♘xf4 ♘xf1 15 ♔xf1 and Black is positionally busted.

7   ♘xf6+

After 7 ♘f2 ♖g8 8 d4 ♗h6 9 ♘c3 ♘c6! White can only achieve a roughly equal game with 10 ♘d3 ♗g4 11 ♗e2 ♗xe2 12 ♘xe2 ♕e7 13 ♗xf4 ♗xf4 14 ♘dxf4

♕xe4 15 ♕d2 0-0-0 16 0-0-0 ♘d5.

7   ...   ♕xf6
8   ♘c3   ♗e6! *(55)*

This is clearly stronger than the old 8 ... c6. As Korchnoi points out, White can then get a strong attacking position by 9 ♗e2 ♖g8 10 ♗f3 ♗h6 11 d4 ♘a6 12 e5! de 13 ♘e4 ♕e7 14 0-0.

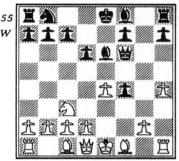

55
W

9   ♕e2!?

With this move, White threatens ♕b5+ and prevents 9 ... ♘c6 (10 ♘d5). A few months earlier the same two players had met in Salamanca where De La Villa chose instead 9 ♕f3 but after 9 ... ♖g8 10 ♕f2 ♘c6! 11 ♗b5 0-0-0! 12 ♗xc6 bc 13 d3 ♗h6, Black had a good position (14 ♕xa7 f3 15 gf ♗xc1 16 ♖xc1 ♕xf3 17 ♖f1 ♕h3 with a clear advantage to Black).

9   ...   ♘d7
10 b3

The only sensible way for White to develop.

10 ...   ♖g8

11 ♗b2   ♗g4!

In this way, Black makes it hard work for White to castle. After 11 ... 0-0-0 12 0-0-0! ♗g4 (of course if Black doesn't accept the offer, he is left with a terrible position) 13 ♕f2 ♗xd1 14 ♕xa7 ♗g4 15 ♗a6! ♘c5 16 ♗b5 ♘d7 (16 ... c6 is a better defence) 17 ♘d5 ♕e6 18 ♗c6! wins.

12 ♕f2   d5!

Black must play actively to compensate for his bad structure.

13 ♗e2!   ♗c5
14 ♕f1

This looks more uncomfortable than it actually is.

14 ...   ♗xe2
15 ♕xe2   0-0-0
16 0-0-0   de
17 ♘xe4   ♕g6
18 ♕c4!

18 ♘xc5 ♘xc5 19 ♕f2 offers Black a chance to solve his problems tactically with 19 ... ♕c6!

18 ...   ♘b6

After this, White's advantage is obvious. 18 ... ♗e7 19 ♘g5 also gives White the better game. 18 ... ♗b6 is recommended by the two players, but 19 ♘g5 still seems to offer White the better chances.

19 ♕xc5   ♕xe4
20 ♖he1   ♕d5

20 ... ♕xg2 is well met by 21 ♕f5+ and 22 ♕xf4.

21 ♕f2   ♖g4
22 ♕f3!?

White opts for the favourable ending.

22 ...   ♕xf3
23 gf   ♖g3
24 ♗f6   ♖f8

The rook ending after 24 ... ♖dg8 25 ♖e7 ♘d5 26 ♖xf7 ♘xf6 27 ♖xf6 ♖xf3 28 ♖f7 is a very difficult one for Black.

25 ♗g5?!

25 c4 would have been an improvement, trying to keep the knight locked out of the game: 25 ... ♘d7 26 ♗b2 ♖xf3 doesn't help because of 27 ♖f1.

25 ...   ♘d5
26 c4?

And this throws away the remaining advantage. After 26 ♖e5! c6 27 ♖f5, Black would still have had a difficult task ahead of him.

26 ...   ♘b4
27 ♔b1   ♘d3

In the last three moves this knight has performed miracles.

28 ♖e7   ♖xf3
29 ♗h6   ♖d8
30 ♖xf7   ♖d7
31 ♖f8+   ♖d8
32 ♖f7   ♖d7
33 ♖f8+   ♖d8
34 ♖f7   ½-½

(notes based on comments by De La Villa and Fernandez in *Informator*).

Game 19
R. Byrne - Keres
USSR - USA 1955

1	e4	e5
2	f4	ef
3	♘f3	g5
4	h4	g4
5	♘e5	♗g7 *(56)*

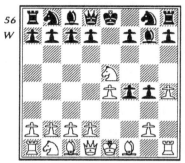

This, the Paulsen variation, was formerly considered one of Black's best defences to the King's Gambit, but recent analysis has cast doubt upon its viability.

6 d4

Schlechter's move, 6 ♘xg4, also deserves consideration: 6 ... d5 7 d4 (not 7 ed?? ♕e7+ and 7 ♘f2 de 8 ♘xe4 ♕e7 9 ♕e2 ♘c6 10 c3 ♘h6 11 ♘g5 ♘e5 12 d4 ♗g4 with advantage to Black) 7 ... de 8 ♗xf4 ♕xd4 9 ♕xd4 ♗xd4 10 c3 and although White has a pawn less, the ending is by no means worse for him, e.g.

(a) 10 ... ♗g7 11 ♗e2 (only 11 ♘f2? was considered in

an analysis by Panov) and 11 ... f5 can be met by 12 ♘e3 with a good game for White. Black probably has to play 11 ... ♗xg4 12 ♗xg4 ♘f6, but after 13 ♗h5 (13 ♗c8 ♘d7 is unclear) White has good play for the pawn.

(b) 10 ... ♗xg4 11 cd ♘c6 12 ♗b5! 0-0-0 13 ♗xc6 bc 14 0-0 f6 15 ♘c3! (Keres) 15 ... ♖xd4 16 ♖ae1. White has a considerable positional advantage, and soon he will be only one doubled (and isolated) pawn down.

6 ... ♘f6 *(57)*

6 ... d6 is the alternative: 7 ♘xg4 ♗xg4 8 ♕xg4 ♗xd4 and now 9 ♘c3! gives White a good game. If Black takes on c3, then the two bishops will far outweigh the ropey pawn structure and after 9 ... ♘f6 10 ♕f5!? ♕e7 11 ♗d3 ♖g8 12 ♗xf4 ♖xg2 13 0-0-0, White had clearly the better game in Gallagher - Sanchi, Paris 1989.

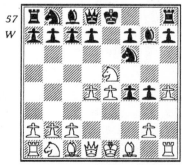

7 ♗c4

7 ♘c3 is the strongest

and most natural move in this position. (I should just mention that I have altered the move order of Byrne – Keres, so that we could use it to examine the variations after 5 ... Bg7. The actual move order was 1 e4 e5 2 f4 ef 3 Nf3 g5 4 h4 g4 5 Ne5 Nf6 6 Bc4 d5 7 ed Bg7 8 d4).

After 7 Nc3 d6 (7 ... 0-0 8 h5 is awkward and 7 ... d5 8 Bxf4 Nxe4 9 Nxe4 de 10 Bc4 is very good for White) 8 Nd3 0-0 (Euwe gave the following variation as good for White: 8 ... Nh5 9 Nxf4 Ng3 10 Rh2 0-0 11 Be2! Nxe2 12 Ncxe2 f5 13 c3 fe 14 Qb3+ Kh8 15 Be3) 9 Nxf4! (This is much better than 9 Bxf4 which runs into trouble against 9 ... Nc6 10 Nf2 Nh5 11 Bg5 f6 12 Be3 Ng3 13 Rh2 f5) 9 ... Nxe4 10 Nxe4 Re8 11 Kf2! Rxe4 12 c3 Qf6 (After any other move 13 Bd3 gives White the advantage) 13 g3 Bh6 14 Bd3 Bxf4 15 Bxf4 Rxf4+ 16 gf Qxf4+, Black's attack looks menacing but Rubinstein demonstrated the correct way for White to continue: 17 Ke2! (17 Kg2 b5!) 17 ... g3 18 Qd2! Bg4+ 19 Ke1 g2 20 Qxg2 Nc6 21 Be2 Re8 22 Rf1! and wins.

7	...	d5
8	ed	Nh5

8 ... 0-0 has been re-commended, but after 9 0-0 White appears to have the better game, e.g.

(a) 9 ... c5 10 dc5 Nh5 11 Nxg4 Qxh4 12 Be2! with advantage to White.

(b) 9 ... Nxd5 10 Bxd5 Qxd5 11 Nc3 (For some reason, only 11 Bxf4 c5! had been considered here) 11 ... Qd8 12 Bxf4 Qxh4 13 Nd5 with a very good game for White.

(c) 9 ... Nh5 10 Nxg4! Qxh4 11 Nh2 Nd7!? (11 ... Qf6 12 Qxh5 Qxd4+ 13 Kh1 Qxc4 14 Bxf4 Bxb2 15 Bh6 with advantage to White) 12 c3 Ndf6 13 Qe1!? (White could also consider keeping the queens on and play something like 13 Nd2 or 13 Qf3. Now a very messy ending is reached) 13 ... Qxe1 14 Rxe1 Bf5 15 Re5 Rfe8 16 Nf3 Bg6 17 Nd2 Rad8 18 Rxe8+ Nxe8 19 Ne5 Nef6 20 Nb3! with a slight advantage to White in Gallagher – Macles, Dijon 1987.

9   0-0

9 Nc3 is rather dubious here: 9 ... 0-0 10 Ne2 c5! 11 Nxf4 (11 ... Bxf4 loses a piece to 11 ... b5, whilst 11 c3 cd 12 cd Nd7 13 Nxd7 Bxd7 was better for Black in Steinitz – Zukertort, Vienna 1882) 11 ... Ng3 12 Ne6 and, as Glaskov points out, Black can gain a clear advantage by 12 ... fe 13 de

♗xe6! 14 ♗xe6+ ♔h8 15 ♕xg4
♕xd4 16 ♕xd4 (16 ♕xg3
♗xe5 17 ♕e3 ♕d6) 16 ... cd 17
♘f7+ ♖xf7 18 ♗xf7 ♘xh1.

9	**...**	**♕xh4**
10	**♕e1!**	

It is time to exchange
queens.

10	**...**	**♕xe1**
11	**♖xe1**	**0–0**
12	**♘c3**	

12 c3 is not sufficiently
active.

12	**...**	**♘d7**

12 ... c5? 13 ♘b5 ♘d7 14
♘c7 ♖b8 15 d6! cd 16 ♘xf7!

13 ♘b5 *(58)*

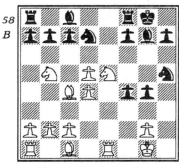

13	**...**	**c6**
14	**♘c7**	

More critical is 14 dc
♘xe5 15 de (15 cb ♗xb7 16
de ♖ac8 17 ♘d6 ♖c5! could
prove dangerous for White)
15 ... bc 16 ♘c7 ♖b8 17 e6
♖b4!. The position is po-
sitively alive with tactical
possibilities, e.g.

(a) 18 e7? ♗d4+ 19 ♔h2 (19
♔h1 ♖xc4 20 ef=♕+ ♔xf8 21
♖e8+ ♔g7 22 ♖xc8 ♘g3+ 23
♔h2 ♘f1+ 24 ♔h1 ♖c5! {Black

may have a rook less, but it
feels like he's a few pieces
up} 25 g3 ♖h5+ 26 ♔g2 f3+
27 ♔xf1 ♖h1 mate) 19 ... g3+
20 ♔h1 ♖xc4 21 ef=♕+ ♔xf8
22 ♖e8+ ♔g7 23 ♖xc8 f3 24
c3 (24 gf ♖xc2) 24 ... f2 25
♗g5 ♗f6 26 ♘e8+ ♔g6 27
♘xf6 ♔xg5 and wins.

(b) 18 ef+ ♔h8 19 ♗e6 (19
♘e6 ♖xc4 20 ♘xf8 ♗xf8 21
♖e8 ♔g7 with advantage to
Black) 19 ... ♗xe6 20 ♘xe6
♖xf7 and White is in
trouble.

White does best to main-
tain the tension and safe-
guard his bishop with 18
♗b3! leaving a very unclear
position on the board.

14	**...**	**cd!**

The exchange sacrifice is
necessary as 14 ... ♖b8 15
d6! is strong.

15 ♘xa8?

This is very optimistic.
Safer was 15 ♗xd5! ♖b8 16
c3 ♘xe5 17 de ♖d8 (17 ...
♔h8 18 ♗d2 ♗f5 19 c4 is
good for White) 18 e6! fe 19
♗xe6+ ♗xe6 20 ♘xe6 ♖e8 21
♗xf4 with about equal
chances (Glaskov).

15	**...**	**dc**
16	**♗d2**	**♘xe5**
17	**de**	**♗f5**
18	**♘c7**	**♗xc2?!**

Keres criticises this
move and gives instead 18
... ♖d8 (taking d5 away
from the knight) 19 ♗c3
♗xc2 and with three pawns

for the exchange, plus active pieces, Black has a clear advantage.

19	♖ac1	♗d3
20	♘d5	b5
21	♗xf4	♖d8

Keres didn't like White's counterplay after 21 ... ♘xf4 22 ♘xf4 ♗f5 23 ♘h5.

22	♘e7+	♔f8
23	♗g5	♖e8
24	♘c6	♘g3

And here Keres thought 24 ... a5 stronger, in order to deprive the knight of the b4-square.

25	♖cd1	♖e6
26	♘xa7	

It was better for White to have played 26 ♘b4 and after 26 ... ♘e2+ 27 ♔f1!, although Black does retain winning chances after 27 ... ♘g3+ 28 ♔g1 ♗g6 29 ♘c6 ♘f5 (Keres).

26	...	♗xe5

Black has a wonderfully centralised position and White's king is feeling the draught.

27	♘xb5	♘e2+
28	♖xe2!	

White bails out, hoping for some drawing chances in the ending.

28	...	♗xe2
29	♖d8+	♖e8
30	♖xe8+	♔xe8 *(59)*

At first glance it seems that the two bishops and an extra pawn should ensure a trivial win for Black,

59
W

but as ever in the King's Gambit, he has trouble mobilising his kingside pawns. Keres, with great skill, eventually broke down White's resistance, and interesting though the ending is, a detailed analysis does not really belong in this book: 31 ♔f2 ♗d3 32 ♘c3 ♔d7 33 ♔e3 ♗h2 34 ♗f4 ♗g1+ 35 ♔d2 h5 36 g3 ♗f2 37 ♘d1 ♗d4 38 ♘c3?! ♔c6?! 39 b4! ♗f6 40 b5+? ♔b7 41 a4 ♗d8 42 ♘d5 ♗e4 43 ♘c3 ♗f3 44 ♔e3 ♗b6+ 45 ♔d2 f6! 46 ♗d6 ♗a5 47 ♗f4 ♗e4 48 ♗d6 ♗d3 49 ♗f4 ♗b4! 50 ♗e3 h4 51 gh g3 52 h5 g2 53 h6 f5 54 ♗f2 f4 55 ♗g1 ♗a5 56 ♗h2 ♗b6 57 h7 ♗xh7 58 ♔e2 g1=♕ 59 ♗xg1 ♗xg1 60 ♘d5 ♗d4 61 ♘xf4 ♗c3 0-1.

Game 20
Gallagher – Hresc
Royan 1989

1	e4	e5
2	f4	ef
3	♘f3	g5

4 h4 g4
5 ♘e5 ♘f6 *(60)*

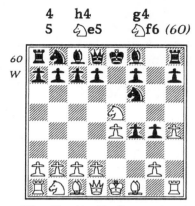

60
W

The Berlin Defence is the most popular answer to the Kieseritzky.

6 ♗c4

The main alternative 6 d4 will be seen in games 22 and 23. White's other possibility, 6 ♘xg4, leads to very sharp play where Black seems to be at least able to hold his own: 6 ... ♘xe4 7 d3 ♘g3 8 ♗xf4 ♘xh1 9 ♕e2+ (9 ♗g5 was refuted in the game Hebden - Stean, Marbella 1982: 9 ... ♗e7 10 ♕e2 h5! 11 ♕e5 f6! 12 ♗xf6 d6 13 ♕e4 ♗xg4 14 ♗xh8 ♔d7 15 ♗d4 ♗xh4+ and White resigned) 9 ... ♕e7 10 ♘f6+ ♔d8 11 ♗xc7+ ♔xc7 12 ♘d5+ ♔d8 13 ♘xe7 ♗xe7 14 ♕g4 d6 15 ♕f4 ♖g8 and Black's pieces should prove stronger than the queen (Hebden - P. Littlewood, Hastings 1982/83).

6 ... d5

Philidor recommended 6 ... ♕e7 but this is not good:

7 d4 d6 8 ♗xf7+ ♔d8 9 ♗xf4 de 10 de+ ♗d7 11 ♗b3 ♕b4+ 12 ♘d2 ♘xe4 13 c3 ♘xc3 14 ♗g5+ with a clear advantage to White (*ECO*).

7 ed ♗d6

7 ... ♗g7 transposes to Byrne - Keres (game 19).

8 d4

8 0-0 is the incredible Rice Gambit, which was once so popular that whole tournaments were devoted to it. Basically, White sacrifices a piece and castles into a raging attack, but according to theory, he miraculously holds the balance. Nevertheless, I still advise you to steer well clear of it.

8 ... ♘h5 *(61)*

61
W

8 ... 0-0! is game 21.

8 ... ♕e7 is doubtful because of 9 ♗xf4 (I once played the rather strange 9 h5 with the idea of preventing the black knight from using this square. After 9 ... ♗xe5 10 de ♕xe5+ 11 ♕e2 ♕xe2+ 12 ♔xe2 f3+ 13 gf gf+

14 ♔xf3 ♗g4+ 15 ♔f4 {Gall-agher – Stevens, Hastings 1988} Black should now have played 15 ... ♘xh5, as after 16 ♔g5? ♘bd7 17 ♖xh5 ♖g8+ he stands very well) 9 ... ♘h5 10 g3! with the idea of meeting 10 ... f6 by 11 0-0.

9   0-0

White has tried other moves:

(a) 9 ♘c3 is best met by 9 ... ♕e7!. Here are a couple of examples from practice:

(a1) 10 ♔f2 (Against 10 ♗b5+, Glaskov gives 10 ... c6 11 dc bc 12 ♘d5 ♕e6 13 ♘c7+ ♗xc7 14 ♗c4 ♕e7 15 ♗xf7+ ♕xf7 16 ♘xf7 as better for Black) 10 ... ♗xe5 11 ♖e1 ♘d7 12 ♗b5 ♕xh4+ 13 ♔g1 0-0 14 de g3 15 ♕d4 c5! 16 dc bc 17 ♗d3 (White dare not leave the f1-a6 diagonal) 17 ... ♖e8 18 b4 ♘xe5! 19 ♖xe5 ♖xe5 20 ♕xe5 ♗g4 21 ♕c5 ♖e8 22 ♘e4 ♖xe4! 23 ♗xe4 ♕h2+ 24 ♔f1 ♕h1+ 25 ♕g1 ♗e2+ and Black won, Murey – Hebden, Paris 1988.

(a2) 10 0-0 ♗xe5 11 ♗b5+ (11 de loses a piece and 11 ♘b5 0-0 12 de a6! is good for Black {Keres}) 11 ... c6 12 dc bc 13 ♘d5 (an ingenious idea) 13 ... ♕xh4! 14 de (14 ♕e1 ♕xe1 15 ♖xe1 f6 16 de cb 17 ♘c7+ ♔f7 18 ♘xa8 ♘a6 19 a4 b4 20 ef ♖d8! is good for Black) 14 ... 0-0 15 ♘xf4 ♘xf4 16 ♗xf4 cb! 17 ♕d5

♕d8!! (This brilliant retreat justifies all Black's previous play, whilst also showing the great power of the queen) 18 ♕xa8 ♕b6+ 19 ♖f2 (19 ♔h1 ♗b7 20 ♗e3 ♕c6! is also terminal) 19 ... ♗b7 20 ♗e3 ♕xe3 21 ♕xb7 g3 22 ♖f1 gf+ 23 ♖xf2 ♕xe5 0-1 Chernakov – Baluyev, Corr. 1977/78.

(b) 9 ♗b5+. This move has been frowned upon for over a century, but it could well be White's best. The reason for its bad reputation is the game Rosanes – Anderssen, Breslau 1863, which went 9 ... c6 10 dc bc 11 ♘xc6 ♘xc6 12 ♗xc6+ ♔f8 13 ♗xa8 ♘g3 with a very strong attack for Black.

However, 11 ♘xc6 is extremely greedy. Instead, the game Carter – Sarfati, Wellington 1985, saw 11 ♗c4! and after 11 ... ♗xe5 12 de ♕a5+ 13 ♘c3 ♘g3? 14 ♕d6 ♘e4 15 ♕d4 White had a very good game. Black should have played 13 ... 0-0!, leaving the situation very unclear.

9   ...   ♕xh4

This is almost universally played, but stronger is 9 ... 0-0! transposing to game 21.

10   ♕e1!   ♕xe1

After 10 ... ♕e7, Keres considers 11 ♕f2! as good for White.

11 ♖xe1 0-0
12 ♘c3 *(62)*

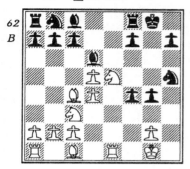

So, the queens are off and White is a pawn down, but that is far from being the whole story. The two d-pawns control a large number of central squares and White's knight can only be removed from its fine outpost by making serious positional concessions. Although Black has a four to one majority on the kingside, it is rather static and the f4-pawn is very weak. If this point falls, then Black's game will probably be in ruins. White will be able to increase the pressure by exchanging the bishop on d6 (♘e4 or ♘b5), and then retreating the knight to d3. This position is more favourable for White than the very similar one reached in Byrne - Keres (game 19), where Black's bishop was better placed on g7 (out of harm's way and exerting some pressure on the long diagonal).

12 ... f6?

Black has two better moves, though White has a fine position in any case:

(a) 12 ... ♘d7 occurred in Gallagher - Boudre, Paris 1990, and White achieved a slight advantage after 13 ♘xg4 (13 ♘b5 ♘xe5 14 de ♗c5+ 15 ♔h1 ♗f2 16 ♖d1 looks risky but could be worth investigation by the reader) 13 ... ♘b6 14 ♗e2 ♗xg4! 15 ♗xg4 ♘f6 16 ♗f3 ♖ae8 17 ♖f1! ♘c4 18 b3 ♘e3 19 ♗xe3 fe 20 ♘e2 ♘e4 21 ♗xe4 ♖xe4 22 c4.

(b) 12 ... ♗f5 is often recommended, but White has at least two ways to get a good position:

(b1) 13 ♗d3 ♗xe5 (13 ... ♗xd3 14 ♘xd3 ♘d7 15 ♘b5 ♖fe8 16 ♗d2 ♘b6 17 b3! is good for White) 14 ♖xe5! (Alapin only considered 14 de with an equal game) 14 ... ♗xd3 15 ♖xh5 ♗xc2 16 ♖g5+ ♗g6 17 ♖xg4 ♘a6 18 ♗xf4 ♖ad8 19 a3 with an edge for White (Mikhalchishin).

(b2) 13 ♘e4 ♗xe4 (In De La Villa - Izeta, Salamanca 1990, Black tried 13 ... ♘d7 but after 14 ♘xd6 cd 15 ♗d3 ♗xd3 16 ♘xd3 ♖fe8 17 ♗xf4 ♘xf4 18 ♘xf4 his pawns were firmly blockaded) 14 ♖xe4 f6 15 ♘xg4 f5 16 ♘h6+ ♔g7 17 ♖e6 ♖f6 18 ♖xf6

♔xf6 19 ♗d3! *(63)*

63
B

Glaskov assesses this position as equal, but at the very least Black has a hard time in front of him, e.g. 19 ... ♘g7 20 c4 c5 21 b4!? cd (Lines like 21 ... b6 22 dc bc 23 ♗b2+ ♔g6 24 ♗xg7 or 21 ... cb 22 c5 leave White clearly better) 22 ♗b2 ♕e5! (If 22 ... ♗xb4 23 ♗xd4+ ♔g6 24 ♘g4 or 22 ... ♔g6 23 ♘g4! are very good for White) and now White can repeat with 23 ♘g8+, but more enterprising is 23 g4!? and after 23 ... fg 24 ♖f1. The position is very hard to judge, but I would certainly take the white pieces in a test case.

13 ♘d3

With his careless twelfth move, Black drove the knight to its ideal square.

13 ... ♗f5

14 ♘b5

White threatens 14 ♘xc7 as well as capturing the bishop.

14 ... ♗xd3

This is a terrible concession to make, but there was little choice.

15 ♗xd3 f5

Otherwise White will play 15 ♗f5.

16 ♘xd6 cd

17 ♖e7

Black can hardly move any of his pieces.

17 ... a5

18 ♖xb7 ♘a6

19 a3 ♖ae8 *(64)*

64
W

Black has managed to bring his queen's rook into the game whilst White has been restoring the material balance. The key factor now is the rather tragic placing of the black knights.

20 ♗d2 ♘b8

21 ♖f1

21 ♖e1 is more accurate.

21 ... ♖e4!

The only chance.

22 ♖e1!?

Taking on e4 gives Black some counterplay as White is unable to blockade the pawns immediately, e.g. 22

♗xe4 fe 23 g3? ♘xg3 24 ♖xf4 ♘e2+.

22	...	♖fe8
23	♗xe4	fe
24	g3!	

But now they can be blockaded. If 24 ... e3, then simply 25 gf.

24	...	f3
25	♔f2	♘f6
26	c4	♘bd7

And now Black's knights are back in the game, but he is too much material down.

27	♗f4	♖c8
28	b3	a4
29	♗xd6	ab
30	c5	b2
31	♖xb2	♘xd5
32	♖xe4	♘7f6
33	♖e5	♘c3
34	♖g5+	♔h8
35	♗e5!	

Offering Black a choice of useless knight forks.

35	...	♘e4+
36	♔e3	♖e8
37	♗xf6+	♘xf6+
38	♖e5	♖d8
39	♔f4	♖f8
40	♔e3	♔g7
41	c6	♘e8
42	♖g5+	♔h8
43	♖xg4	♘d6
44	♖f4	1-0

Game 21
De La Villa – Am. Rodriguez
Bayamo 1991

1	e4	e5
2	f4	ef
3	♘f3	g5
4	h4	g4
5	♘e5	♘f6
6	♗c4	d5
7	ed	♗d6
8	d4	0-0 (65)

65 W

| 9 | 0-0 | |

The only alternative worth considering is 9 ♗xf4, although it is certainly of a dubious nature, e.g. 9 ... ♘h5 and now:

(a) 10 g3 f6 11 ♘d3 ♘xg3 12 ♗xg3 (12 ♖g1 could be a try to keep the variation alive) 12 ... ♗xg3+ 13 ♔f1 ♕e8 with advantage to Black, Pillsbury – Chigorin, Vienna 1903.

(b) 10 0-0. The only theory I've seen on this position is an incredibly inaccurate piece of analysis by Levenfish which runs 10 ... ♘xf4 11 ♖xf4 f6 12 ♖xg4+ ♔h8! winning for Black. However, after 13 ♘g6+ it is White who wins as 13 ... hg 14 ♖xg6 leads to mate. Instead of 12 ... ♔h8, Black had to play 12 ... ♗xg4 even though after 13 ♕xg4+ ♔h8 14 ♘f3 White has good compensation for the exchange.

Unfortunately, the one thing Levenfish appears to have got right is his conclusion: Black is winning, but by playing 10 ... ♕xh4! *(66)*.

66
W

At first I held out some hope for 11 ♗h6, checking variations such as 11 ... ♗xe5 12 de g3 13 ♖f3! ♕h2+ (13 ... ♕xc4? 14 ♗xf8 ♔xf8 15 ♖xf7+! and White should win) 14 ♔f1 ♕h1+ 15 ♔e2 ♕xg2+ 16 ♔e3 when the outcome is unclear. But the feeling that I was trying to defend a lost cause never deserted me, and indeed after 11 ♗h6 the simple 11 ... ♖e8 seems decisive. There are numerous threats: 11 ... ♖xe5 12 de ♗c5+; 11 ... ♘g3; 11 ... g3; and 11 ... ♗xe5 followed by 12 ... g3.

9 ... ♘h5
10 ♘xg4

10 ♗xf4 transposes to the previous note.

10 ... ♕xh4
11 ♘h2

Up until now, this position has been thought of as good for White. Of course, Black has attacking chances, but his structural problems were deemed to be more important. As we shall see, the play of Rodriguez casts serious doubts on that assessment.

11 ♘e5 is certainly not an improvement: 11 ... ♘g3 12 ♖e1 f6 13 ♘f3 ♕h1+ 14 ♔f2 ♘e4+ 15 ♖xe4 ♕xd1 16 ♘c3 ♕h1 and White was a queen down in Hebden – Lima, Hastings 1988/89.

11 ... ♘g3!

Alapin considered the position after 11 ... ♖e8 12 ♘c3 a6 13 ♕f3 ♘g3 14 ♗xf4 ♘xf1 15 ♖xf1 to be in White's favour.

12 ♖e1 *(67)*

67
B

12 ... ♗f5!

This is the new move which causes White so

much trouble. Previously 12 ... ♘d7 with the idea of quickly transferring the knight to g4 had been played, but after 13 ♘d2! ♘f6 14 ♘df3 ♕h5 15 ♖e5!, or 14 ... ♕h6 15 ♘e5, the complications favour White.

By playing 12 ... ♗f5 Black intends to calmly develop his pieces, whilst at the same time ensuring that his knight will remain on d7 to hinder any White counter-play based on something to e5.

I should just mention that the attempt to mate White by brute force is in-sufficient: 12 ... f3 13 ♘xf3 ♕h1+ 14 ♔f2 ♘e4+ 15 ♔e3 ♕h6+ 16 ♔d3 ♕g6 17 ♖xe4 ♗f5 18 ♘bd2 ♖e8 19 ♔c3! ♗xe4 20 ♘xe4 ♕xe4 21 ♕h1! and White has some dan-gerous attacking chances as well as a relatively safe king (Pliester - Korning, London 1983).

13 ♘d2

White decides on the normal plan of bringing his knight to f3 in order to re-inforce the kingside: 13 ♗d3 ♘d7 14 c4 ♖ae8 or 14 ♗xf5 ♘xf5 15 ♘f3 ♕h5 16 c4 ♖ae8 are better for Black.

13	...	♘d7
14	♘df3	♕h5
15	♗e2	

White tries to close the e-file until he has managed

to connect his rooks and hopes that the advance of his c-pawn might disturb Black's smooth progress. As this plan doesn't really work out, White should look for an improvement here, possibly 15 ♗f1 or 15 ♗d2, but Black must stand well.

| 15 | ... | ♖ae8 |
| 16 | c4 | ♖e4! |

This strong move pre-vents 17 c5 on account of 17 ... ♖fe8.

17	♗d2	♖fe8
18	♗d3	♖xe1
19	♗xe1	

If 19 ♘xe1 then 19 ... ♘e2+ or 19 ... f3 are dangerous.

19	...	♗xd3
20	♕xd3	♘e2+
21	♔f1	♖e3!

There are still sufficient pieces for a very strong attack.

22	♕d1	♘f6
23	♗f2	♘g3+
24	♔g1	♘e2+

The professional app-roach.

25	♔f1	♘g3+
26	♔g1 *(68)*	
26	...	♘g4!

This forces White to ex-change off into a bad end-ing as after 27 ♗xe3 fe the threat of ... ♘e2+ or ... ♘xh2 followed by ... ♘e2 gives Black a mating att-ack.

27 ♗xg3 fg

28 ♘xg4 ♛xg4

Black is in control of the only open file and his bishop will become very active once it arrives at f4.

29 ♖c1

29 ♛d2 ♛e4 30 ♖e1 ♗f4! illustrates the strength of Black's position.

29 ... ♛e4!

Centralisation.

30 ♛c2 f5!
31 ♛xe4 fe
32 ♘e5

32 ♖e1 is refuted by 32 ... ♗f4.

32 ... ♖e2
33 c5

At last White finds time to get this advance in, but after ...

33 ... ♗f8

... ♗h6 - e3 is in the air.

34 ♘g4

After 34 ♘c4 b5! is strong.

34 ... e3
35 ♘f6+ ♔f7
36 ♘e4 ♖xb2
37 ♘xg3 ♔g6!

Of course Black doesn't

allow ♘f5.

38 ♖f1 ♗g7
39 ♖f4 ♖d2!

Now the d-pawn can't be defended (40 ♘f5 ♖d1+ and ... e2). White tries a last trick.

40 ♖g4+ ♔f7
41 ♖f4+ ♔g8
42 ♖g4 h5!

42 ... ♖xd4?? 43 ♖xg7+!

43 ♘xh5

If 43 ♖g5 h4 is similar.

43 ... ♖d1+
44 ♔h2 e2
45 d6 cd
46 cd e1=♛
47 d7 ♛g1+
0-1

Game 22
Hellers - Ernst
Swedish Ch 1985

1	e4	e5
2	f4	ef
3	♘f3	g5
4	h4	g4
5	♘e5	♘f6
6	d4	*(69)*

This is a far more positional approach to the Berlin Defence than 6 ♗c4. White is happy to exchange his e-pawn for Black's f-pawn in order to obtain classic King's Gambit style compensation.

6 ... d6

This is the normal move, but 6 ... d5 transposes to game 17 and 6 ... ♗g7 to game 19.

7 ♘d3

♘xf7 sacrifices never really work in the Kieseritzky, as Black hasn't had to waste time on h6.

7 ... ♘xe4

8 ♗xf4

8 ♕e2 ♕e7 9 ♗xf4 transposes back to the main lines, but by adopting this move order White misses out on the chance to play 9 ♗e2!?

You may have been wondering what this classic compensation actually is? The answer is Black's dreadful pawn structure on the kingside which will make it very difficult for him to utilise his extra pawn. Meanwhile, White has some fine outposts (especially f4) and potentially strong pressure on the f-file. White is also not bothered by an exchange of queens as this by no means lessens the pressure.

8 ... ♕e7

This seems the most logical. Black plans to develop his queenside as quickly as possible and then castle long.

8 ... ♗g7 has also been seen quite frequently. White now has:

(a) 9 ♘c3?! (This occurred in the famous first encounter between Spassky and Fischer, Mar del Plata 1960). After 9 ... ♘xc3 10 bc c5! (nibbling at the centre - Fischer) 11 ♗e2 cd 12 0-0 ♘c6 13 ♗xg4 0-0 14 ♗xc8 ♖xc8 15 ♕g4 f5 (or 15 ... ♔h8) Black had the better game.

(b) 9 c3 ♕e7 (It would be dubious to castle short, for example 9 ... 0-0 10 ♘d2 ♖e8 11 ♘xe4 ♖xe4+ 12 ♔f2 ♕f6 13 g3 ♗h6 14 ♕d2! with advantage to White) 10 ♕e2 (10 ♗e2!?) 10 ... h5 11 ♘d2 ♘xd2 12 ♕xe7+ (12 ♔xd2!?) 12 ... ♔xe7 13 ♔xd2 and White has good play for the pawn.

9 ♕e2

This move has usually been the automatic response here, but 9 ♗e2 is certainly deserving of attention. Due to the current state of the main line (see game 23) I have decided to examine this in some detail. After 9 ♗e2 Black has a large number of replies, of which the most important are seen below:

(a) 9 ... h5. Black secures his g-pawn once and for all, but in doing so neglects his development. 10 ♘d2 (The knight on e4 is immediately challenged) 10 ... ♗f5 11 0-0! (One of the main ideas behind 9 ♗e2 is to castle kingside, and often this has to be done even at the cost of another pawn) 11 ... ♕xh4 (Black could conceivably decline the offer with 11 ... ♘d7, but White can obtain good chances with 12 ♘xe4 ♗xe4 13 ♕d2) 12 ♘xe4 ♗xe4 13 ♘f2!. White's lead in development assures him of a powerful attack. Black's first problem is to find a good retreat for the bishop:

(a1) 13 ... ♗c6 14 d5!? ♗d7 15 ♕d4 ♖g8 16 g3 followed by 17 ♖ae1 looks very menacing.

(a2) 13 ... ♗f5 14 ♗d3!?

(a3) 13 ... ♗g6 14 ♗b5+ c6 (14 ... ♘d7 is more resilient) 15 ♕d2!. Now the bishop cannot be taken: 15 ... cb 16 ♗g5 ♕g3 17 ♖ae1+ and 18 ♖e3 nets the queen, whilst 15 ... g3 16 ♘h3 cb leads to a similar conclusion after 17 ♖ae1+ ♔d7 18 ♗g5 ♕g4 19 ♖f4; Black can try 15 ... ♕f6 but after 16 ♖ae1+ ♔d7 17 ♗g5 ♕g7 18 ♗a4 he will do well to survive the coming onslaught.

(a4) It should also be mentioned that 13 ... g3 only serves to worsen the black position. Either the simple 14 ♘h3 or 14 ♗xg3 ♕xg3 15 ♘xe4 ♕e3+ 16 ♔h1 ♕xe4 17 ♗b5+ should win for White.

(b) 9 ... ♘c6 10 c3 (10 d5 ♘d4) 10 ... ♗f5 11 d5 (The natural move 11 ♘d2 fails to 11 ... ♘xc3! 12 bc ♗xd3; 11 0-0 is also interesting, but I feel that by playing 11 d5 White reduces Black's options. For example, after 11 0-0 ♕xh4 12 ♘d2 Black could consider giving back one of his pawns with 12 ... 0-0-0, in order to reduce White's initiative) 11 ... ♘b8 (Other squares look worse. If 11 ... ♘e5 then 12 ♗xe5 de 13 ♗xg4) 12 0-0 (12 ♘d2 still fails to 12 ... ♘xc3!; however, 12 ♕b3!? is an alternative as 12 ... b6 13 ♘d2 looks fine for White and 12 ... ♘g3!? 13 ♗xg3 ♗xd3 14 0-0 ♗xe2 15 ♖e1 ♗h6 16 ♕c2 (16 ♕xb7!? can be investigated by the reader) 16 ... 0-0 17 ♖xe2 ♕f6 {17 ... ♕d7!?} 18 ♖e4 ♕g6 19 ♕e2 gives good compensation for the pawn) 12 ... ♕xh4 13 ♘d2 and now:

(b1) 13 ... g3 14 ♘f3. Where does the queen go? If 14 ... ♕h5 then 15 ♕a4+ ♘d7 16 ♖ae1 with the threat of ♗d1 looks good for

White; 14 ... ♕e7 15 ♘d4 ♕h4 (15 ... ♗g6!?) 16 ♗xg3! (White is not obliged to repeat) 16 ... ♘xg3 17 ♘xf5 ♕h1+ 18 ♔f2 ♘xf1 and now 19 ♕a4+ ♔d8 20 ♗g4! looks bone-crushing.

(b2) 13 ... ♘xd2 14 ♕xd2 ♗e7 15 ♖ae1 ♘d7?! 16 g3! ♕f6 (16 ... ♕h3 17 ♖f2 or 16 ... ♕h5 17 ♖f2 ♕g6 18 ♗f1 with the idea of doubling on the e-line) 17 ♗xg4! and as 17 ... ♗xg4 is met by 18 ♗g5! Black is in deep trouble.

(c) 9 ... ♗f5 10 ♘c3!? (10 ♘d2? ♘c6! causes White problems with his d-pawn – 11 d5 ♘d4 or 11 c3 ♘xc3. 10 c3 can be considered as an alternative to the text) 10 ... ♘xc3 11 bc. This position is very similar to the Spassky – Fischer game (examined above in variation 'a' to Black's eighth move) with the important difference that Black has developed his queen's bishop to f5, rather than his king's bishop to g7. This means that counter-attacking against the centre with ... c5, as Fischer did, will be less productive. Also the bishop on f5 could find itself in an exposed position after White brings a rook to the f-file.

Practical tests are awaited on 9 ♗e2.

9	...	♘c6
10	c3	♗f5
11	♘d2	♘xd2

For 11 ... 0-0-0 see game 23.

| 12 | ♔xd2 | ♕xe2+ |
| 13 | ♗xe2 | (70) |

70
B

We have reached an ending typical of the Kieseritzky, with the sort of compensation outlined above. White's rooks are now ready to occupy the two open files.

13	...	♗g7
14	♖hf1	♘e7
15	♖ae1	h5
16	♗d1!	

White's bishop heads for its most attractive diagonal, whilst simultaneously unblocking the e-file for the rook.

16	...	♔d7
17	♗b3	♖af8
18	♗g5	

White is willing to invest some time to force Black to advance his f-pawn, thereby weakening e6.

| 18 | ... | f6 |

19 ♗f4   ♘g6?!

Black lets the white pieces in without a struggle. 19 ... ♘g6 20 ♗g3 ♗h6+ 21 ♔c2 ♗xd3+ 22 ♔xd3 is also good for White; Black had to wait and play something like 19 ... ♖e8. White then has a number of ideas (for example, 20 ♖f2 to prepare the doubling of rooks or 20 ♗g3!? threatening ♖xe7+) but it's not clear if they will be strong enough to break down the black position.

20 ♗e6+   ♔d8
21 d5?!

21 ♗e3, with the idea of ♘f4, was an interesting alternative. The text unnecessarily weakens e5.

21 ...   ♗f7
22 c4   ♘g6
23 g3   ♗xe6
24 ♖xe6   ♘e5
25 ♗xe5!   fe
26 ♖xf8+   ♗xf8

With some exchanges Black has relieved most of the pressure from his position, but he is still left with the inferior minor piece and weak kingside pawns. On the other hand, he does still have an extra pawn, which should be enough to hold the balance.

26 ... ♖xf8 27 ♖g6 ♖f7 28 ♔e3 intending ♔e4 would have given White good play.

27 ♘f2

He knows where he is going.

27 ...   ♗e7?!

27 ... ♖h6 was more sensible. After 28 ♖xh6 ♗xh6+ 29 ♔d3 ♔e7 30 ♘e4 a draw seems very likely although White might be able to create some slight problems for Black by advancing his queenside pawns.

28 ♘e4   ♔e8
29 b4   ♔d7
30 ♖g6   c6
31 ♖g7   ♖f8

Black realises that he cannot leave his rook passively on h8 for ever, so he switches to the f5-square, from where he might have a chance of active counterplay one day.

32 ♖h7   cd
33 cd   ♖f5
34 a4!

Although Black is tied down on the kingside, White will be unable to win without opening another front which will make his greater mobility tell.

34 ...   a6
35 b5   ab
36 ab   ♔d8?

36 ... b6! would have offered drawing chances.

37 b6! *(71)*

Black is beginning to run out of space.

37 ...   ♔d7
38 ♔e2

Zugzwang.

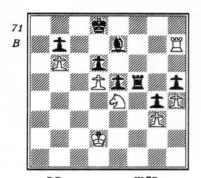

56	Rf8+	Ke7
57	Rb8	Kf6
58	Kh4	e4?

After this, White has no trouble containing the pawns. Better was 58 ... Rc5, followed by pushing the d-pawn. White should still win, however.

59	Ng4+!	Ke7
60	Ne3	Rc5
61	Kg4	d5
62	Nf5+	Kd7
63	Kf4	Kc7
64	Ra8	b4
65	Ra1	Kb6
66	g4	Rc2
67	Ne3	Rd2
68	g5	Kb5
69	g6	Rf2+
70	Ke5	Rf8
71	Nxd5	b3
72	Kxe4	Kc5
73	Rc1+	Kd6
74	Nf4	Re8+
75	Kf5	Re5+
76	Kf6	Re4
77	Rd1+	Kc5
78	Ne6+	Kb4
79	g7	Rg4
80	Ng5	Rf4+
81	Ke5	1-0

38 ... Rf3

38 ... Kd8 39 Rh8+ wins at least a pawn.

39	Rxh5	Rb3
40	Rh7	Rxb6
41	Nf6+	Kd8
42	Nxg4	

Black has managed to activate his rook, but White has won back his pawn and his kingside pawns are about to start marching.

42	...	Rb2+
43	Kf3	b5
44	h5	Rb3+
45	Kg2	Rb2+
46	Kh3	Rb1
47	h6	Bf8
48	Rh8	Ke7
49	h7	Bg7
50	Rg8	Rh1+
51	Nh2	Kf7
52	h8=Q	Bxh8
53	Rxh8	Rd1
54	Rb8	Rxd5
55	Kg4?!	

It would have been better to play 55 Kh4, leaving the g-pawn's route free.

| 55 | ... | Kf6 |

**Game 23
D. Holmes – Hebden
British Championship,
Plymouth 1989**

1	e4	e5
2	f4	ef
3	Nf3	g5
4	h4	g4

5	♘e5	♘f6
6	d4	d6
7	♘d3	♘xe4
8	♕e2	♕e7
9	♗xf4	♘c6
10	c3	♗f5
11	♘d2	0-0-0
12	0-0-0	

Bangiev considers that 12 ♘xe4 ♕xe4 13 ♔d2 deserves attention.

12 ... ♖e8 *(72)*

12 ... ♗g7 is an alternative, with the idea of bringing the king's rook to e8. Gallagher – Bachmayr, Zug 1991 continued: 13 ♘c4?! h5! 14 ♖e1 ♖he8 15 ♕c2?! ♕d7 16 g3 ♗xd4! 17 cd ♘xd4 18 ♕d1 ♕c6 (Black has tremendous compensation for the piece) 19 ♘b4 ♕c5 20 ♗e3 ♕xb4 21 ♗xd4 ♘xg3 22 ♖xe8 ♖xe8 23 a3 ♕e1 24 ♖g1 ♘xf1 25 ♖xf1 ♕e4! 26 ♘e3? ♕b1+ 27 ♔d2 ♕d3+ 28 ♔e1 (28 ♔c1 ♖xe3) 28 ... c5 (28 ... ♖xe3+ wins easily) 29 ♕a4 (Up to this point, my opponent had played a fantastic game, but fortunately for me he had less than a minute to reach move 40) 29 ... ♕e4? (29 ... ♗d7! wins at once) 30 ♖f4! ♕e6 31 ♔d2 cd 32 ♕xd4 ♗e4 33 ♕xa7 (I began to have some hope) 33 ... ♗c6 34 ♘c4! (The best move under the circumstances) 34 ... ♕e1+ 35 ♔c2 ♕e6?! 36 ♔c3! g3? 37 ♖xf7! ♕e1+ 38 ♔b3 ♕e6 39 ♕a8

mate. An absolute scandal!

Instead of 13 ♘c4?! White can play 13 d5. After 13 ... ♘xd2 14 ♕xd2 (14 dc ♕xe2 15 ♗xe2 ♘e4 is fine for Black) 14 ... ♘e5 15 ♕f2 (15 ♘b4!? deserves attention) 15 ... ♘xd3+ 16 ♗xd3 ♗xd3 17 ♖xd3 ♔b8 18 ♗g5 f6 19 ♖e3 (19 ♖e1 ♕d7 is about equal) 19 ... ♕d7 (19 ... ♕f7 20 ♖e6 with good compensation for the pawn) 20 ♗xf6 ♗xf6 (20 ... ♖hf8 21 ♖e6) 21 ♕xf6 ♖hf8 22 ♕g5 (22 ♕e6) 22 ... ♖f2 23 ♖e7 ♕b5 24 ♖e2! ♖ff8 25 ♖he1 with an edge for White. Of course there may be improvements for either side as this analysis is untested.

13 ♖e1?!

This is just one of several mistakes White can make in this position. For example:

(a) 13 g3? (13 ♕e3? meets a similar accident) 13 ... ♘xc3! 14 ♕xe7 ♘xa2+ 15 ♔b1 ♖xe7 16 ♔xa2 ♗xd3 17 ♗xd3 ♘b4+ 18 ♔b3 ♘xd3

0-1 Hajek - Bures, Corr. 1962.

(b) 13 d5?. Glaskov and Estrin considered this to lead to a good game for Black after 13 ... ♘xd2 14 ♕xd2 ♘e5 15 ♗xe5 de 16 ♕f2 ♕d7. This is a very strange assessment as after 17 ♕xa7 ♗h6+ (17 ... ♕xd5 18 ♘f4!) 18 ♔b1 ♕xd5 19 ♔a1! Black is in deep trouble. 19 ... e4 is met by 20 ♕a8+ ♔d7 21 ♘c5+! and 19 ... c6 20 ♗e2 ♕d6 21 ♘f2!? ♕c7 (21 ... ♕b8 22 ♕a4) 22 ♗xg4 ♗xg4 23 ♘xg4 ♗f4 (23 ... ♗g7 24 ♘e3 is good for White) 24 ♘f6 ♖d8 25 ♘d7!! ♖xd7 26 ♕a8+ ♕b8 27 ♕xb8+ ♔xb8 28 ♖xd7 with a winning ending for White.

Unfortunately, after doing this analysis the truth was discovered. White does indeed lose, and very quickly. If you have read 'a' you should have no problem working out the solution: 13 ... ♘xc3! 14 ♕xe7 ♘xa2+ 15 ♔b1 ♘xe7 16 ♔xa2 ♘xd5 and White must lose a piece, leaving him at least three pawns behind.

(c) 13 ♘c4 is well met by 13 ... ♕d7 14 ♘e3 h5 when White does not have enough for the pawn.

(d) 13 ♘xe4 (This is relatively best) 13 ... ♕xe4 14 ♕xe4 ♗xe4 15 ♘f2 f5 and it will be very difficult for Black to convert his material advantage into a full point.

| 13 | ... | ♕e6! |

This attack on a2 proves rather embarrassing as 14 ♔b1 fails to 14 ... ♘xd2+ 15 ♗xd2 ♕xe2 16 ♗xe2 ♖xe2.

| 14 | a3 |

14 ♘xe4 ♕xa2.

| 14 | ... | ♕a2 |

White is suddenly in all sorts of trouble.

| 15 | ♕d1 | h5 |

This move emphasises White's helplessness, but the immediate 15 ... ♗g7 was probably more precise.

| 16 | g3 | ♗g7 |
| 17 | ♖h2 | ♘xc3! |

This neat sacrifice ends the game.

| 18 | bc | ♕xa3+ |
| 19 | ♔c2 |

19 ♔b1 ♖xe1 20 ♕xe1 ♕xc3 wins.

| 19 | ... | ♗xd4 |
| 20 | ♕a1 |

If 20 cd ♘b4+ 21 ♔b1 ♖xe1 22 ♕xe1 ♕a2+ 23 ♔c1 ♕c2 is mate. Now, it's almost as strong.

| 20 | ... | ♘b4+ |

0-1

4) Modern Defence

1	e4	e5
2	f4	ef
3	♘f3	d5 (73)

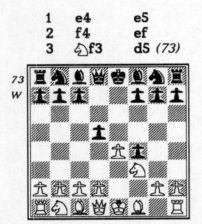

73
W

Black makes no attempt to keep the gambit pawn and concentrates on opening lines for his pieces and joining in the battle for the initiative.

As a King's Gambit player, you should make sure that you are thoroughly acquainted with the lines arising from the Modern Defence, not least because it has been recommended by several publications as a simple way to equalise against the King's Gambit. But of course this is not the case, even when the position becomes simplified White often maintains a slight, but persistent advantage. This can usually be attributed to the extra central pawn in his possession, or to the activity of his major pieces on the open files of the kingside.

After 4 ed ♘f6, I have selected two of the most interesting lines for White (at least in my opinion): 5 ♗c4 and 5 ♗b5+. The latter is normally regarded as the main line, but recently Black has been finding life more difficult against 5 ♗c4. Let's have a look at some games.

Game 24
Spassky – Bronstein
Leningrad 1960

1	e4	e5
2	f4	ef
3	♘f3	d5
4	ed	♗d6 (74)

Normally in this variation, Black captures the pawn on d5 and White the one on f4. With 4 ... ♗d6, however, Black intends a different sort of game, but one in which he will have to be careful to avoid being steam-rollered by the white centre.

Apart from 4 ... ♘f6 (the subject of subsequent games), there are a number of other rarely played alternatives:

(a) 4 ... ♕xd5 (This can't be good) 5 ♘c3 ♕e6+ (Other queen moves are no better, e.g. 5 ... ♕h5 6 ♗e2; or 5 ... ♕a5 6 ♗c4 ♘f6 7 ♕e2+ ♗e7 8 d4; 5 ... ♕d8!?) 6 ♗e2 ♗d6 7 0-0 ♘e7 8 d4 0-0 9 ♘g5 with a clear advantage to White.

(b) 4 ... ♗e7 5 ♗c4 (or 5 ♗b5+ c6 6 dc bc 7 ♗c4 ♗h4+ 8 ♔f1 with a good game for White) 5 ... ♗h4+ 6 ♔f1. This position could also be reached via the Cunningham. It seems to me that Black has wasted too much time. The game Blaess – Schoppmeyer, Bundesliga 1986/87, continued: 6 ... ♗f6 7 d4 ♘e7 8 ♘c3 0-0 9 ♗xf4 b5 10 ♘xb5 ♗a6 11 d6! cd 12 a4 and Black has no compensation for the pawn.

(c) 4 ... c6 5 d4 ♗d6 (After 5 ... cd 6 ♗xf4 White's favourable pawn structure will guarantee a slight advantage). Now 6 ♘c3 leads to the Nimzowitsch Counter-Gambit (which we consider later), but 6 dc ♘xc6

7 ♗d3 is also interesting.

74
W

5   ♘c3

Spassky has a liking for an early ♘c3 in many lines of the King's Gambit, but here it only serves to limit White's options by blocking the c-pawn.

After the natural 5 d4, Black normally chooses from 5 ... ♘f6 or 5 ... ♘e7:

(a) 5 ... ♘f6 6 c4 (Against 6 ♕e2+ Black should play 6 ... ♗e7!. It would then be dangerous for White to try and win a pawn as Black can create awkward threats on the e-file, e.g. 7 c4 0-0 8 ♗xf4 ♖e8 9 ♘c3 ♗d6 10 ♘e5 c5!) 6 ... 0-0 (6 ... ♗g4 7 ♗d3 0-0 8 0-0 and White's central pawns are strong). In this position, 7 ♘e5 is normally recommended, but with the rest of his pieces still at home, this knight foray looks premature, e.g. 7 ... ♖e8 8 ♗xf4 ♘bd7 9 ♗e2 (9 ♕e2 ♘xe5 10 de ♘g4) 9 ... ♘xe5 10 de ♗xe5 11 ♗xe5 (or 11 0-0

♗xb2) 11 ... ♖xe5 12 0-0 ♕e7 13 ♘c3 ♕c5+ 14 ♔h1 ♗d7 and Black controls the dark squares and the e-file.

Instead of 7 ♘e5, 7 ♗e2 looks better. After 7 ... ♖e8 8 0-0 c5 9 ♘c3 (9 b4!?) 9 ... ♗g4 10 ♔h1 White has the better chances.

(b) 5 ... ♘e7 6 c4 ♘g6 7 ♗e2!? (7 ♗d3 0-0 8 0-0 c5 9 b4 b6 10 bc bc 11 ♘c3 ♗g4 Hebden – Johansen, London 1982, and now 12 ♗xg6!? fg 13 ♘e4 is a recommendation of Bangiev's) 7 ... 0-0 8 0-0 b6 9 ♘c3 c6 10 dc ♘xc6 11 ♘b5 ♗e7 12 d5 ♗c5+ 13 ♔h1 ♘ce7 14 ♘fd4 a6 15 ♘c3 ♗d6 16 ♘e4 ♗e5 17 ♘f3 ♗b8 18 b4 with a clear advantage to White in Gallagher – Boulard, Paris 1990.

| | 5 | ... | ♘e7 |

5 ... ♘f6 6 ♗c4 transposes to the notes of game 26.

	6	d4	0-0
	7	♗d3	♘d7
	8	0-0	h6?

This move is a serious waste of time and serves merely to weaken the kingside. Spassky demonstrated two ways for Black to achieve rough equality:

(a) 8 ... ♘f6 9 ♘e5 ♘exd5 10 ♘xd5 ♘xd5 11 ♗xf4 ♘xf4 12 ♖xf4 ♕g5;

(b) 8 ... ♘g6 9 ♘e4 ♘f6 10 ♘xd6 ♕xd6 11 c4 ♗g4.

| | 9 | ♘e4! |

Preparing the advance of the c-pawn.

	9	...	♘xd5
	10	c4	♘e3
	11	♗xe3	fe
	12	c5	♗e7
	13	♗c2!	

This strong move is the point behind White's play. If instead 13 ♕e2, then 13 ... ♘f6 gives Black satisfactory play, e.g. 14 ♕xe3 ♘d5 or 14 ♘xf6+ ♗xf6 15 ♕xe3 ♖e8.

| | 13 | ... | ♖e8 |

Black vacates f8 for his knight.

| | 14 | ♕d3 | e2 (75) |

75
W

| | 15 | ♘d6!? |

Whilst probably not the strongest move in the position (15 ♖f2 gave White the better game with no risk), it certainly came as a shock for his opponent, who was already short of time.

| | 15 | ... | ♘f8? |

And immediately Bronstein makes a decisive mistake. It was essential to remove the lone intruder with 15 ... ♗xd6. After 16 ♕h7+ ♔f8 17 cd ef=♕+ 18 ♖xf1 cd 19 ♕h8+ ♔e7 20 ♖e1+ ♘e5 21 ♕xg7 ♖g8 22 ♕xh6 ♕b6 23 ♔h1 ♗e6 24 de d5; White has some play for the exchange, but the outcome is far from clear.

16 ♘xf7!

This must have been the reason that Spassky could not resist the risky combination.

16 ... ef=♕+
17 ♖xf1 ♗f5

17 ... ♔xf7 18 ♘e5++ ♔g8 19 ♕h7+! ♘xh7 20 ♗b3+ ♔h8 21 ♘g6 mate is why Black can't take the knight. 17 ... ♕d5 is another try, but 18 ♗b3 is very strong, e.g. 18 ... ♕h5 19 ♘xh6+ ♔h8 20 ♘f7+ ♔g8 21 ♘g5+ ♔h8 22 ♗f7! and wins. 18 ... ♕xf7 doesn't save Black either: 19 ♗xf7+ ♔xf7 20 ♕c4+ ♔g6 21 ♕g8 and Black is defenceless.

After 17 ... ♗f5 White has only a minimal material deficit, but his attack is still raging.

18 ♕xf5 ♕d7
19 ♕f4 ♗f6
20 ♘3e5 ♕e7

If 20 ... ♗xe5, 21 ♘xe5 ♕e7 22 ♕e4! is very strong.

21 ♗b3

Black has disastrous white squares.

21 ... ♗xe5

22 ♘xe5+ ♔h7
23 ♕e4+ 1-0

Game 25
Gallagher – Ferretti
Chiasso 1991

1	e4	e5
2	f4	ef
3	♘f3	d5
4	ed	♘f6
5	♗c4	*(76)*

5 ♗b5+ will be seen in games 29–31.

Although 5 ♗c4 is less forcing than 5 ♗b5+, it certainly doesn't contain less venom. White calmly develops his bishop, anticipating the opening of the a2-g8 diagonal after 5 ... ♘xd5 (games 27–28). In this game, however, we shall be examining various alternatives for Black apart from 5 ... ♗d6, which is game 26.

5 ... ♘bd7

Black borrows a plan from the Caro-Kann Panov Attack, but he will soon realise that White has a c-pawn (instead of just doubled isolated d-pawns). Another dubious move is 5 ... ♕e7+ which is answered by 6 ♗e2! leaving the black queen very badly placed. The game Gallagher–Orlov, Royan 1988, continued: 6 ... ♘xd5 7 0-0 ♕f6 8 c4 ♘e7 9 d4 c5? (I must admit that around about here I was finding it hard to believe my opponent's 2400 rating) 10 ♘c3 cd 11 ♘xd4 ♗g6 12 ♘d5 ♕d8 13 ♖e1 ♗c5 14 ♗f3+ ♗e6 15 b4 ♗b6 16 c5 0-0 17 ♘xf4 and Black lost on time (fortunately).

6 d4 ♘b6

6 ... ♗d6 occurred in the game Hebden – Boudre, Le Touquet 1987, which continued: 7 0-0 0-0 8 ♗b3 b5 (otherwise 9 c4) 9 ♘c3 a6 10 a4 b4 11 ♘e2 ♘b6 12 ♘xf4 ♗b7 13 ♘e5 ♗bxd5 14 ♘fd3 ♘d7 15 ♕g4 ♘5f6 16 ♕h4 ♗xe5?! (Black's position was already difficult, but after the coming exchanges his queenside will be too weak) 17 de ♘e4 18 ♕xd8 ♖axd8 19 ♗e3 a5? 20 e6 fe 21 ♗xe6+ 1-0.

7 ♗b5+ ♗d7
8 ♕e2+ (77)

In order to cover the c4-square.

8 ... ♗e7?

Black had to play 8 ... ♕e7, and after 9 ♗xd7+, 9 ... ♘fxd7 so that White can't

77
B

play c4. After 10 ♘c3 ♕xe2+ 11 ♔xe2 ♘f6 (or 11 ... ♗d6 12 ♘e4 with an edge) 12 ♗xf4 ♘bxd5 13 ♘xd5 ♘xd5 14 ♗g3, White has preserved a slight advantage.

For the more adventurous, 9 ♘e5 is also worth looking at.

9 ♗xd7+ ♕xd7
10 c4!

White's pawns are secure and strong, whilst there is nothing Black can do to save his f-pawn.

10 ... 0-0
11 0-0 c5

11 ... ♖e8 is answered by 12 ♕d3 and 11 ... c6 loses to 12 d6!

12 dc6 bc
13 ♗xf4 ♖fe8
14 ♕d3 ♗c5

Obviously Black has to seek some sort of complications.

15 ♘bd2!

From b3 the knight will take the pressure off d4.

15 ... ♖ad8
16 ♘b3 ♗f8

17 ♖ae1?!

This extremely natural move gives Black a chance to complicate. Instead, 17 ♘e5 would have left White a pawn up for nothing.

17 ... ♖xe1
18 ♖xe1 c5!
19 ♗g5!

The main point is that after 19 d5 Black plays 19 ... ♘fxd5! 20 cd c4 with good drawing chances. With 19 ♗g5, White gives back the pawn but seriously weakens the black kingside.

19 ... cd
20 ♗xf6 gf
21 ♖e4!

White is not interested in entering into some cross-pins by capturing on d4.

21 ... ♛c8

The only move as Black had to meet the threat of ♖xd4 whilst keeping g4 covered.

22 ♖h4 h6
23 ♘bd2

I spent some time considering 23 c5, but after 23 ... ♘a4! couldn't see a way to a clear advantage.

23 ... ♘a4 *(78)*
24 b4!

White meets the threats of ... ♘xb2 and ... ♘c5.

24 ... ♗xb4?!

Black came to the conclusion that he was lost and decided his best chance

was to try and survive the coming onslaught. I think I would have preferred 24 ... a5, although 25 ♖xd4 leaves White a pawn up.

25 ♖xh6 ♗xd2
26 ♘xd2 ♛e6

Black had to meet the threats of ♛h7+, ♛h8+ and ♛xf6+.

27 ♘e4 ♔g7
28 ♖h7+ ♔g8

After 28 ... ♔xh7 29 ♘g5+ ♔g7 30 ♘xe6+ fe, White wins with 31 ♛a3!. Well, he saw through that one, so it's over to 'plan B'.

29 ♖h6 ♔g7
30 ♖xf6 ♛g4

This loses at once. 30 ... ♛e5 caused me some concern, until I found the following variation: 31 ♛f3 d3 32 ♖xf7+ ♔g8 33 ♘f6+ ♔xf7 34 ♘g4+ ♔e6 35 ♘xe5 d2 (35 ... ♔xe5 is better but White will win) 36 ♛f7+! ♔d6 37 ♛d5+ ♔c7 38 ♛c6+ ♔b8 39 ♘d7+ ♖xd7 40 ♛xd7 and the pawn is stopped.

31 ♖f3! ♘b2?

32	♕e2	♕h4
33	♘g3	1-0

Game 26
Gallagher - Metzger
Lenk 1989

1	e4	e5
2	f4	ef
3	♘f3	d5
4	ed	♘f6
5	♗c4	♗d6

This move is slightly illogical as White's d5-pawn should be stronger than Black's f4-pawn.

6 ♕e2+

Black's main chances lie in some sort of kingside attack, therefore White offers to exchange queens.

6 ♘c3 is an interesting alternative, e.g. 6 ... 0-0 7 0-0 and now Black has several ways to try and complete his developement:

(a) 7 ... c6 8 d4 cd (8 ... ♗g4 should be met by 9 ♕d3 with ideas of ♘e5; 8 ... b5 is dubious, e.g. 9 ♗d3 cd 10 ♘xb5 ♘c6 11 ♘xd6 ♕xd6 12 ♘e5! ♘xe5 13 ♗xf4! with advantage to White) 9 ♘xd5! ♗e6 10 ♘xf6+ ♕xf6 and, according to *ECO*, 11 ♗e2 gives White the edge.

(b) 7 ... ♘bd7 8 d4 ♘b6 9 ♗b3 ♗g4 10 ♕d3 a5 11 a3 a4 12 ♗a2 ♗xf3 13 ♕xf3 with a good game for White, Spielmann - Fahrni, Baden 1914.

(c) 7 ... ♗g4 8 d4 ♘bd7 9 ♕d3 ♗h5 (9 ... ♖e8 10 ♗b3 ♗h5 11 ♘g5 ♗g6 12 ♕f3 is better for White; 9 ... ♘b6 10 ♗b3 transposes to 'b') 10 ♘g5 ♗g6 11 ♕h3 h6 12 ♘e6! fe 13 de ♔h8 14 ed ♘xd7 (Heuer - Uusi, Tallinn 1964) 15 ♗d3! with a good game for White.

6 ... ♕e7

Black has been known to give up the right to castle in this position with 6 ... ♔f8. After 7 d4 ♗g4 8 ♘c3 a6 I found the wrong plan in the game Gallagher - Cladouras, Luxembourg 1989, which continued 9 0-0? ♘bd7 10 a4 h6 11 ♗d2 g5 12 ♖ae1 ♔g7 13 ♕d3 ♖e8 14 ♖xe8 ♕xe8 15 ♖e1 and a draw was agreed.

Much better would have been 9 ♗d2 followed by castling long, which would enable White to attack on the kingside.

6 ... ♗e7 was played against me in the game Gallagher - Chudinovski, Lenk 1991. Play continued 7 d4!? (7 ♘c3 could well be best, but I was hoping to steer the game into familiar lines with an extra tempo) 7 ... ♘xd5 8 ♗xd5 ♕xd5 9 ♗xf4 c6 (9 ... ♕d8? 10 ♕e5!) 10 0-0 (10 ♘c3 ♕e6!) 10 ... ♗e6 11 ♘c3 ♕a5? (It was better to play 11 ... ♕d8 in order to defend his bishop on e7) 12

♘e4! 0-0 13 ♘eg5 ♗xg5 14 ♘xg5 ♖e8 15 ♕d3 (15 ♕h5 was also strong as 15 ... h6 loses to 16 ♗e5 hg 17 ♕xg5 f6 18 ♖xf6!) 15 ... ♗f5? (The last chance was 15 ... g6) *(79)*.

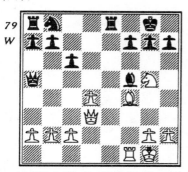

16 ♕b3 ♖e7 17 ♗d6 ♗e6 (17 ... ♖d7 loses to 18 ♗b4) 18 ♘xe6 ♖xe6 19 ♕xe6! 1-0.

7   ♕xe7+

7 ♘c3 is also possible. Hebden - Lein, New York 1983 continued 7 ... a6 8 ♕xe7+ (8 ♘e5!?) 8 ... ♔xe7 9 0-0 ♖e8 10 d4 b5 11 ♗b3 ♘bd7, and now 12 ♘g5 would have given White the better game.

7   ...   ♔xe7
8   d4   ♗f5
9   ♗b3   b5?!

Naturally, Black is worried about White playing c4, but ... b5 seriously weakens the queenside.

10   ♘c3   a6
11   ♘e5

This is a beautiful square for the knight. Of course it is unthinkable to play ...

♗xe5 and if Black plays ... ♘bd7 he has to contend with ♘c6. Meanwhile, the f-pawn is under attack.

11   ...   ♘h5

11 ... g5 12 h4.

12   0-0   f6
13   ♘c6+   ♔f7

Taking on c6 would liberate White's queenside pieces - a long diagonal for the bishop and a beautiful outpost on d5 for the knight.

14   ♗d2   ♖e8
15   ♖ae1   ♘d7
16   a4!

White wants to lure the black pawn to b4 so that he can play c4 and create a mobile pawn mass.

16   ...   b4
17   ♘d1   a5
18   ♖xe8   ♔xe8
19   c4   ♘b8

Black is in a desperate state with his knight and rook tied down defending weak pawns.

20   ♖e1+   ♔d7
21   c5   ♗f8 *(80)*

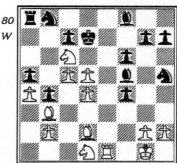

Black is in a desperate state with his knight and rook tied down defending weak pawns.

22 ♘xa5!?

This little combination is not strictly necessary, but it does lead to an endgame where White's queenside pawn majority will be decisive.

22	...	♖xa5
23	♗xb4	♖a8
24	c6+	♘xc6
25	dc+	♔xc6
26	♗xf8	♖xf8
27	♘c3!	

White threatens to transfer his bishop to the long diagonal, after which his a-pawn will become the star of the show. Meanwhile, Black's knight on h5 continues to look rather sad.

| 27 | ... | ♖b8 |

If 27 ... ♖d8 then 28 ♗d1 is strong.

28	♗d5+	♔d7
29	♗f3	g6
30	a5	♗d3
31	♘a4	♗c4
32	a6	1-0

Game 27
Gallagher – Balashov
Lenk 1991

(One might be forgiven for thinking that Lenk is a modern day theme tournament for this variation, but I assure you it is just a normal international open!)

1	e4	e5
2	f4	ef
3	♘f3	d5
4	ed	♘f6
5	♗c4	♘xd5 (81)

Black's most popular choice.

6 0-0

It is quite possible that White can achieve an edge with the naïve-looking 6 ♗xd5 ♕xd5 7 ♘c3. Black has a number of squares for his queen:

(a) 7 ... ♕h5 8 d4 ♗d6 9 ♕e2+ ♔d8 10 ♘e5 (10 0-0!?) and White had the advantage in Leonhardt – Szekely, Abbazia 1912.

(b) 7 ... ♕d8 8 d4 ♗d6 9 ♕e2+ ♕e7 10 ♕xe7+ ♔xe7 11 ♘d5+ and White has a promising ending.

(c) 7 ... ♕f5 8 ♕e2+ ♗e7 9 d4 c6 (9 ... ♗e6 10 d5! ♗xd5 11 ♘d4 ♕d7 12 ♗xf4 0-0 13 0-0-0 is dangerous for Black) 10 0-0 (also good is 10 d5!? cd 11 ♘d4) 10 ... ♗e6 11 ♘e5 g5 12 g3 ♖g8 (or 12 ... ♘d7 13 gf g4 14 ♘e4) 13 gf gf+ 14 ♔h1 ♘d7 (14 ... ♗b4 15 ♖xf4! ♕h3 16 ♖f3 ♕h5 17

♘xf7) 15 ♗xf4 0-0-0 16 ♗g3 ♛h3 17 ♘xc6 ♖xg3 18 ♘xe7+ ♔b8 19 ♛f2 with a clear advantage for White (Glaskov).

6 ... ♗e7

The main alternative, 6 ... ♗e6, will be seen in game 28.

7 d4

Again White should consider taking on d5: 7 ♗xd5 ♛xd5 8 d4 0-0 9 ♗xf4 and we have transposed to the text. However, Black does have the extra possibility of 8 ... g5!?

7 ... 0-0

Black can also play 7 ... ♗e6. Plans with ♗b3 and c4 are not so effective when White has already played d4 as Black will be able to answer c4 with ♘e3. 8 ♛e2 looks best and after 8 ... 0-0 9 ♘c3 Black has several moves:

(a) 9 ... ♘xc3 10 bc ♗xc4 11 ♛xc4 ♗d6 12 ♛b5 b6 13 ♘g5! with a good game for White.

(b) 9 ... c6 10 ♘xd5 ♗xd5 11 ♗d3! (This is Glaskov's improvement on the old 11 ♗xd5 cd 12 ♗xf4 with rough equality. I should just mention that 10 ... cd is not so good as Black remains with the bad bishop) 11 ... ♗xf3 12 ♖xf3 ♛xd4+ 13 ♔h1 ♗d6 14 ♗d2! (White's bishops are lining up for a direct

assault on the black king. If now 14 ... ♛xb2 15 ♗c3!) 14 ... ♘d7 15 ♗c3 ♛c5 16 ♖h3 g6 17 ♗xg6 fg 18 ♛e6+ ♖f7 19 ♖xh7! and White wins.

(c) 9 ... ♘c6!. White seems to have nothing better than 10 ♗xd5 ♗xd5 11 ♘xd5 ♛xd5 12 ♗xf4 ♗d6! 13 ♗xd6 (13 c4? ♘xd4) 13 ... ♛xd6 14 c3 with only the slightest of edges.

8 ♗xd5 ♛xd5
9 ♗xf4 (82)

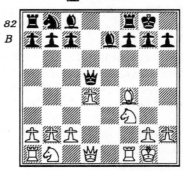

9 ... c5?

It is natural for Black to want to open the centre for his two bishops, but White's lead in development will prove too much to cope with.

In the game Bangiev - Aleksandrov, Minsk 1987, Black played 9 ... c6, but after 10 ♘c3 ♛h5 11 ♛d2 h6 12 ♖ae1 ♗e6 13 ♘e5 ♖e8 14 ♘e4 ♘d7 15 ♘g3 ♛h4 16 ♘g6! fg 17 ♖xe6 White had clearly the better chances. Maybe 9 ... ♛d8 is Black's best, but White has the freer game.

10 ♘c3   ♛c4

This suspicious-looking move is virtually forced as any other queen move (apart from the horrible ... ♛f5) would allow 11 d5 with a marked positional superiority.

11 ♛e1!

The main idea behind this 'creeping' queen move is to defend the knight on c3, thereby creating the threat of 12 b3. Instead, in the game Wall – Morris, British Ch 1989, White played 11 ♘e5 and after 11 ... ♛xd4+ 12 ♛xd4 cd 13 ♘b5 ♘a6 White's slight initiative never really troubled Black.

11 ...   ♗f6

Forced, as 11 ... cd 12 ♛xe7 dc 13 ♗d6 ♘d7 14 ♘e5! is decisive.

12 ♗d6   ♗xd4+

12 ... ♖d8 13 dc is clearly better for White.

13 ♔h1

This game against Balashov was in fact the third time I'd reached this position. One of the previous occasions was against the very same Morris who drew with such consumate ease against Wall (see above). However, on coming face to face with the truth about his position, Morris decided not to put up any resistance at all and played

13 ... ♛e6. After 14 ♗xf8 ♛xe1 15 ♖axe1 ♔xf8 16 ♘xd4 cd 17 ♘b5 ♘c6 18 ♘c7 he resigned (Gallagher – Morris, Hastings 1990/91).

13 ...   ♖d8 *(83)*

14 ♘e4

The first time I had this position (Gallagher – Campora, Biel 1990) I thought over an hour here. I was fascinated by the variations arising from 14 ♛h4!? ♖xd6. White can now play 15 ♘e4 or 15 ♖ae1:

(a) 15 ♘e4. Black has to stay defending d8 so he has a choice of 15 ... ♖d5, 15 ... ♖d7 or 15 ... ♛d5:

(a1) 15 ... ♖d5. This ugly move meets with a swift refutation: 16 ♛e7!

(a2) 15 ... ♖d7 is more resilient but also loses: 16 ♖ae1!. Black is now faced with the threat of 17 ♘eg5 and has 16 ... h6 or 16 ... f6.

(a21) 16 ... h6 17 ♘xd4 and now each of the three recaptures lose: 17 ... cd 18 ♘f6+ gf 19 ♖e8+ ♔h7 20

♕e4+ ♔g7 21 ♕g4+ and
mate; 17 ... ♕xd4 18 ♘f6+ gf
19 ♖e8+ ♔h7 20 ♕g3 mating;
17 ... ♖xd4 is a little
tougher but 18 ♘f6+ is
again good: 18 ... gf 19 ♖e8+
♔h7 20 ♕xf6 ♕xf1+ 21 ♕xf1
♗e6 22 h3 ♔g7 and now 23
♕e1! is very strong.

(a22) 16 ... f6. If you've
studied the above variat-
ions, the first move should
be obvious: 17 ♘xf6+! gf 18
♖e8+ ♔f7 19 ♕h5+ (19 ♘e5+
wins the queen, but White
will have virtually no pieces
left. 19 ♖fe1 ♕f1+!! is not so
clear) 19 ... ♔g7 20 ♕g4+
♔h6 21 ♘d2! ♕f7 22 ♖g8!
and Black has to play 22 ...
♕xg8 to avoid mate (22 ...
♕g6 23 ♕h4+! ♕h5 24 ♖xf6+
♗xf6 25 ♕xf6+ ♕g6 26 ♕f4+
♔h5 27 g4+ ♔h4 28 ♘f3+
♔h3 29 ♕g3 mate). After 23
♕xg8 ♘c6 24 ♖f4 ♖g7 25
♖h4+ ♔g6 26 ♕e8+ White
has a winning attack.

(a3) 15 ... ♕d5!. This is a
far superior defence to
either of the rook moves
and, in fact, I can't find any
way for White to obtain the
advantage.

(a31) 16 ♘xd4!? (16 ♕e7
♖e6) 16 ... cd (not 16 ...
♕xd4? 17 c3! ♖h6 {17 ... ♕e5
18 ♘xd6 ♕xd6 19 ♖ad1} 18
♕xh6 ♕xe4 19 ♕d6 ♕h4 20
♖f4 ♕g5 21 h4 winning) 17
♕e7 ♖d8 18 ♖xf7! ♕xf7 19
♕xd8+ ♕f8 20 ♕d5+ ♕f7 21

♕d8+ with a draw by per-
petual. If Black tries to win
with 20 ... ♔h8, White gets
a very strong attack, e.g. 21
♘g5 h6 22 ♘f7+ ♔h7 23
♕e4+ ♔g8 24 ♖f1 ♕c5 25
♘xh6+.

(a32) 16 ♘xd6 ♕xd6 and
White has several tries:

(a321) 17 ♘g5 ♕g6! and
now both 18 ♖xf7 (18 ♘xf7
♗f6) 18 ... ♘c6 19 c3 (19 ♖af1
♗e6) 19 ... ♗f6 20 ♕c4 ♘e5
and 18 ♖ae1 ♗d7 (18 ... f6 19
♕xh7+!) 19 ♖xf7 h6 20 ♖ef1
♘c6 21 ♖xd7 hg lead no-
where.

(a322) 17 ♖ae1 ♗d7 18
♕d8+ ♕f8 19 ♕c7 ♗c6 and
Black has no worries.

(a323) 17 ♖ad1 ♕f6! 18
♘g5 ♗f5 19 c3 (19 g4 ♕c6+)
19 ... h6 20 ♘f3 ♕xh4! (20 ...
♗e5? 21 ♖d8+ ♔h7 22 ♖d5
♘c6 23 ♕xf6 gf 24 ♘xe5 fe
25 ♖xf5 winning) 21 ♘xh4
♗g4 22 cd ♗xd1 23 ♖xd1 cd
24 ♖xd4 ♘c6 25 ♖d7 ♖d8!
with a winning ending.

So, 15 ♘e4 only seems to
offer equality (Line a31).
Returning to the position
after 14 ... ♖xd6 *(84)*:

(b) 15 ♖ae1! and now
Black has:

(b1) 15 ... h6? 16 ♘d2! ♕b4
(or 16 ... ♕a6 17 ♖e8+ ♔h7
18 ♖xc8) 17 a3 ♕xb2 18 ♘c4
♕xc3 19 ♖e8+ ♔h7 20 ♘xd6
and White has a crushing
attack.

(b2) 15 ... f6 16 ♖e8+ ♔f7

17 ♘e5+ ♗xe5 18 ♕xc4+
♔xe8 19 ♕g8+ ♔d7 20 ♘e4
with advantage to White.

(b3) 15 ... ♗e6 16 ♕e7 (a
strange way to win a rook)
16 ... ♘c6 17 ♕xd6 ♖d8 18
♕c7 and although Black has
some compensation for the
exchange, White's chances
are to be preferred.

Let's return to the game
after 14 ♘e4.

14 ... f5?!

This is an understand-
able reaction as Black
wasn't too keen on having
his kingside shattered after
14 ... ♘c6 15 c3 ♗f6 but
nevertheless this is his
best course. In fact it is
not so easy for White to
win and maybe his best line
is 16 ♘fd2!? ♕e6 17 ♘xf6+
gf 18 ♕g3+ ♕g4 (18 ... ♔h8
19 ♖ae1 ♕xd6 20 ♖e8+) 19
♕xg4+ ♗xg4 20 ♖xf6 and
Black's weakened dark
squares give White the advantage.

15 ♕h4! ♘c6 *(85)*

15 ... ♖e8 16 ♘fg5 h6 17

♘f6+ wins.

16 ♘e5!!

It's rare that one gets a
chance to play such a move,
but to play the same one
twice against grandmasters
is really too much.

16 ... ♗xe5

The best practical chance.
Of course, 16 ... ♘xe5 allows 17 ♕xd8+ and 16 ...
♕xf1+ 17 ♖xf1 fe 18 ♕xd8+
♘xd8 19 ♖f8 is mate. 16 ...
♕e6 17 ♘xc6 ♖xd6 18 ♘e7+
♔h8 19 ♘g5 also wins. During the game I actually saw
19 ... ♕g6 20 ♕xh7+! ♕xh7
21 ♘f7 mate without notic-
ing that the queen on g6 is
en prise.

17 ♘f6+ ♗xf6
18 ♕xc4+ ♔h8
19 ♗xc5 ♘e5
20 ♕e2 b6

At last the twin games
go their separate ways as
Campora played 20 ... ♗e6
here. In that game, due to
my long think on move 14, I
had only a few minutes until the time control so I

tried to simplify as much as possible (almost too much). The game went: 21 ♖fd1 f4 22 ♖xd8+ ♖xd8 23 ♗e7 f3 24 gf ♗c4 25 ♕xe5 ♗xe5 26 ♘xd8 ♗xb2 27 ♖b1 ♗d4 28 ♖xb7!? ♗d5 29 ♖b3 ♗xb3 30 ab ♔g8 31 ♔g2 ♔f7 32 f4 ♔e6 33 ♔f3 ♔f5 34 ♗c7 ♗g1 35 h3 ♗h2 36 c4 g5 37 ♗b8 a6 38 b4! gf 39 b5 ab 40 ab ♔e6 41 b6 ♔d5 42 ♗xf4 1-0.

	21	♗e7	♗xe7
	22	♕xe5	♗f6
	23	♕c7	

Occasionally, two bishops can make life difficult for a queen, but here White is very active.

	23	...	h6
	24	♖ae1	♗a6
	25	♖xf5	♗xb2
	26	h3!	

Playing safe.

| | 26 | ... | ♖dc8 |
| | 27 | ♕e7! | |

Now Black can't take on c2 because of 28 ♖f8+ ♖xf8 29 ♕xf8+ ♔h7 30 ♕f5+.

| | 27 | ... | ♗c4 *(86)* |

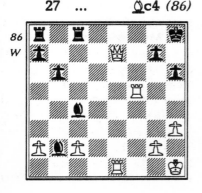

28 ♕b4!

The start of a fine sequence of moves leading to victory.

28 ... ♗d4

The bishop does not have the f6-square at its disposal, as White could then sacrifice an exchange with a mating attack.

| | 29 | ♖e4! | a5 |
| | 30 | ♕d2 | |

White's queen eyes up the kingside.

| | 30 | ... | ♗b2 |
| | 31 | ♖h5! | ♖c6 |

Black tries to stop ♖xh6+. But ...

	32	♖xc4!	♖xc4
	33	♖xh6+!	gh
	34	♕xh6+	♔g8
	35	♕e6+	1-0

Game 28
Hebden – Geller
Moscow 1986

	1	e4	e5
	2	f4	ef
	3	♘f3	d5
	4	ed	♘f6
	5	♗c4	♘xd5
	6	0-0	♗e6 *(87)*

By defending his knight with the bishop, Black makes it less attractive for White to capture on d5, as there is no longer any time to be gained by pushing around the black queen.

7 ♗b3

White gives up any idea

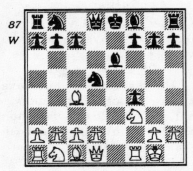

87
W

of playing ♗xd5 followed by ♗xf4, judging that this would lead only to an equal game. Instead, he wishes to set his central pawns in motion. This prospect is even more enticing now that the black bishop has developed to e6, as the white pawns will be given something to bite on when they advance.

White does have other plans though, for example 7 ♕e2 and after 7 ... ♗e7 he can play 8 d4 transposing to the note to Black's seventh move in Game 27.

8 ♘c3 is also deserving of attention, when Black shouldn't play 8 ... ♘xc3 because of 9 dc!, but instead 8 ... ♘c6 with a decent game.

7 ... ♗e7

Black has a couple of other tries:

(a) 7 ... ♘c6 8 d4 (8 c4 is not good now because of 8 ... ♘b6 9 d4 ♗xc4) 8 ... ♘e3 9 ♗xe3 ♗xb3 10 ♗xf4 ♗e6 11

♘c3 and White's game is preferable, Gallagher – Murey, Metz 1990.

(b) 7 ... ♗d6 8 c4 and now:

(b1) 8 ... ♘b6 9 d4 ♘xc4 (Black has little choice but to take) 10 ♕e2 b5 11 a4 0-0 (There is no time for 11 ... c6 12 ab cb 13 ♘c3 ♕b6 because of 14 ♘xb5!) 12 ab ♘e3?! (12 ... ♘b6 would have kept White's advantage within tolerable proportions) 13 ♗xe6 ♘xf1 14 ♗d5! c6 15 bc ♗c7 16 ♘c3! ♘e3 17 ♗xe3 fe 18 ♕xe3 and White has tremendous play for the exchange. Even so, Black managed to draw in Gallagher – Greenfeld, Tel Aviv 1988.

(b2) 8 ... ♘e7 (Black intends to bring his knight around to g6 to reinforce his f-pawn) 9 d4 ♘g6 10 c5?! ♗e7 11 ♗xe6 fe 12 ♖e1 0-0 13 ♖xe6 ♗xc5? (This loses at once, whilst after 13 ... ♘c6 or 13 ... ♕d5 the game is roughly level) 14 ♕b3 ♗xd4+ 15 ♘xd4 ♕xd4+ 16 ♗e3! 1-0 Bronstein – Zaitsev, Moscow 1969.

Rather than the hasty 10 c5, 10 ♘c3 looks better. Now 10 ... c5 is met by 11 ♘e4 and after 10 ... 0-0 11 c5 (11 ♔h1 is also interesting) 11 ... ♗e7 12 ♗xe6 fe 13 ♕b3 is possible.

8 c4 ♘b6

If 8 ... ♘f6 then 9 d4 will

leave White with an edge.

9   d4! *(88)*

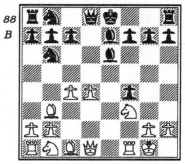

9   ...   ♞xc4

In the game Gallagher – Dutreeuw, San Bernardino 1991, Black decided not to accept the pawn. Play continued 9 ... 0-0 10 d5 ♗g4 11 ♗xf4 ♗d6 12 ♕d4 (12 ♕d2 may be better) 12 ... ♗xf3 13 ♖xf3 ♞8d7 14 ♗xd6 (with the queen on d2 this wouldn't be necessary) 14 ... cd 15 ♗c2! ♞e5 16 ♖h3 g6 17 ♞d2 ♖c8 18 b3 f5 19 ♖f1 ♞bd7 20 ♖g3! ♔h8 21 ♞f3 ♕b6 and now 22 ♔h1! would leave White with the advantage. Instead, I played the unfortunate 22 ♕xb6 overlooking the *zwischenzug* 22 ... ♞xf3+ which equalises at once (White needed his knight to exploit the weak squares such as e6).

10   ♗xf4

That Mark Hebden learnt about this position the hard way can be seen from the following miniature: 10 ♕e2?! ♞e3! 11 ♗xe6 ♞xf1 12 ♕b5+ c6 13 ♕xb7 fe 14 ♕xa8 ♕b6! 15 ♗xf4 0-0 16 ♞c3 ♞d7 17 ♕xf8+ ♗xf8 18 b3 e5 0-1 Hebden – Toth, Biel 1983.

There remain a couple of untested moves for White in this position: 10 ♖e1 with the threat of ♖xe6; and 10 ♞c3 with the idea of d5.

10   ...   0-0?!

This is the source of most of Black's serious problems. It's better to retreat the knight immediately with 10 ... ♞b6. After 11 ♗xe6 fe 12 ♕e2 ♞c6 13 ♞c3!? an unclear position is reached. Bangiev – Flomin, Corr. 1986/87, continued: 13 ... ♕d7 14 ♞e5 ♞xe5?! 15 ♗xe5 ♗d6 16 ♗xd6?! (Better is 16 ♞b5! ♞d5 17 ♗xd6 cd 18 ♖ae1 with a small advantage for White) 16 ... cd 17 ♖ae1 ♖f8 18 ♖xf8+ ♔xf8 19 ♕xe6 ♕xe6 20 ♖xe6 ♖d8 21 ♞e4 ½-½.

11   ♕e2   b5

Now it is a little late for Black to retreat his knight, e.g. 11 ... ♞b6 12 ♗xe6 fe 13 ♕xe6+ ♔h8 14 ♞e5!? ♕xd4+ 15 ♔h1 with a strong attack. 15 ... ♖xf4 should be met by 16 ♞c3! (not 16 ♖xf4?? ♕d1+).

12   ♞c3   a6

12 ... c6 is also met by 13 a4.

13 a4!

The queenside is now under heavy pressure as 13 ... c6 fails to 14 ab cb 15 ♘xb5. Black has no choice but to seek counterplay against d4.

13	...	♘c6
14	ab	♘xd4
15	♘xd4	♕xd4+
16	♔h1	♖ab8

16 ... ab is bad because of 17 ♖xa8 ♖xa8 18 ♘xb5 ♕xb2 (otherwise 19 ♘xc7 wins) 19 ♗xc4.

The point of 16 ... ♖ab8 is to pin the b-pawn so that White can't achieve a powerful passed pawn on a6.

17 ♖xa6 ♗d6

18 ♖xe6 was threatened.

18 ♖a4!

18 ♗xd6 was an alternative: 18 ... cd loses to 19 ♖d1!; after 18 ... ♘xd6 19 ♗xe6 fe 20 ♕xe6+ White has some advantage but Black maintains good drawing chances.

The text sets in motion a series of forced moves which leads to a position where White has an extra pawn.

18	...	♗xf4
19	♗xc4	♕d6!
20	♖d1	♕e5
21	♗xe6	fe
22	♖e4	♕g5
23	g3	♗d6
24	♖xe6	♕f5
25	♔g2	♗c5

26	♖d5	♕f2+
27	♕xf2	♖xf2+
28	♔h3	♗d6
29	♖e2	♖xe2
30	♘xe2	♖e8
31	♘c3	♖e6 (89)

89
W

This endgame is of course clearly better for White although in the end Hebden had to fight for the draw: 32 ♔g2 ♔f7 33 ♖f5+ (Why not 33 ♔f3?) 33 ... ♔g6 34 g4 ♖e3 35 ♖h5 h6 36 ♔f2 ♖d3 37 ♔e2 ♖d4 38 h3 ♖b4 39 ♘d1 ♔f6 40 ♔d3 ♗e5 41 ♘c3 ♖xb2 42 ♘e4+ ♔e6 43 g5 g6 44 ♖xh6 ♔f5 45 ♖h7 ♖xb5 46 ♖f7+ ♔e6 47 ♖h7 ♖d5+ 48 ♔e3 ♖a5 49 ♔d3 ♖a3+ 50 ♔c4 ♔f5 51 ♘c5 ♖c3+ 52 ♔b4 ♖c1 53 ♘d7 ♗g3 54 ♘f6 ♖b1+ 55 ♔c4 ♖h1 56 ♔d3 ♗e5 57 ♘g4 ♗g3 58 ♘f6 ♖a1 59 h4 ♖a3+ 60 ♔e2 ♖a4 61 ♖f7 ♗h2 62 ♔f3 ♖f4+ 63 ♔g2 ♖xh4 64 ♘h7+ ♔g4 65 ♘f8 ♗d6 66 ♘xg6 ♖h2+ 67 ♔f1 ♔xg5 68 ♘e7 ♖d2 69 ♘f5 ♗f4 70 ♘g7 ½-½.

Game 29
Spassky – Sakharov
Leningrad 1960

1	e4	e5
2	f4	ef
3	♘f3	d5
4	ed	♘f6
5	♗b5+	*(90)*

90
B

This is often thought of as the critical test of the Modern Defence.

    5 ... c6

Other moves are inferior:
(a) 5 ... ♘bd7 6 c4 (6 0-0!?) 6 ... a6 7 ♗xd7+! ♗xd7 8 0-0 and White is clearly better.

(b) 5 ... ♗d7 6 ♗xd7+ (This is the simplest, although 6 ♗c4 deserves attention) 6 ... ♘bxd7 (6 ... ♕xd7 7 c4 c6 8 ♕e2+ ♗e7 9 ♘e5 ♕c7 10 d4 cd 11 ♗xf4 is good for White) 7 0-0 ♘xd5 8 ♖e1+ ♗e7 9 c4 ♘b6 10 ♕e2 with advantage to White.

    6 dc bc

This capture is quite commonly played although it seems inferior to 6 ... ♘xc6 (see games 30 and 31).

    7 ♗c4 *(91)*

7 ♗e2 is an alternative which leaves White free to advance his central pawns, e.g. 7 ♗e2 ♗d6 8 d4 0-0 9 c4 ♖e8 10 ♘c3 ♘bd7 (There is nothing to be gained by 10 ... ♘g4 11 0-0 ♘e3 12 ♗xe3 fe 13 c5 ♗c7 14 d5 with advantage to White) 11 c5 ♗c7 12 0-0 and Black's position is very passive: 12 ... ♘d5 is bad because of 13 ♘xd5 cd 14 ♗b5!; so Black can try 12 ... ♘f8, but after 13 ♘e5! ♗xe5 14 de ♘6d7 15 b4 a5 16 ♘e4 ♖xe5 17 ♘d6 ♖d5 White could gain the advantage by 18 ♕a4!

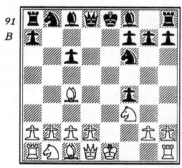

91
B

    7 ... ♘d5

This move was prepared by Botvinnik for the World Championship tournament of 1948, but he had to wait until 1952 before having a chance to test his novelty.

The alternative is 7 ... ♗d6, after which White should play 8 ♕e2+!. This move typifies the modern treatment of the King's Gambit, where White is not afraid to exchange queens when the situation demands so.

The endgame (I have to admit to being one of those people who regard virtually everything after a queen exchange as an endgame) after 8 ... ♛e7 9 ♛xe7+ ♚xe7 is better for White as several examples from practice have illustrated:

(a) 10 0-0 ♗e6 11 ♖e1! (Stronger than the 11 ♗xe6 played in Illescas – Smyslov, Spain – USSR 1987) 11 ... ♞bd7 12 d4 ♖he8 13 ♗xe6 fe 14 ♞bd2 h6 15 ♞c4 and Black is positionally busted, Bhend – Barcza, Zurich 1959.

(b) 10 ♞c3 ♖e8 11 0-0 ♚f8 12 d4 h6 13 ♞e5! ♗xe5 14 de ♞g4 15 ♗xf4 ♗e6 16 ♗xe6 ♖xe6 17 ♖ad1 g5 18 h3 ♞xe5 19 ♗xe5 ♖xe5 20 ♖d6! with advantage to White, Tripolsky – Tsayek, 1987.

After 8 ♛e2+, Furman has recommended 8 ... ♚f8, but here too White can gain the advantage: 9 d4 ♗g4 10 0-0 ♞bd7 11 ♗b3! (White vacates the c4-square for his queen's knight) 11 ... ♛c7 12 ♞a3 ♖e8 13 ♛d3 g5 14 ♞c4! ♗xf3 15 ♛xf3 ♖g8 16 ♞xd6 ♛xd6 17 c3 ♞d5 18 ♗d2 ♞7f6 19 ♖ae1 with the

better game for White in Glaskov – Poromsnyuk, Moscow 1972.

8 0-0 *(92)*

92
B

It is possible that 8 ♞c3 is the most accurate move, as Black is then prevented from developing his bishop to d6, thereby rendering the f-pawn even weaker than usual. Black has a number of replies:

(a) 8 ... ♞xc3 9 dc! ♗d6 (9 ... ♛xd1+ 10 ♚xd1 ♗d6 11 ♖e1+ is good for White) 10 ♛d4! 0-0 11 ♗xf4 ♛e7+ 12 ♚d2 ♖d8 13 ♗d3 c5 14 ♗xd6 ♖xd6 15 ♖ae1 ♗e6 16 ♛e4 1-0 Krustan – Endre, Corr. 1970.

(b) 8 ... ♗e7 9 d4 is good for White, e.g. 9 ... ♞xc3 10 bc ♗d6 11 ♛e2+.

(c) 8 ... ♗e6 9 ♛e2 (This prevents ... ♗d6 again, but 9 ♗b3 is an interesting alternative) 9 ... ♗e7 10 0-0 ♞d7 (Black leaves his king in the centre as he intends to support the f-pawn with g5. After 10 ... 0-0 11 d4

♘xc3 12 bc ♗xc4 13 ♕xc4 ♗d6 14 ♘e5! White is assured of the better game) 11 d4 g5 12 ♘xd5 cd 13 ♘xg5!! (A beautiful refutation of Black's plan) 13 ... ♗xg5 (13 ... dc 14 ♘xe6 fe 15 ♕h5+ ♚f8 16 ♗xf4 gives White a winning attack) 14 ♗xd5 0-0 (If 14 ... ♖c8, then 15 ♗xe6 fe 16 ♕h5+ ♚f8 17 ♗xf4) 15 ♗xa8 ♕xa8 16 ♗xf4 with a clear advantage for White in Votova-Rantanen, Warsaw 1989.

8 ... ♗d6

Against 8 ... ♗e6, White should play 9 ♗b3 with the idea of c4 and d4.

9 ♘c3

In the stem game of the variation, Bronstein - Botvinnik, USSR Ch 1952, White played the inferior 9 d4. After 9 ... 0-0 10 ♘c3 ♘xc3 11 bc ♗g4 (11 ... ♘d7!?) 12 ♕d3 ♘d7 White could have obtained equal chances with 13 ♗d2, but instead played the reckless 13 g3 and was duly punished: 13 ... ♘b6 14 ♗b3 c5 15 c4 ♕f6 16 ♘e5 ♗xe5 17 de ♕xe5 18 ♗xf4 ♕h5 19 ♖fe1 ♖fe8 20 a4 ♗e2 21 ♕c3 ♘d7! 22 a5 ♘f6 23 ♗a4 ♖e6 24 ♚g2? ♘e4 25 ♕b3 g5 0-1.

9 ... ♗e6

If Black plays 9 ... 0-0, White can safely take on d5: 10 ♘xd5 cd 11 ♗xd5 ♗c5+ 12 d4 ♕xd5 13 dc ♕xc5+ 14

♖f2! with advantage to White.

10 ♘e4 ♗e7

Understandably, Black want to keep his bishop, but this retreat means that he will only be able to defend f4 with drastic measures. 10 ... ♗c7 is also unattractive: 11 ♘eg5 0-0 (The complications arising from 11 ... ♘e3 favour White) 12 ♘xe6 fe 13 ♕e2 (13 d4!?) 13 ... ♕f6 14 ♖e1 ♖e8 15 ♘e5 with a good game for White in Kuznetsov - Zhuravlev, Kalinin 1970.

11 ♗b3

This rules out any tactical tricks based on ... ♘e3.

11 ... 0-0

In the radio game Tal - Winter, 1960, Black omitted castling, but was soon in trouble: 11 ... ♘d7 12 d4 ♘7f6? 13 ♘eg5 ♗g4 14 ♕d3 ♘d7 15 ♗xd5 cd 16 ♗xf4 h6 17 ♘xf7!

12 d4 ♘d7
13 ♕e2 *(93)*

White is now threatening

to win a pawn by 14 c4.

13 ... g5?

So Black defends f4, but it is indeed a rare event when you can get away with moves like this. There is, in fact, a reasonable defence here, 13 ... ♖e8! as after 14 c4 Black has the surprising move 14 ... ♗f8!. Kuznetsov - Holmov, Smolensk 1981, continued: 15 cd ♘xd5 16 ♘fd2 f5 17 ♖xf4 fe 18 ♖xe4 ♘f6 and Black has some compensation for the pawn, although White's chances remain preferable.

14 c4 ♘5b6

15 h4!

White begins to open up the kingside.

15 ... h6

15 ... g4 16 ♘fg5.

16 hg hg *(94)*

94 W

17 ♘fxg5!

For the piece, White receives two pawns and permanently damages Black's king position. Although there is no immediate win, his greater mobility will allow him to feed more pieces into the attack than Black can into the defence.

17 ... ♗xg5

18 ♗xf4 ♘f6

Exchanging bishops would leave the black king completely naked.

19 ♖ad1!

The d-pawn is given protection and the rook is ready to swing.

19 ... ♗f5

20 ♘e5!

White is happy to exchange all the minor pieces around the black king as this will leave the way clear for his major pieces to come and finish the job.

20	...	♗xe4
21	♕xe4	♗xe5
22	de	♕g5
23	♖f5	♕g7
24	♕f4	

It's all over now.

24	...	♖fe8
25	♖g5	♘xe5
26	♖xg7+	♔xg7
27	♖d6	♘g6
28	♕f6+	♔g8
29	♗c2	♘xc4
30	♖d7	1-0

Game 30
Frances - Cornell
New Jersey 1986

1	e4	e5
2	f4	ef
3	♘f3	d5
4	ed	♘f6

5	♗b5+	c6
6	dc	♘xc6 *(95)*

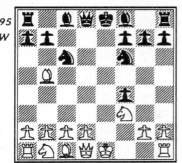

This is the best way for Black to recapture, developing a piece and not messing up his queenside. In fact, even the time gained by 6 ... bc is illusory as the bishop is not well placed on b5.

7 d4 ♗d6

7 ... ♕a5+ has also been seen. After 8 ♘c3 ♗b4 9 0-0 ♗xc3 10 ♕e2+ ♗e6 11 bc White stood clearly better in Pachmann - Vymetal, Prague 1953.

8 ♕e2+

8 0-0 is game 31.

8 ... ♗e6

8 ... ♕e7 walks straight into a bad ending: 9 ♕xe7+ ♔xe7 10 0-0 ♗g4 11 ♗xc6 bc 12 ♘e5.

8 ... ♔f8 was tried in Illescas - Murey, Holon 1986, and Black soon achieved a good position after 9 ♗xc6? bc 10 ♘e5 ♕b6! and the threat of ... ♗a6 persuaded White to part com-

pany with his d-pawn. But after 11 ♘c4 ♕xd4 12 ♘xd6 ♕xd6 13 0-0 g5 14 ♗d2 ♕c5+ 15 ♔h1 ♗g4 there was a distinct lack of compensation. However, all of White's difficulties can be traced back to the unnecessary 9 ♗xc6. After the simple 9 0-0 White's position looks preferable to me.

9 ♘g5

This looks risky, but in reality White hasn't much choice. If he didn't feel like playing this move, he shouldn't have played 8 ♕e2+ in the first place.

The alternative attempt to grab material, 9 ♘e5, is dubious as can be seen from the course of the game Hartston - Spassky, Hastings 1965/66, which continued: 9 ... 0-0! 10 ♗xc6 bc 11 ♗xf4 ♘d5 12 ♗g3 f6 13 ♘f3 ♗xg3+ 14 hg ♖e8 with a very good game for Black.

9 ... 0-0!
10 ♘xe6 fe

In the game Petrovic - Petran, Novi Sad 1981, Black played 10 ... ♕b6 and after 11 ♘xf8? ♘xd4 12 ♘d7 ♘xd7 13 ♗xd7 ♘xe2 14 ♔xe2 ♖d8 had a clear advantage. Instead of 11 ♘xf8, White should play 11 ♗xc6 as after 11 ... bc 12 0-0 (even 12 ♘xf8 can be considered) 12 ... ♖fe8 13 ♕d3 ♖e6 14 ♘d2! he has the better chances

(Glaskov).

11   &xc6   bc *(96)*

12   0-0

It is far too dangerous to take the pawn as after 12 &xe6+ &h8 13 0-0 f3! Black has a very strong attack.

With the text, White attacks two pawns.

12   ...   &c7

Of course, Black defends his f4-pawn (rather than the e6-one) and threatens to push ... f3; 12 ... &d5 is well met by 13 c4!

13   &xe6+?!

White finally succumbs to the temptation. The alternative is 13 &d2, with the idea of blockading the weak pawns instead of capturing them. Unfortunately, Black doesn't have to fall in line with White's noble intentions and can play 13 ... e5!. After 14 de &xe5 15 &c4 (15 &f3 &d6 16 &d2 &ae8 17 &c4+ &h8 18 &ae1 was about equal in Gross - Plachetka, Stary Smokovec 1973) 15 ... &d4+

16 &h1 &d5 17 &e4 Glaskov considers the position to be in White's favour. However, after 17 ... &c5 Black's activity should compensate for his positional weaknesses.

13   ...   &h8

14   &d2

White hurries his knight to the kingside.

14   ...   &ae8

15   &h3

15 &c4 led to swift defeat in Hahn - Class, Bundesliga 1984: 15 ... f3! 16 &xf3 &g4 17 h3 &h2+ 18 &h1 &xf3 19 gf &g3 (or 19 ... &g1) 20 fg &xh3 21 &e2 &d6+ 0-1.

15   ...   c5

Naturally, Black wants to open up the position as soon as possible. 15 ... &e2 looks a little premature as after 16 c4 &fe8 17 c5 &f8 18 &f3 Black's bishop is no longer able to participate in the attack. White will be able to diffuse the attack with moves such as &f2 or &d2 and &ae1.

16   &c4 *(97)*

With the imminent opening of the g1-a7 diagonal, White sees his first task as removing the dangerous bishop.

16   ...   f3!

Black's rook on f8 is brought into the game with what could prove to be

97
B

devastating effect. Previously, the position had been considered as unclear:

(a) 16 ... ♘e4 17 d5 ♗e5 18 ♘xe5 ♕xe5 19 ♕d3 and White should be able to defend.

(b) 16 ... ♖e2 17 ♕f3 ♖fe8 18 ♗d2 cd 19 b3 with an unclear position in Hay – Hamilton, Australia 1971.

17 ♘xd6

17 gf ♖e2 is very unpleasant, as is 17 ♖xf3 ♖e1+ 18 ♖f1 ♗xh2+.

17 ... ♕xd6

Black has no time to play 17 ... fg because of 18 ♖xf6.

18 gf

18 ♕xf3 occurred in Carroll – Cornell, Corr. 1986 and the two players agreed to a draw. This was rather a strange decision as after 18 ... ♘e4! Black has a winning attack, e.g.

(a) 19 ♕d1 ♖xf1+ 20 ♔xf1 ♕xh2 or 20 ♕xf1 ♕xd4+.

(b) 19 dc ♕xc5+ 20 ♕e3 ♖xf1+ 21 ♔xf1 ♕xc2.

(c) 19 ♗f4 (relatively best) 19 ... ♕xd4+ 20 ♔h1 (20 ♕e3 ♖xf4!) 20 ... ♘d2 21 c3 ♕d8 and Black wins the exchange.

18 ... ♕xd4+
19 ♔h1 ♖e2
20 ♕f5 ♖fe8

This gives White the respite he needed. Either 20 ... ♘d7 or 20 ... ♕h4 would have kept up the pressure.

21 ♗g5 ♕xb2
22 ♖ac1 ♕b8
23 ♗f4 ♕b7
24 ♕xc5

White is clearly over the worst. The remaining moves were: 24 ... ♘d5 25 ♕d4 ♕f7 26 ♗d2 ♘e3 27 ♗xe3 ♖8xe3 28 ♕d8+ ♖e8 29 ♕g5 h6 30 ♕g3 ♕xa2 31 c4 ♖8e5 32 ♖g1 ♖g5 33 ♕b8+ ♔h7 34 ♖xg5 hg 35 ♕g3 ♕d2 36 ♖g1 ♕e3 37 ♖f1 a5 38 h4 g4 39 ♕xg4 ♕e5 40 f4 ♕e4+ 41 ♕f3 ♕xf3+ 42 ♖xf3 ♖c2 42 ♖a3 ½-½.

Game 31
Kinlay – Nunn
New Malden 1977

1	e4	e5
2	f4	ef
3	♘f3	d5
4	ed	♘f6
5	♗b5+	c6
6	dc	♘xc6
7	d4	♗d6
8	0-0	0-0 (98)
9	♘bd2	

The white knight heads

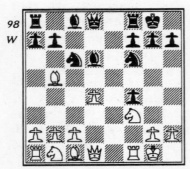

for c4, from where it will help to exert pressure on the black f-pawn by either capturing the bishop on d6 or hopping into e5 at an appropriate moment. 9 ♘a3, with the same idea, is also playable.

9 ♘c3 is bad because of 9 ... ♕b6! and White is already feeling strong pressure against d4 (as c3 is no longer possible). Westerinen - Boey, Skopje 1972 continued: 10 ♔h1 ♗g4 11 ♗xc6 ♕xc6! 12 ♕d3 ♖ad8 13 ♗d2 g6 with advantage to Black.

It is surprising that 9 c4 has never been played. There is, however, a short analysis by Muchnik which runs 9 c4 ♗g4 10 ♘c3 ♖c8 11 ♘e2 a6 (11 ... ♖e8 12 ♘xf4; 11 ... ♘h5 12 c5 ♗b8 13 d5) 12 ♗a4!. Unfortunately, as I don't read Russian, I can't understand his assessment, but anyway it looks worth a try!

9   ...   ♗g4

Black has a number of alternatives:

(a) 9 ... ♕b6? 10 ♘c4 ♕xb5 (I would like to congratulate a certain Mr Butler who found the courage to play 10 ... ♕c7 here) 11 ♘xd6 ♕b6 12 ♗xf4 ♕xb2 (12 ... ♗g4 was probably better, although after 13 ♘c4 ♕b4 14 ♕d3! ♗xf3 15 ♖xf3 b5! 16 ♘d6 ♕xd4+ 17 ♕xd4 ♘xd4 18 ♖f2 White has a clearly better ending according to Bangiev) 13 d5 ♕b6+ 14 ♔h1 ♘e7 15 c4 ♘g6 16 ♗g3 ♖d8 17 ♕d4! ♘h5?! (99)

18 ♘xf7! ♔xf7 19 c5! ♕b5 20 d6 (White shows admirable restraint in keeping his discovered check in reserve) 20 ... ♘xg3+ 21 hg ♘f8 22 ♘g5++ ♔g8 23 ♖f7! ♘e6 24 ♘xe6 ♔xf7 25 ♕xg7+! (And to cap it all, we have a classic chase) 25 ... ♔xe6 26 ♖e1+ ♔d5 27 ♖d1+ ♔xc5 28 ♕d4+ ♔c6 29 ♖c1+ ♔d7 30 ♖c7+ ♔e6 31 ♖e7+ ♔f5 32 g4+ ♔g5 33 ♖g7+ 1-0 Bangiev - Mglo-

siek, Corr. 1985/86.

(b) 9 ... ♘e7. This leaves the bishop stranded on b5, but it is rather slow and gives White time to man-oeuvre his knight to e5: 10 ♘c4 ♗c7 11 ♘ce5 ♘ed5 12 c4 (Bangiev considers 12 ♗c4, with the idea of ♗b3 and c4, as stronger) 12 ... a6 13 ♗a4 b5 14 cb ♘g4 (Bangiev – Bezman, Simferopol 1985) and now 15 ♘xg4 ♗xg4 16 ba ♖xa6 17 ♗b3 with the better game for White (Bangiev).

(c) 9 ... ♘d5 can be met by 10 ♘e4 ♗c7 11 c4.

(d) 9 ... ♗c7. This pro-phylactic retreat keeps Black's options open: 10 c3 (10 ♘c4 ♗g4 transposes to Kinlay – Nunn) 10 ... ♗f5 11 ♘c4 ♘d5 12 ♗xc6 bc 13 ♘fe5 g5 *(100)*.

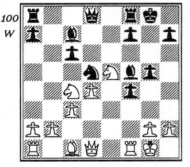

100
W

This position has been considered to be clearly in Black's favour, but this seems a little excessive to me. Whilst Black does have good attacking chances,

White's material advantage is not to be underestimated, e.g. 14 ♘xc6 ♕e8 15 ♘6e5 f6 16 ♘d3 (16 ♕f3 ♖d8 17 ♘d3 ♗e4) 16 ... ♕g6 17 ♘c5 g4 18 ♗d2 and it will not prove easy for Black to break through.

10 ♘c4 ♗c7

In the game Renet – van der Sterren, Budel 1987, Black played 10 ... ♗xf3 11 ♖xf3 ♗c5 with the idea of 12 c3 ♘xd4!. But after 12 ♗xc6! ♕xd4+ 13 ♕xd4 ♗xd4+ 14 ♔h1 bc 15 ♗xf4 White's better pawn struc-ture gave him a slight but persistent edge.

11 c3

It's quite possible that White should remove the knight on c6 before it runs away. After 11 ♗xc6 bc 12 ♕d3 ♗xf3 (otherwise the knight will come to e5) 13 ♖xf3 ♘h5 (13 ... ♘d5 was played in Arnason – Kris-tiansson, Reykjavik 1984, but this is less good as it interferes with Black's play on the d-file. White should have replied 14 ♗d2) 14 ♗d2 ♕d5 15 ♖e1, the position is difficult to assess and re-quires practical testing. White has to aim for ex-changes in order to make pawn structures the do-minant factor in the posi-tion. Thus 15 ... ♖ad8 is met by 16 ♗b4!

11 ...   ♘e7!
12 ♗a4

There is very little else to do against the threat of ... a6 and ... b5.

12 ...   b5!?

Black sacrifices a pawn with the worthy idea of transporting his queen to the kingside as quickly as possible.

13 ♗xb5   ♛d5
14 ♘a3   ♛h5
15 ♗d3

This is one of the positions where we can see the strength of the pawn on f4, which severely cramps White and gives Black a big space advantage on the kingside.

With the text, White tries to get his queenside pieces back into play, but it turns out that he has no time for this. 15 h3 would have been a more critical test of Black's sacrifice.

15 ...   ♘ed5
16 ♘c4   ♖ae8
17 h3 *(101)*

101
B

17 ...   ♘e3!

Black has timed the attack to perfection.

18 ♗xe3   fe
19 hg?

This loses by force. Better was 19 ♘ce5 after which Black could speculate with moves like 19 ... ♗xh3. However, 19 ... ♗xe5! assures him of some advantage, e.g.

(a) 20 hg? ♘xg4 21 de ♖e6! and there is nothing to be done about ... ♖h6 and ... ♛h1 mate.

(b) 20 de ♗xf3 21 ♛xf3 ♛xe5 and Black's advanced pawn gives him a good game.

19 ...   ♘xg4
20 ♘ce5

20 ♖e1 is no defence either as 20 ... ♗g3! wins.

20 ...   ♖xe5!
21 de   e2!

Black's last two moves have cleared the a7–g1 diagonal which, in combination with the open h-file, give a decisive attack.

22 ♗xe2   ♗b6+
23 ♛d4

Black's next move destroys any lingering hopes White might have had.

23 ...   ♛h6!
24 ♖ae1   ♖d8!
25 ♗c4

Or 25 ♛xb6 ♛xb6+ and the white king is too weak.

25 ...   ♖xd4!
0-1

5) 3 ... ♘c6

Game 32
Glaskov – Soloviev
Moscow 1971

1	e4	e5
2	f4	ef
3	♘f3	♘c6 *(102)*

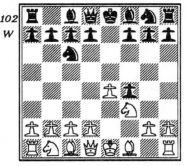

102
W

This variation has never really caught on, probably because it does nothing to address Black's immediate problems. In fact, it is rather similar to the idea behind the Fischer Defence - a waiting move. Black wants to see White's next move before he makes his mind up.

4   ♘c3

I should just mention that the position is more often reached via the Vi-

enna Game (1 e4 e5 2 ♘c3 ♘c6 3 f4 ef 4 ♘f3). The King's Gambit move order offers White an additional possibility, namely 4 d4. In fact, this move has been frowned upon by theoreticians, but I decided to look at it in some detail, as I found it hard to believe that such a natural move leads to a good game for Black. My conclusion is that it leads to rough equality (or unclarity) and I present my analysis in order to open the debate on 4 d4:

4 ... d5 (4 ... g5 5 d5) 5 ed (5 ♘c3 is bad because of 5 ... de 6 ♘xe4 ♕e7! 7 ♕e2 ♗f5 8 ♘c3 ♕xe2+ 9 ♗xe2 0-0-0; and 5 e5 can be met by 5 ... g5 6 h4 g4 7 ♘g1 ♗h6 and the early closing of the centre is not in White's favour) 5 ... ♕xd5 6 ♗xf4 (6 ♘c3 ♗b4 7 ♗xf4 ♗g4 transposes, but maybe Black can try 7 ... ♕a5) 6 ... ♗g4 7 ♘c3 (This is better than taking on c7. Glaskov gives 7 ♗xc7 ♗xf3 8 ♕xf3 ♕xf3 9 gf

♞xd4 as good for Black. This is not true as 10 ♞c3! gives White a dangerous attack. Unfortunately, however, Black can play instead 7 ... ♖c8! and then 8 ... ♗xf3 which does offer him good chances of an advantage) 7 ... ♗b4 (better than 7 ... ♕e6+ 8 ♕e2! and White retains an edge, e.g. 8 ... ♗xf3 9 ♕xe6+ fe 10 gf 0-0-0 {10 ... ♞xd4 11 0-0-0} 11 0-0-0 ♖xd4 {11 ... ♞xd4 12 ♗h3 is strong} 12 ♖xd4 ♞xd4 13 ♗h3 and White will win back his pawn with a good game; or 8 ... ♕xe2+ 9 ♗xe2 ♗xf3 10 ♗xf3 ♞xd4 11 ♗xb7 ♖b8 12 0-0-0 with advantage) 8 ♗e2 (8 a3 also deserves attention. Although slightly time consuming, it does force Black to exchange on c3, thereby considerably bolstering the defences of d4) 8 ... 0-0-0 9 0-0 ♕d7 (Other squares are not so good, e.g. 9 ... ♕a5 10 ♞g5 ♗xe2 11 ♞xe2 or 9 ... ♕h5 10 h3 in both cases with advantage to White) 10 d5!? (10 ♞e5 ♗xe2 11 ♕xe2!? is a pawn sacrifice Black shouldn't accept. Instead, after 11 ... ♞xe5 12 ♗xe5 f6 13 ♗g3 ♗xc3 {13 ... ♕xd4+ 14 ♗f2! is still very dangerous for Black} 14 bc ♞e7, the position is roughly level) 10 ... ♗xc3 (Moving the knight is obviously dis-astrous {11 ♞e5} and 10 ... ♗xf3 11 ♕xf3 ♗c5+ 12 ♔h1 ♞d4 13 ♗e3 or 13 ♗g4 f5 14 ♗e3 are clearly better for White) 11 dc ♕xc6 (103) (It would be wrong for Black to exchange queens, e.g. 11 ... ♕xd1 12 ♖xd1 ♞f6 {Black has little choice as after 12 ... ♖xd1 13 ♖xd1, 14 ♖d7 is in the air} 13 cb+ ♔xb7 14 ♖xd8 ♗xd8 15 ♗c4 with a clear advantage to White).

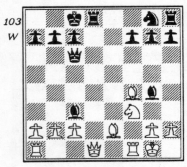

103
W

12 ♞e5. Suddenly, the board is ablaze. If Black now manages to avoid a few nasty traps he can reach a roughly level game:

(a) 12 ... ♗xe5?? 13 ♗xg4+.

(b) 12 ... ♖xd1?? 13 ♗xg4+ ♔b8 14 ♞xc6+.

(c) 12 ... ♗xe2. This gives rise to some fascinating complications. White now has:

(c1) 13 ♕xe2 ♗xe5 14 ♗xe5 (14 ♕g4+ ♔d7) 14 ... f6. It seems unlikely that White's slight initiative will fully compensate for the pawn.

(c2) 13 ♕xd8+ ♔xd8 14

♘xc6+ bc 15 bc! (15 ♗xc7+? is met by 15 ... ♔c8!) 15 ... ♗xf1 16 ♖xf1 and a draw is the likely outcome.

(c3) 13 ♘xc6! and now:

(c31) 13 ... ♗xd1. White now has a most elegant way to achieve an advantage: 14 ♘xa7+ (14 ♘xd8 ♗d4+ 15 ♔h1 ♗h5! is good for Black) 14 ... ♔b8 15 ♘b5! (The black pieces remain *en prise* and White will collect in the most favourable fashion) 15 ... ♗e2 (15 ... ♗d4+ 16 ♘xd4 ♖xd4 17 ♗e5! wins) 16 ♗xc7+ ♔c8! 17 ♘xc3 (17 bc ♗xb5) 17 ... ♗xf1 18 ♗xd8 ♗xg2 19 ♔xg2 (19 ♗b6!?) 19 ... ♔xd8 20 ♖d1+ ♔c8 21 ♘d5 and White is very active.

(c32) 13 ... ♖xd1 14 ♘xa7+ ♔b8 15 ♖fxd1 ♗xd1 (If 15 ... ♔xa7 then 16 ♖d8 is strong) 16 ♘b5!? (16 ♖xd1 ♔xa7 17 bc ♘f6 18 ♗xc7 leads to a slght edge) 16 ... ♗xc2 17 bc and White will restore material equality whilst retaining a sizeable initiative.

(d) 12 ... ♕c5+ (Along with variation 'e', Black's best choice) 13 ♔h1 ♗xe2 (13 ... ♖xd1 loses to 14 ♗xg4+ ♔b8 15 ♖axd1 ♘f6 16 bc; and 13 ... ♗e6 is met by 14 ♘d3) 14 ♕xe2 ♗xe5 (14 ... ♗xb2 15 ♘d3! and there is no time for 15 ... ♖xd3: 16 cd ♗xa1 17 ♕e8 mate!) 15 ♗xe5 ♘f6 (15 ... f6 16 ♕g4+ is good for White) 16 ♗xf6 gf 17 ♖xf6 with approximate equality.

(e) 12 ... ♕b6+ 13 ♔h1 ♗xe2 (13 ... ♗e6!? 14 ♘d3! ♘f6 15 a4 gives White a dangerous initiative. Black's queen is rather awkwardly placed; 13 ... ♖xd1? is the same as in 'd') 14 ♕xe2 ♗xe5 15 ♕g4+ ♕e6 16 ♕xe6+ fe 17 ♗xe5 ♘f6 18 ♖xf6! gf 19 ♗xf6 ♖hf8 20 ♗xd8 ♖xd8 (20 ... ♔xd8 21 ♔g1 is a little better for White) 21 ♖f1. A difficult rook ending has arisen in which White's chances shouldn't be inferior. A straight race seems inadvisable for Black, e.g. 21 ... ♖d2 22 h4 (22 g4 is also good) 22 ... ♖xc2 23 ♖f7 ♖xb2 24 ♖xh7 c5 25 h5 c4 26 h6 c3 27 ♖h8+ ♔d7 28 h7 and wins: if 28 ... c2 then 29 ♖d8+ ♔c7 30 ♖c8+; or 28 ... ♖b1+ 29 ♔h2 c2 30 ♖d8+ ♔xd8 31 h8=♕+ ♔c7 32 ♕h7+ and ♕xc2.

4   ...   g5

Now that ... d5 has been ruled out, Black's most obvious plan is to hang on to his f-pawn.

4 ... ♘f6 has also been played, but by replying 5 ♗c4 the game has transposed into a variation of the Bishop's Gambit known to be favourable for White. e.g. 5 ... ♗b4 6 ♘d5! 0-0 7 0-0 ♘xe4 (or 7 ... ♘xd5 8 ed ♘e7 9 ♘g5 h6 10 ♘e4

♘g6 11 c3 ♗a5 12 d4 with advantage to White) 8 d4. White will soon win one of his pawns back and Black's development looks particularly ineffective. Here are a couple of examples from practice:

(a) 8 ... ♗e7 9 ♗xf4 d6 10 ♕d3 ♘f6 11 ♘g5 g6 12 ♘xe7+ ♘xe7 13 ♘xf7! ♖xf7 14 ♗xf7+ ♔xf7 15 ♗g5 ♘eg8 16 ♖xf6+ ♘xf6 17 ♖f1 with a winning position for White in Spielmann - Grünfeld, Innsbruck 1922.

(b) 8 ... ♘f6 9 ♘g5!? (9 ♘xb4 and 10 ♗xf4 also looks good) 9 ... h6 (Against 9 ... ♘xd5, Bogoljubov recommended 10 ♘xf7 with a crushing attack) 10 ♘xf7! ♖xf7 11 ♘xf6+ gf 12 ♕h5 with a winning attack Khlusevich - Verkhovtsev, USSR 1973.

5 h4

With this move White signals his intention of playing an Allgaier (or a Hamppe-Allgaier as it is known with the queen's knights already out). 5 d4 can be seen in game 34.

5 ... g4
6 ♘g5 *(104)*
6 ... h6

Black naturally forces the sacrifice on f7. Other continuations are dubious:

(a) 6 ... f6 7 ♕xg4 fg 8 ♕h5+ ♔e7 9 ♕xg5+ ♘f6 10

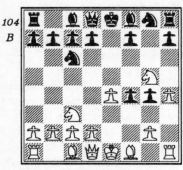

104
B

♘d5+ ♔f7 11 ♗c4 (Chigorin).

(b) 6 ... d5 7 d4 h6 8 ed with a good game for White.

7 ♘xf7 ♔xf7
8 d4!

This is the strongest, opening more lines and holding the check at c4 in reserve. The first time I came across Allgaier-type positions, I could not take them seriously. White gives up a piece for a pawn and then calmly continues as if nothing had happened. But after a little (in fact a lot of) study, I began to understand that Black's defensive task is by no means easy.

Black's main problem is that his king will never find a safe haven and if White manages to complete his development, picking up a pawn or two along the way, he will have very good compensation.

The Hamppe-Allgaier is probably more favourable

for White than the normal version (the inclusion of ♘c3 means that White is one step nearer to evacuating his king to the queenside, whilst the knight on c6 can sometimes be attacked by d5 or ed5). Of course, Black does have defensive resources, including suddenly switching to an attack against the white king if circumstances permit.

8 ... d5 *(105)*

105
W

For 8 ... f3 see game 33.

8 ... d6 has also been played, but it does little to hinder White's smooth development, e.g. 9 ♗xf4 ♘f6 (or 9 ... ♗g7 10 ♗e3 ♘f6 11 g3 ♘ge7 12 ♗c4+ ♔g7 13 ♕d2 ♗d7 14 0-0-0 with excellent attacking chances) 10 ♗c4+ ♔g7 11 a3!? (White waits to see where the black pieces are deployed before deciding on the continuation of the attack) 11 ... ♗e7 12 0-0 ♘xe4?! 13 ♘xe4 d5 14 ♘f2 dc 15 d5

♗xh4 16 dc ♕xd1 17 ♖axd1 ♖d8 18 ♖xd8 ♗xd8 19 cb ♗xb7 20 ♘xg4 with a clear advantage to White in Triguda - Tarasov, Corr. 1982/83.

9 ♗xf4!

White doesn't waste any time before opening the f-file.

9 ... ♗b4

There are a number of other defensive tries:

(a) 9 ... ♔g7 10 ♘xd5 ♗d6 11 e5 ♕e8 12 ♕d2 with advantage to White.

(b) 9 ... ♗g7 10 ♗e3 ♘f6 11 g3 de 12 ♗c4+ ♔g7 13 0-0 ♗xd4 14 ♖f7+ ♔g6 15 h5+ ♔xh5 16 ♖g7! with a mating attack. This occurred in a blindfold simultaneous exhibition of Pillsbury's in 1900.

(c) 9 ... ♘f6 10 ♗d3 (10 ♗e2!? or 10 ♘xd5 ♘xd5 11 ♗c4 deserve attention) 10 ... de (or 10 ... ♗b4 11 0-0 ♗xc3 12 bc ♔g7 13 ed ♕xd5 14 ♕d2 ♗d7 15 ♖ab1! ♖ae8 16 ♖b5 ♕xa2 17 ♗xh6+! with a winning attack) 11 ♗c4+ ♔e8 12 d5 ♘a5 (12 ... ♘e7 13 ♘b5) 13 ♗e2 ♗d6 14 ♕d2 h5 15 0-0 and White has a strong attack. In Romashkevich - Shabelsky, Corr. 1895, Black lost his extra piece after 15 ... ♕e7 16 ♗xd6 cd 17 ♕d4!

10	♗e2	♗xc3+
11	bc	♘f6
12	0-0	♔g7

13   c4! (106)

106
B

Now Black is unable to maintain a foothold in the centre and the opening of the position will give added power to the white bishops.

13   ...   de

13 ... ♘xe4 loses in spectacular fashion: 14 cd ♘c3 (14 ... ♕xh4 15 dc g3 is too slow: 16 ♗e5+ ♔g6 17 ♗h5+ wins; 14 ... ♕xd5 15 c4 followed by 16 d5 gives White a strong attack) 15 dc!! ♘xd1 16 ♗e5+ ♔g6 (16 ... ♔g8 loses to 17 ♗c4+ ♔h7 18 ♖f7+ ♔g6 19 ♖g7+ ♔f5 {19 ... ♔h5 20 ♗f7+ ♔xh4 21 ♔h2} 20 ♖xd1 ♖f8 21 ♖f1+ ♔e4 22 ♖e1+ ♔f5 23 d5 and White wins) 17 ♗d3+ ♔h5 18 cb! ♗d7 19 ba=♕ ♕xa8 20 ♖axd1 ♖f8 21 ♖xf8 ♖xf8 22 ♖f1 ♕b4. So far all this analysis was carried out by a character named Trumberg in 1893. Here he went astray with 23 g3 but Glaskov has pointed out the way to victory: 23 ♗g3! and Black is powerless against the threat of ♖e1-e5.

14   d5   ♘e7
15   ♗e5   ♖f8 (107)

107
W

Keres considered this position to be favourable for Black, but Glaskov's forceful play shows that the opposite is in fact true.

16   ♕d4!   ♘g6
17   ♗xf6+   ♖xf6
18   h5   ♘f8
19   ♖f4!

White calmly prepares to double on the f-file. Black is unable to untangle his pieces in time.

19   ...   ♘h7
20   ♖af1   ♗d7
21   ♗xg4   ♗xg4
22   ♖xg4+   ♔f7

On 22 ... ♘g5, Glaskov intended 23 ♕e5! followed by ♖xg5+.

23   ♕xe4   ♖xf1+
24   ♔xf1   ♘g5
25   ♕g6+   ♔e7
26   ♕g7+   ♘f7
27   ♖e4+   ♔d6
28   ♕g3+   ♔c5
29   ♕f2+   1-0

Game 33
Gallagher – Hresc
Geneva 1991

1	e4	e5
2	f4	ef
3	♘f3	♘c6
4	♘c3	g5
5	h4	g4
6	♘g5	h6
7	♘xf7	♔xf7
8	d4	f3 *(108)*

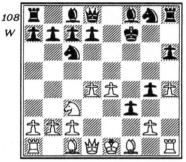

108
W

The main purpose of this move is to ensure that the f-file stays closed for as long as possible. The move also has disruptive qualities which could especially be seen after 9 gf ♗e7.

9   ♗c4+

White can also consider various other moves, such as 9 ♗e3 or 9 ♗f4, but the text is the most logical. Black is forced to make the difficult decision between ... ♔g7 or ... ♔e8, but first ...

9   ...   d5

... lines are opened for his undeveloped pieces.

10   ♗xd5+

10 ed is inadvisable, offering Black the pleasant choice of 10 ... ♘a5 or 10 ... fg!?

10   ...   ♔g7

By placing his king on g7, Hresc opts for the most common way. The main problem with 10 ... ♔e8 is that, with the king stuck in the centre, White will have long-term compensation for the piece, even if his attack may be initially less strong. It is quite probable that, theoretically speaking, White doesn't have enough for the piece, but over the board (or even through the post) the position is very hard to defend, e.g. 11 gf ♗e7 (Chigorin considered that after 11 ... ♘f6 12 f4 ♗b4 13 ♗xc6+ bc 14 ♕d3 {with the threat of e5} White has a strong attack) 12 ♗e3 ♗xh4+ 13 ♔d2 ♗g5 14 f4 ♗f6 15 ♕g1! and Black has a difficult defence in front of him (don't forget he can't castle!).

11   gf   ♗b4

11 ... ♗e7 looks like the critical test, e.g. 12 0-0 ♗xh4 13 f4 (13 fg ♘f6) and the position is very hard to assess.

Against 11 ... ♘f6, Tarrasch gave the following variation: 12 ♗f4 ♘e7 13 ♗e5 ♘g6 14 f4! with a dangerous attack.

12 ♗e3 *(109)*

I spent a long time here wondering about the best square for the bishop. I eventually settled for the solid ♗e3. My reasoning was along the following lines: I've got two pawns for the piece, a big centre and my opponent's king is not too happy. All that remains to be done is to defend the d-pawn so that I can retreat my light-squared bishop, castle long and mate will follow shortly. It is, of course, necessary to think positively when you play the King's Gambit!

12 ...   ♘f6
13 ♗c4   ♛e7

13 ... ♖e8 could well be better. My opponent didn't like it because it weakened his h6-pawn.

14 ♛e2

14 ♛d2 also came into consideration but I preferred to keep my f-pawn

defended and I didn't wish to have my knight on c3 still pinned after I castled.

14 ...   gf

Black needs the g4-square for his minor pieces.

15 ♛xf3   ♗g4?

But this is the wrong one. 15 ... ♘g4 offered better chances. Of course 15 ... ♛xe4 loses to ♖g1+.

16 ♖g1   h5
17 e5!

Now Black realises that if he moves the knight the exchange sacrifice on g4 will be murderous (probably White should castle first). There is little choice but to give back the piece.

17 ...   ♘xe5
18 de   ♛xe5 *(110)*

19 0-0-0

This was a most enjoyable move to play for two reasons. Firstly, it was pleasant to have my king out of the centre; and secondly, because I found it very artistic to use my queen as a shield in order to provide the move with its legality.

19 ... ♗c5?

Black overlooks the threat, but his position was pretty hopeless anyway, e.g. 19 ... ♖ad8 (19 ... ♗xc3 20 bc ♕xc3 21 ♗h6+) 20 ♘d5! followed by ♗d4 will prove decisive.

20 ♖d7+! ♘xd7

Obviously this is not the best, but 20 ... ♗e7 21 ♗d4! or 20 ... ♔f8 21 ♗xc5+ ♔e8 22 ♖e7+ (there are also other ways e.g. 22 ♕f2!?) 22 ... ♕xe7 23 ♗xe7 ♗xf3 24 ♗xf6 win for White.

21 ♕f7 mate

Game 34
Motwani – Kula
Berlin 1991

1	e4	e5
2	f4	ef
3	♘f3	♘c6
4	♘c3	g5
5	d4	*(111)*

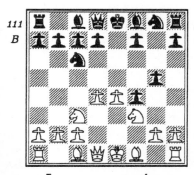

111
B

5 ... g4

Black has no other good

way of meeting the threat of d5, e.g.

(a) 5 ... ♗g7 6 d5 ♘e5 7 d6! with the advantage.

(b) 5 ... d6 6 d5 (6 h4 g4 7 ♘g5 h6 8 ♘xf7 ♔xf7 9 ♗xf4 with a Hampe-Allgaier position favourable for White) 6 ...♘e5 7 ♗b5+ ♗d7 8 ♗xd7+ ♔xd7 (8 ... ♘xd7 is clearly weaker, e.g. 9 ♕d4 f6 10 h4 g4 11 ♘g5! ♘c5 12 ♘e6 ♘xe6 13 de c6 14 ♗xf4 ♕b6 15 ♕d3 0-0-0 16 0-0-0 h5 17 ♕g3 ♕c7 18 ♖d3 ♕e7 19 ♖hd1 ♕xe6 20 ♗xd6 ♗xd6 21 ♖xd6 with a clear advantage, Arnason - Adams, Manila (ol) 1992) 9 h4 ♘xf3+ 10 ♕xf3 gh 11 ♗xf4 and White is better.

6 ♗c4 gf

We are now in the so-called Pierce Gambit.

7 0-0 *(112)*

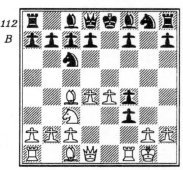

112
B

It has been known for a long time that 7 ♕xf3 ♘xd4 is good for Black, but maybe White can try 7 ♗xf4!? here. One important point being that 7 ... fg 8 ♗xf7+ ♔xf7 9 ♕h5+ ♔g7 10 ♖g1 wins for White. 7 ... ♗g7 8 0-0 transposes to the note to Black's seventh move, whilst avoiding the 7 ... d5 variation.

7 ... ♕g5?!

Of course, Black has a large number of alternatives. I would just like to remind the reader that it will be of more benefit to study the variations in order to get a feel for the attack, rather than to remember them in rote fashion. If the latter approach is adopted, you will find yourself at sixes and sevens when faced with a novelty or, heaven forbid, when you forget the theory.

(a) 7 ... fg (This is suicidal) 8 ♗xf7+ ♔xf7 9 ♕h5+ ♔g7 10 ♕g4+ ♔f7 11 ♖xf4+ ♘f6 12 ♘d5 (Analysis by Lange, 1856).

(b) 7 ... ♗g7 8 ♗xf4 ♗xd4+ (Against 8 ... ♕f6 9 ♗e3 is strong as 9 ... ♘xd4 10 ♘d5 ♕g6 11 ♖xf3! ♘xf3+ 12 ♕xf3 ♕c6 13 ♗b5 ♕d6 14 ♖f1 wins; 8 ... ♘xd4 9 ♗e3 {9 ♗xf7+ deserves attention} 9 ... c5 10 ♘b5 ♘xb5 11 ♗xb5 ♕b6 12 ♕xf3 f6 13 ♕h5+ ♔d8 14 ♗xc5 and White has a very strong attack) 9 ♔h1 ♗xc3 (As usual in this variation capturing on g2 only serves to open further lines for White) 10 ♗xf7+ (The second piece sacrifice is a ty-

pical way of strengthening the attack) 10 ... ♔xf7 11 ♕d5+ ♔e8 (11 ... ♔g7 is worse: 12 ♖xf3 ♗f6 13 e5 ♗e7 14 ♖g3+ ♔f8 15 ♖xg8+ 1-0 is Keres – Wilkins, Corr. 1933) 12 ♕h5+ ♔e7 and now Glaskov's and Estrin's suggestion of 13 e5 looks very strong.

(c) 7 ... d6 8 ♕xf3 ♗e6 9 ♗b5! ♗d7 10 ♕xf4 ♕f6 11 ♕xf6 ♘xf6 12 ♖xf6 ♗g7 13 ♗g5 0-0 14 ♖af1 with advantage to White (Tseitlin).

(d) 7 ... ♘xd4!? 8 ♗xf4! (Not 8 ♕xd4?? ♕g5 and White can resign) 8 ... ♗c5! (An improvement on the old 8 ... ♕f6 9 ♘d5 ♕g7 10 ♘xc7+ ♔d8 11 g3 with a winning position for White). After 8 ... ♗c5, Polaksek – Karolyi, Prague 1988, continued: 9 ♗xf7+ ♔xf7 10 ♗e3 ♔e8! 11 ♗xd4 ♗xd4 12 ♕xd4 ♕f6 13 ♕d3 ♘e7 14 ♖xf3 ♕e5 and Black eventually beat off the attack and converted his material advantage. A better try for White would have been 9 ♔h1!

(e) 7 ... d5 (This is the most common move) 8 ed ♗g4 *(113)*.

Now White has two possibilities:

(e1) 9 ♕e1+ ♗e7! (9 ... ♘ce7 10 ♗b5+ ♗d7 11 ♕e5) 10 ♗xf4 ♘xd4 11 ♗e5 ♘e2+ 12 ♘xe2 fe 13 ♗xe2 ♗xe2 14

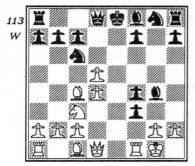

♕xe2 f6 and now White's best is to force a draw with 15 ♖xf6! ♘xf6 (15 ... ♕xd5? 16 ♕h5+ ♔d8 17 ♖d1 wins) 16 ♗xf6 ♖f8 17 ♕h5+ ♖f7 (17 ... ♔d7 18 ♕f5+ is also a draw) 18 ♖e1 ♔f8 19 ♕h6+ ♔e8 20 ♕h5.

(e2) 9 ♕d2. White wishes to capture with the queen on f4, hoping that this will create decisive threats on the f-file. Black has a number of defensive tries, e.g.

(e21) 9 ... ♗g7 10 ♕xf4! ♗xd4+ 11 ♔h1 fg+ 12 ♔xg2 ♕h4 13 dc (Estrin also gives 13 ♕xf7+ ♔d8 14 ♕f8+ ♔d7 15 dc+ bc 16 ♕f4 ♗h3+ 17 ♔h1 ♕xf4 18 ♖xf4 ♗xc3 19 bc ♘e7 20 ♗a3! with advantage to White) 12 ... 0-0-0 14 cb+ ♔xb7 15 ♕g3 ♕xg3+ 16 hg ♗e6 17 ♗xe6 fe 18 ♖f7 with advantage to White.

(e22) 9 ... ♘a5 10 ♗b5+ c6 (Weaker is 10 ... ♗d7 11 ♕xf4 ♗xb5 12 ♘xb5 ♗d6 13 ♕xf3 ♕d7 14 ♘xd6+ cd 15 b4 and White is better) 11 ♕xf4 ♘f6 (After 11 ... cb probably

best is 12 ♕xg4 with a very strong attack) 12 ♖e1+ (Lepeshkin has shown that 12 ♘e4 ♗g7! is good for Black, e.g. 13 ♘d6+ ♔f8 14 gf ♗h5 with every chance of a successful defence or 13 ♘xf6+ ♕xf6 14 ♕xg4 ♕xd4+) 12 ... ♔d7 13 ♘e4 (114)

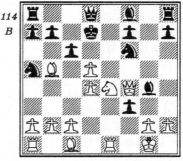

Here Lepeshkin gives 13 ... f2+ as clearly better for Black. This assessment doesn't seem correct, e.g. 14 ♕xf2! (14 ♘xf2 is less good, on account of 14 ... ♗d6!) 14 ... ♘xe4 (After 14 ... ♗e7, the simple 15 dc+ bc 16 ♗d3 leaves White with excellent play for the piece, whilst 15 ♘g5 could also be worth investigation) 15 ♖xe4 (15 ♕xf7+ ♕e7 16 dc+ bc 17 ♕d5+ ♔c7 18 ♗f4+ ♔b6 is a false trail, although 18 ♕xe4 may not be completely hopeless) 15 ... f5 16 ♖e6! cb 17 h3!

Now Black will lose one of his extra pieces (17 ... ♗h5 or 17 ... ♗d1 lose to 18 ♕xf5) and on top of this he will be unable to prevent the infiltration of the white queen to f5. In the game Gallagher - Kamber, Olten 1992, Black ran away with his king, but after 17 ... ♔c8 18 hg b6 19 ♕xf5 ♔b7 20 ♗g5, White had an overwhelming position.

17 ... ♗xh3 fares no better: 18 gh ♖g8+ (or 18 ... ♕c7 19 ♕xf5! ♕g3+ 20 ♔h1) 19 ♔h1 ♖g6 20 ♕xf5 ♖xe6 21 ♕xe6+ (21 de+ is also better for White) 21 ... ♔c7 22 ♗f4+ ♗d6 23 ♖f1! ♘c4 24 b3 ♗xf4 25 bc ♕h4 26 d6+ and White wins. Relatively best for Black is to bring his knight back into play. After 17 ... ♘c4 18 hg ♘d6 19 gf White's position remains clearly preferable.

Instead of 13 ... f2+ Black can play 13 ... ♘xe4. There could then follow 14 ♕xg4+ ♔c7 15 ♕xe4 cb 16 ♗f4+ ♔b6 (16 ... ♗d6 loses to 17 ♕e7+!) and White obviously has some compensation for the piece but it is difficult to say how much. 17 a4 looks a tempting continuation.

(e23) 9 ... ♘ce7 10 ♕xf4 ♕d7 (10 ... ♘h6 is well met by 11 ♘e4! ♘eg8 {11 ... ♗g7? 12 ♕xh6} 12 ♗b5+ ♗d7 13 ♕e5+ ♕e7 14 ♗xd7+ ♔xd7 15 ♘c5+ ♔c8 16 ♕xh8 fg 17 ♖d1 b6 18 ♗xh6 ♘xh6 19 ♖e1 and White had the advantage in Zuckerman - Markov, Corr.

1985/86) 11 d6! ♘g6 (Lepeshkin considers 11 ... 0-0-0 to be better for Black, but after 12 dc! ♖e8 {12 ... ♕xd4+ loses to 13 ♗e3 ♕xf4 14 cd=♕+!} 13 ♗xf7 and White's position is clearly preferable) 12 ♕e4+ ♔d8 13 h3 ♗e6 14 ♗xe6 ♕xe6 15 ♕xb7 ♖c8 16 dc+ ♖xc7 17 ♕a8+ ♖c8 18 ♕xf3 and White has more than enough for the piece.

Let us return to Motwani - Kula after 7 ... ♕g5.

8 ♖xf3 ♘xd4
9 ♗xf7+!

Of course not 9 ♕xd4 ♗c5. Now Black is unable to take the bishop, e.g. 9 ... ♔xf7 10 ♖xf4+ ♘f6 11 ♘d5 ♕e5 12 ♖xf6+ ♔g8 13 ♕g4+ and wins.

9 ... ♔d8
10 ♖f2

10 ♖xf4 is also possible but Motwani's move threatens to take the knight.

10 ... ♕g7
11 ♗xf4 ♘e7

11 ... ♗c5 could also be met by 12 ♕h5.

12 ♕h5

White's attack is already decisive.

12 ... d6
13 ♗g5 ♘xc2

Faced with the threat of ♗f6, Black plays a move reeking of desperation.

14 ♖af1

White is not going to be side-tracked by a mere

knight.

| 14 | ... | ♛e5 *(115)* |
| 15 | ♗g8! | |

If Black takes the bishop, mate follows very shortly.

15	...	♛c5
16	♔h1	♔d7
17	♖xf8	♘g6
18	♖d8+	♔c6
19	♗d5+	1-0

115
W

6) Becker Defence

Game 35
Gallagher – Spyrsl
Fribourg 1987

1	e4	e5
2	f4	ef
3	♘f3	h6 *(116)*

116
W

The Becker Defence signals Black's intention to hold on to the gambit pawn, but without the weaknesses inherent in the Kieseritzky. By playing ... h6 first, Black won't be forced into playing ... g4 if White decides to undermine the pawn chain with h4. But, as we shall see, White has other ways to develop his initiative.

4   d4

4 b3, in order to dissuade Black from playing ... g5, is interesting, and can be seen in game 36; whilst 4 ♗c4 g5 leads to the Classical which is not part of our repertoire (5 ♘e5 ♖h7! doesn't disturb Black).

4   ...   g5
5   ♘c3

5 h4 ♗g7 6 g3 is another, but less promising, method.

5   ...   d6

5 ... ♗g7 caught me napping a little in the game Gallagher – Nunn, Islington 1990. I just continued in the normal fashion: 6 g3 fg 7 h4 g4 8 ♘g1 but was then very surprised by 8 ... d5!. Previously this idea hadn't been considered at all, theory normally stating that whether Black plays 5 ... d6 or 5 ... ♗g7 doesn't make any difference as play simply transposes. After 8 ... d5!, 9 ♘xd5 is bad because of 9 ... c6, so play continued: 9 ed ♘e7 10 ♘ge2 c6! 11 ♗g2 cd 12 ♘f4 ♘c6 13 ♕d2 ♕a5 with advantage to Black.

However, all is not doom and gloom. White has a very interesting possibility on his seventh move: 7 hg *(117)*, instead of 7 h4.

117
B

Now 7 ... d6 looks normal for Black. 8 ♗c4 (White can even consider the speculative 8 ♘xg5!?, e.g. 8 ... hg 9 ♖xh8 ♗xh8 10 ♕h5 ♗xd4 11 ♗xg5! ♕d7 {11 ... ♗f6 12 ♕h7 ♗xg5 13 ♕xg8+ ♔d7 14 ♕xf7+ ♕e7 15 ♗h3+} 12 ♗c4 followed by 13 0-0-0 and ♖f1 with a dangerous attack) 8 ... ♘f6 (Black has to watch his step. For example, 8 ... ♘c6? 9 ♘xg5 hg 10 ♖xh8 ♗xh8 11 ♕h5; or 8 ... ♘e7 9 ♘xg5! hg 10 ♖xh8+ ♗xh8 11 ♕h5 ♘g6 12 ♗xg5 ♕d7 {12 ... ♗f6 13 ♗xf7+ ♔xf7 14 ♕h7+} 13 0-0-0 with a crushing attack) 9 ♕d3 ♘c6 10 ♗e3 ♗g4 11 ♖f1. This is a little inconvenient, but White maintains a firm grip on the centre. Black now has to decide which way to castle.

a) 11 ... ♕d7 12 0-0-0 0-0-0 13 ♗b5! causes Black serious problems.

b) 11 ... 0-0 12 0-0-0 ♕d7 (12 ... ♕e7 13 ♖de1 {13 ♘xg5!?} 13 ... ♖ae8 14 ♘xg5 hg 15 ♗xg5 ♗e6 16 ♗b3 {or 16 ♘d5!?} with excellent compensation for the piece) 13 ♖f2 and White plans to double rooks on the f-file. Black has difficulties in countering this plan, e.g. 13 ... ♖ae8 14 a3! and now 14 ... ♗xf3 15 ♖xf3 ♕g4 16 ♖df1 ♘xe4 17 ♖xf7 is good for White.

6   g3!

White has to take action against the pawn chain before Black has time to consolidate.

6   ...   fg

6 ... g4 doesn't fit in with the Becker system (3 ... h6 was played to hold the kingside): 7 ♘g1 f3 8 h3 is good for White, whilst 7 ♗xf4 is also highly tempting, e.g. 7 ... gf 8 ♕xf3 ♘c6 9 0-0-0 with a strong attack.

More critical is 6 ... ♗g7 7 gf g4 8 ♘g1 ♕h4+ 9 ♔e2 g3 10 ♘f3 ♗g4, but after 11 ♗e3 White has the better game, e.g. 11 ... gh 12 ♔d2 ♕g3 13 ♗e2 ♘c6 14 ♘xh2 or 11 ... ♘c6 12 ♔d2! ♕h5 13 ♗e2 g2 14 ♖g1 ♕h3 15 d5 ♘e7 16 ♘d4 (Bhend).

7   h4

This is the normal way of

continuing the attack but, in view of the analysis above, 7 hg can also be considered.

    7 ... g4

7 ... ♗g4 is not good because of 8 hg ♘c6 (8 ... ♗g7 9 gh ♗xh6 10 ♗g2!) 9 ♘d5! ♗xf3 10 ♕xf3 ♘xd4 11 ♕c3 ♗g7 12 ♘xc7+ ♔f8 13 ♘xa8 ♕xa8 14 gh with a clear advantage for White (Glaskov).

If 7 ... gh, 8 ♘xh4 and White will soon pick up the g-pawn and remain with excellent compensation for the other one sacrificed.

    8 ♘g1 ♗g7?!

8 ... ♗e7 9 ♗g2 (9 h5!?) 9 ... ♗xh4 10 ♘f4 ♕f6 11 ♕d2 and Korchnoi considers that Black's three extra pawns are no match for White's strong centre and lead in development.

8 ... g2 9 ♗xg2 ♗e7 10 h5 ♗h4+ 11 ♔e2 is also pleasant for White, e.g. 11 ... ♗g5 12 ♗xg5 ♕xg5 13 ♕d2 ♕xd2+ (13 ... ♘f6 14 ♖f1 ♘xh5 15 ♖xh5 ♕xh5 16 ♘d5 is good for White) 14 ♔xd2 ♘e7 15 ♘ge2 and White has the better ending in spite of Black's extra pawn.

    9 ♗e3

Black has no counterplay and is suffering terribly from a lack of space.

    9 ... ♘c6
    10 ♘ge2 ♕f6?

Black must have overlooked that after 11 ♘d5 ♕f3 the bishop on e3 would be defended by the knight. 10 ... ♗f6 looks best, but after 11 ♗g2 (11 h5!?) 11 ... ♗xh4 12 ♕d2 with 0-0-0 to follow is similar to 8 ... ♗e7 in the note to Black's eight move.

    11 ♘d5 ♕d8
    12 ♘xg3 ♘f6
    13 ♘f4

White avoids exchanges and has the option of playing ♘h5.

    13 ... ♕e7
    14 ♕d3 ♗d7
    15 0-0-0 h5
    16 ♗g2

White is in no rush and calmly continues developing.

    16 ... 0-0-0
    17 ♕a3!? a6
    18 ♖he1 ♖de8
    19 ♔b1 ♗h6
    20 ♕c3! ♔b8 *(118)*

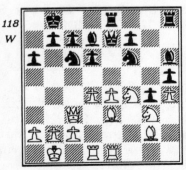

118
W

    21 e5!

The preparation is over – now it is time for the

attack; White's bishop on g2 comes forcefully into the game.

21 ...   ♘h7

Unpleasant though it may be, Black should have taken on e5. After 21 ... de 22 de ♕xe5 (22 ... ♘xe5 23 ♗c5 ♕d8 24 ♕b4! wins for White) 23 ♗a7+ ♔xa7 24 ♖xe5 ♘xe5 25 ♕xc7 White has a clear advantage but Black can soldier on.

22 ♗xc6

22 ♘d5 ♕f8 23 ♘xc7 is also good.

22 ...   ♗xf4?

The final error. To avoid immediate capitulation Black had to play 22 ... bc (22 ... ♗xc6 23 ♘f5 wins quickly).

23	♗xf4	♗xc6
24	ed	♕xh4
25	d5	♗xd5
26	dc+	♔c8
27	♘f5	1-0

Game 36
Bangiev – Karolyi
Kecskemet 1987

1	e4	e5
2	f4	ef
3	♘f3	h6
4	b3 *(119)*	

Over the past few years, this has become an increasingly popular way of dealing with the Becker Defence. White prevents g5, or at least makes it un-

attractive, and thereby leaves 3 ... h6 looking like a waste of time.

White's plan is to develop his queenside pieces as quickly as possible, castle long, and then play g3 to open lines on the kingside. He should then receive the sort of compensation one normally associates with the Benko Gambit, with the added bonus of having the black king to aim at. Nevertheless, a quick mate is unlikely and it is the long lasting pressure which should make Black suffer.

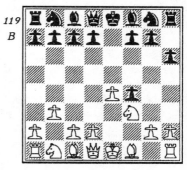

119
B

4 ...   d6

After this, White has no difficulty in carrying out his plan.

4 ... ♘f6 is interesting, when White has normally played 5 ♕e2 (5 e5 could well be stronger when we arrive in a strange sort of Schallop Defence. Admittedly, 3 ... h6 is marginally more useful than 4 b3, but then again I'm sure that

God would never choose the Schallop against the King's Gambit) 5 ... d5!. By the opening of the centre, White's development is made to look rather clumsy. Hebden - Pein, London 1987 continued: 6 ed+ ♗e7 7 ♗b2 (7 c4 is too slow) 7 ... 0-0 8 ♘c3 ♖e8 9 0-0-0 ♘xd5 10 ♕e5 ♘xc3 11 dc ♗d6 12 ♕h5 ♘d7?! (This is where Black starts going downhill. The knight is fated never to arrive at its destination, leaving behind it an undeveloped queenside. Better was 12 ... ♘c6, after which White is hard pressed to justify his pawn minus, e.g. 13 ♗c4 ♕f6 14 ♖he1 ♗d7; or 13 c4 ♕e7 14 ♗d3 ♗a3 15 ♖he1 ♗xb2+ 16 ♔xb2 ♕f6+) 13 ♗c4 ♕f6 14 ♖he1 ♖e3 15 ♖xe3 fe 16 ♖f1 g6 17 ♕a5 ♕f5 18 ♕a4 c6 19 ♘d4 e2 20 ♘xf5 ♘b6 21 ♗xe2 1-0.

5	♗b2	♘f6
6	♘c3	♗e7
7	♕e2	0-0
8	0-0-0	♘c6 *(120)*

In the game Hebden - Romanishin, Moscow 1986, Black chose instead 8 ... c6. Play continued 9 g3! fg 10 ♖g1 ♖e8 (Of course, taking another pawn is incredibly risky) 11 ♖xg3 ♗f8 12 d3 (12 ♕e3 looks more precise) 12 ... ♘bd7 13 ♕d2 ♘e5 14 ♗e2 g6 and now 15 ♖dg1 would have given good play for the pawn.

120
W

9	**g3!**	♗g4

Black aims to simplify the position but this won't relieve the pressure. 9 ... fg 10 ♕g2 also gives White a strong attack.

10	♕f2	♘e5
11	♗e2	fg
12	♕xg3	♘h5

Black's activity is of a temporary nature.

13	♕f2	♗xf3
14	♗xf3	♗h4
15	♕f1	♘f4
16	♖g1	

The open g-file and long diagonal are the most important aspects of the position. White also has, in reserve, the option of playing d4 at a good moment.

16	...	c6
17	♗g4!	

The bishop sets off for the active f5-square and Black's minor pieces begin to look as if they are in a tangle.

17	...	♘fg6
18	♗f5	♗g5

19 ♔b1   ♘e7
20 d4!

Black's knights are driven back and, after the exchange of dark-squared bishops, the open files on the kingside look even more menacing.

20 ...   ♘5g6
21 ♗c1!   ♗xc1
22 ♔xc1   d5

Black should probably try to complicate the issue with something like 22 ... ♕a5 23 ♔b2 c5, although White should still be better. After 22 ... d5 the situation is close to being beyond repair.

23 e5   ♘xf5
24 ♕xf5   ♘e7

24 ... ♕c8 25 e6!

25 ♕g4   g6

Now the kingside pawns have been fatally weakened.

26 ♖df1   ♕c8
27 ♕h4   ♘f5
28 ♕f6   ♔h7
29 ♘e2!

It just remains for the knight to be transferred to the kingside.

29 ...   ♕e6 *(121)*

What can Black do? Waiting passively is out of the question and 29 ... ♕d8 allows 30 ♖xf5.

30 ♖xg6! ♕xf6

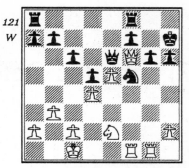

121
W

31 ♖xf6   ♘g7
32 ♖xf7

32 ♖1f3 looks even stronger.

32 ...   ♔g8
33 ♖xf8+ ♖xf8
34 ♖xf8+ ♔xf8

Black fought well in the coming endgame, but he eventually had to bow to the inevitable. The remaining moves were: 35 ♔d2 ♘e6 36 ♔e3 ♔f7 37 c4 ♘c7 38 ♘f4 b5 39 ♔d3 a5 40 cd cd 41 a4 b4 42 ♔e3 ♔e8 43 ♘d3 ♘e6 44 ♘c5 ♘d8 45 ♘d3 ♘c6 46 ♘f4 ♘e7 47 ♘e2 ♔f7 48 ♔f4 ♔g6 49 ♘g1 ♘c6 50 ♘f3 ♔f7 51 ♔f5 ♘e7+ 52 ♔g4 ♔e6 53 ♘h4 ♘c8 54 ♘f5 ♘b6 55 ♘d6 ♘d7 56 ♘b5 ♘b8 57 ♔f4 ♘c6 58 h4 ♘e7 59 ♘d6 ♘c6 60 ♘f5 h5 61 ♔g5 ♘xe5 62 ♘g7+ ♔d6 63 de+ ♔xe5 64 ♘xh5 ♔d4 65 ♘f4 ♔c3 66 h5 ♔xb3 67 h6 ♔a2 68 h7 b3 69 ♘d3 1-0.

7) Schallop Defence

1	e4	e5
2	f4	ef
3	♘f3	♘f6 (122)

Black intends to hold on to his f-pawn, defending it with his knight from h5. In this way he avoids weakening his kingside pawns, but h5 is hardly the sort of outpost that knights dream about. Apart from having very little mobility, its exposed position offers White some tactical possibilities.

Game 37
Glaskov – Shapoval
Corr. 1985/86

1	e4	e5
2	f4	ef

3	♘f3	♘f6
4	e5	

Obviously this is the critical continuation. 4 ♘c3 is met by 4 ... d5. If now 5 ed, play has transposed into a variation of the Modern Defence, where White has little hope of gaining the advantage, whilst 5 e5 ♘h5 is less favourable than the text.

4	...	♘h5

Averbakh's move 4 ... ♘e4 is seen from time to time, a recent example being Illescas – Motwani, Thessaloniki 1988: 5 d3 ♘g5 6 ♗xf4 ♘e6 7 ♗g3 d6 8 d4 de 9 d5 (9 ♗xe5) 9 ... ♘f4 10 ♘xe5 ♘xd5 11 ♗c4 ♗e6 12 ♕e2 ♗e7 13 ♘c3 with an unclear position.

White does better to follow the recommendation of Keres and play 5 d4. After 5 ... d5 6 ♗xf4 c5 7 ♘bd2 ♘c6 8 ♗d3 he has the better game.

5	♗e2!?	

White prepares to castle quickly which will enable him to move his knight from f3, thereby causing embarrassment to the knight on h5. 5 d4 is game 38.

    5 ... g5

There are a number of alternatives:

a) 5 ... d5 6 0-0 g5 7 ♘xg5!

b) 5 ... g6 6 d4 ♗g7 7 0-0 d6 8 ♘c3 0-0 and, as Chigorin pointed out, 9 ed! cd (9 ... ♕xd6 10 ♘e5) 10 ♘e1.

c) 5 ... d6 6 0-0 (In the game Camarra - Sayed, Lucerne 1982, White decided to throw the kitchen sink at his opponent and won in spectacular fashion: 6 d4?! de 7 0-0 ed {7 ... e4 8 ♘e5 f3 9 gf ef 10 ♗c4 ♗e6 11 ♗xe6 fe 12 ♗e3 gives White good compensation} 8 ♗c4 ♗e6 9 ♗xe6 fe 10 ♕e2 ♘c6? {Here Black could have cast serious doubts upon the correctness of White's idea with 10 ... ♕d5!} 11 ♕xe6+ ♕e7 12 ♕h3 ♕c5 {12 ... ♕f7 13 ♖e1+ ♗e7 14 ♘g5 ♕g6 15 ♘e6, with the threat of ♕xh5, is good for White} 13 b4! ♘xb4 {13 ... ♕d5 14 c4!} 14 ♖e1+ ♗e7 15 ♖e5 ♕xc2 16 ♕xh5+ g6 17 ♖xe7+ ♔xe7 18 ♕e5+ ♔d7 19 ♕xd4+ ♔e7 20 ♕xb4+ c5 21 ♕xb7+ ♔e6 22 ♘g5+ ♔e5 23 ♗b2+ ♔f5 24 ♕d5+ ♔g4 25 h3+ 1-0) 6 ... de 7 ♘xe5 and Black's two main choices don't seem to give him equality:

c1) 7 ... ♕d4+ 8 ♔h1 ♘f6 9 ♘d3 and White wins back the f-pawn with a good game as 9 ... g5 10 b3! is strong.

c2) 7 ... ♗c5+ 8 ♔h1 ♘f6 (The attempt to play for a snap mate fails, e.g. 8 ... ♘g3+ 9 hg fg 10 ♗b5+ {10 ♘f3} 10 ... c6 11 ♕h5 g6 12 ♘xc6 ♘xc6 13 ♕e5+ ♕e7 14 ♕xh8+ ♔d7 15 ♕xh7) 9 c3 ♗d6 (9 ... ♘bd7 10 ♘xd7 ♗xd7 11 d4 ♗d6 12 ♗xf4 ♗xf4 13 ♖xf4 0-0 14 ♘d3 is clearly in White's favour. In the game Verdikhanov - Ilyin, Corr. 1982, Black tried 9 ... g5 but after 10 d4 ♗d6 11 ♘d2! ♘bd7 12 ♘df3 h6 13 ♗c4 ♕e7 14 ♕b3 White stood clearly better) 10 d4 ♗xe5 11 de ♕xd1 12 ♗xd1 (12 ♖xd1 ♘e4 is unclear) 12 ... ♘d5 13 ♗f3! ♘e3 14 ♗xe3 fe 15 ♘a3! and White's chances are to be preferred. The e-pawn is not long for this world and the bishop exerts strong pressure on the long diagonal.

    6 0-0 *(123)*

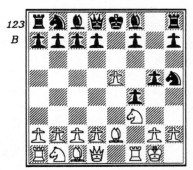

123
B

6 ... ⬜g8

In former times, this position was believed to be favourable for Black, but recent examples show this assessment to be incorrect.

Apart from 6 ... ⬜g8 Black has tried:

a) 6 ... ♘c6 7 d4 (7 ♘xg5? would be disastrous: 7 ... ♗c5+ 8 ♔h1 ♘g3+! 9 hg ♕xg5) 7 ... ⬜g8 and now Lasker demonstrated a very fine way for White to continue: 8 ♘fd2! ♘g7 (8 ... g4 9 ♗xg4 ♕g5 10 ♗f3 ♘xd4 11 ♘e4 ♘xf3+ 12 ♕xf3 ♕xe5 13 ♘bc3 with the threat of ♕xh5) 9 ♘e4 ♗e7 10 ♘bc3 d5 11 ed cd 12 ♘d5 with dangerous attacking chances.

b) 6 ... d6 7 ♘xg5! ♕xg5 8 ♗xh5 de 9 d4! (Keres).

c) 6 ... ♘g7 7 d4 d5 8 c4 c6 9 ♘c3 ♗e6 10 cd cd 11 ♕b3 ♘d7 12 ♘xd5 ♗e7 13 ♕xb7 0-0 14 ♘c7 with a clear advantage to White in Lutikov – Kuzmin, Sochi 1970.

7 d4 g4?!

As Black doesn't achieve a strong attack, he should avoid this self-destructive move and play 7 ... d5. White still gets a good game in an unusual fashion for the King's Gambit: 8 c4! c6 9 ♘c3 ♗e6 (9 ... g4 10 cd gf 11 ♗xf3 is good for White) 10 cd cd 11 ♕d3 (Glaskov also suggests 11 ♕b3 ♕d7 12 g4!) 11 ... ⬜g6 12 ♘h4! ⬜h6 13 ♘f5 ♗xf5 14 ♕xf5 ♘g7 15 ♕d3 ♘c6 and, according to Glaskov, White gains the advantage after 16 g3! fg 17 hg.

8 ♘c3!?

Although this piece sacrifice is very strong, the simple 8 ♘e1 leaves Black in a bad way, e.g. 8 ... d5 (8 ... f3 9 ♗xf3 gf 10 ♕xf3) 9 ♘d3! and 9 ... f3 is again met by ♗xf3.

8 ... gf?!

It's probably better to try 8 ... d5. Glaskov gives 9 ♘e1 ♗h6 10 ♘d3! ♕h4 11 ♘xf4 g3 12 ♗b5+ c6 13 ♕xh5 as clearly better for White.

9 ♗xf3 *(124)*

White's big mobile pawn centre and active pieces give him a positional bind which Black will be unable to shake off.

9 ... ♕g5

9 ... ♘g7 is more resilient. White can then play 10 ♘e4 (10 ♕d3!?) 10 ... ♗e7

11 ♗xf4 ♘e6 12 ♗e3 with very strong pressure.

| 10 | ♘e4 | ♕f5 |

10 ... ♕g6 11 ♕e2.

11	♗xh5!	♕xe4
12	♗xf7+!	♔xf7
13	♖xf4+	♕xf4
14	♕h5+	♔g7
15	♗xf4	

Although Black has sufficient material for the queen, his chronic lack of development obviously renders him defenceless.

| 15 | ... | ♔h8 |
| 16 | ♗g5 | d6 |

It is a little late to start worrying about the queenside.

17	♗f6+	♗g7
18	♖f1	♗xf6
19	♖xf6	♘d7
20	♖f7	♖g7

20 ... ♘f8 21 ♕h6.

| 21 | e6 | 1-0 |

Game 38
Bangiev – Podrezov.
Corr. 1986/87

1	e4	e5
2	f4	ef
3	♘f3	♘f6
4	e5	♘h5
5	d4	(125)

White's most direct move. Black's choices are rather limited as 5 ... g5 6 ♘fd2! is very strong.

| 5 | ... | d5 |

The main alternative is 5 ... d6, after which White

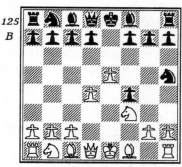

does best to reply 6 ♕e2, virtually forcing Black's reply, 6 ... d5 (6 ... de 7 ♘xe5 {or 7 ♕xe5+ ♕e7 8 ♗e2} 7 ... ♕h4+ 8 g3 ♘xg3 9 hg ♕xh1 10 ♗xf4 is very favourable for White; 6 ... ♗e7? loses a piece to 7 ed and 8 ♕b5+. This might not be such an obvious trap as it has occurred in two of my games, including one against the Soviet master Huzman) 7 c4! (It is important for White to gain space on the queenside) 7 ... ♗e6 8 cd (8 ♘c3!?) 8 ... ♗xd5 9 ♘c3 ♘c6 10 ♗d2! ♗b4 11 ♘xd5 ♕xd5 12 0-0-0! ♕xa2 (If 12 ... 0-0-0 then 13 ♕c4 ♗xd2+ 14 ♖xd2 ♕xc4+ 15 ♗xc4 is favourable for White as 15 ... f6 can be met by 16 ♗e6+ ♔b8 17 ♗g4!) 13 d5!. Analysis by Korchnoi shows that White stands better after 13 ... ♗xd2+ 14 ♘xd2 ♕xd5 15 ♕xh5 ♕xe5 16 ♕xe5+ ♘xe5 17 ♖e1 f6 18 ♘c4 0-0-0 19 ♘xe5 fe 20 ♖xe5 and White's bishop is stronger than Black's pawns.

6 c4

Again we have the 'Queen's Gambit' variation of the King's Gambit. White can also consider 6 ♗e2 when after 6 ... g5 7 0-0 ♖g8 play has transposed to the seventh move note of Glaskov - Shapoval. After 6 ♗e2, the game S. Bucker - S. Nikolic, Biel 1984, took an independent course: 6 ... ♗g4 7 0-0 g6 8 ♖e1 ♗e7 9 c3 c5 10 ♕b3 b6 with a complicated struggle ahead. Instead of the strange 8 ♖e1, 8 ♘e1 seems more to the point, and after the exchange of bishops White can play ♘d3 and ♘xf4.

6 ... g5 *(126)*

Black has a large number of alternatives:

a) 6 ... ♗b4+ 7 ♘c3 ♘c6 8 ♗e2 0-0 9 0-0. *ECO* considers White to be slightly better, e.g. 9 ... ♗xc3 10 bc ♗g4 11 ♘e1 ♗xe2 12 ♕xe2 g6 13 ♗xf4 with advantage to White in Muchnik - Dzhalalov, Moscow 1952.

b) 6 ... ♘c6 7 cd ♕xd5 8 ♘c3 ♗b4 9 ♗e2 (9 ♔f2!?) 9 ... ♕a5 (9 ... g6 10 0-0 ♗xc3 11 bc ♗g4 12 h3 ♗f5 13 ♘h4 was slightly better for White in Gragev - Chernakov, Corr. 1972) 10 ♗d2 ♗g4 11 a3 ♗xc3 12 bc 0-0 13 ♘g5! (White starts a lethal attack) 13 ... ♗xe2 14 ♕xe2

g6 15 g4! fg 16 hg ♘xg3 17 ♘xh7! and White won, Glaskov - Malyuzhinets, Moscow 1950.

c) 6 ... c6. White can now exert strong pressure with ♘c3 and ♕b3.

d) 6 ... ♗e7 7 ♗e2 ♗h4+ 8 ♔f1 ♗g4 (8 ... ♗e7 9 cd ♕xd5 10 ♘c3 ♕d8 11 d5 and the threat of ♘d4 gives White the advantage, e.g. 11 ... ♗g4 12 ♘d4 ♗xe2 13 ♕xe2 g6 14 ♕e4) 9 cd 0-0 10 ♘c3 and White's powerful centre is more important than his misplaced king.

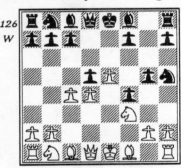

126
W

7 g4!

This incredible looking move guarantees White a clear advantage.

7 ... ♘g7

If 7 ... ♗xg4 8 ♖g1 gives White a good game, e.g. 8 ... ♗xf3 9 ♕xf3 ♘g7 10 cd; or 8 ... ♕d7 9 cd.

8 ♘c3 ♗b4

9 ♖g1

9 cd allows Black counterplay with 9 ... h5!

9 ... h5

10 h3

By holding the g4-point White seriously restricts the mobility of Black's minor pieces.

10 ... dc?!

It is, however, inadvisable to give up the centre in this fashion; Black should have prepared to dig in for a sturdy defence with 10 ... c6.

11 ♗xc4 c5

In for a penny...

12	d5	♘d7
13	♗d2	♘b6
14	♕e2	hg
15	hg	♗d7

White's pawns control the whole board and Black is reduced to moves like this.

16	a3	♗a5
17	♘e4	♗xd2+
18	♘fxd2	♕e7
19	d6 *(127)*	1-0

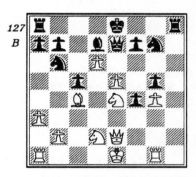

Black, rather prematurely, decided to call it a day (although one can sympathise with him).

8) Rare Third Moves

Game 39
Spassky – Seirawan
Montpellier 1985

1	e4	e5
2	f4	ef
3	♘f3	♘e7 *(128)*

128
W

The so-called Bonsch-Osmolovsky variation. Black plans to bring his knight around to g6 in order to give protection to his extra pawn. But 3 ... ♘e7 doesn't really put any pressure on White's position and g6 turns out to be not such a solid base.

4	d4	d5

Black has to stake a claim in the centre. After 4 ... ♘g6 5 h4! gives White a good game, e.g. 5 ... h5 6 ♘c3 ♗e7 7 ♘d5 ♘xh4 (7 ... ♗xh4+ 8 ♘xh4 ♘xh4 9 ♗xf4 d6 10 ♗g3 ♘g6 11 ♖xh5 is good for White) 8 ♗xf4 with a clear advantage.

5	♘c3	

Blocking the centre with 5 e5 unnecessarily concedes control of the white squares, e.g. 5 ... ♘g6 6 ♗d3 ♗e7 7 ♗xg6 fg 8 ♗xf4 g5 9 ♗g3 g4 and Black already had the upper hand in Naftalan – Martiroshan, Corr. 1985/87.

5	...	de
6	♘xe4	♘g6
7	h4!	

Spassky's improvement on his game against Novopashin, 23 years earlier, where he played 7 ♗c4.

7	...	♕e7 *(129)*

7 ... ♗e7 8 h5 ♘h4 9 ♗xf4 ♗g4 10 h6! with advantage to White in Kuznetsov – Bonsch-Osmolovsky, Moscow 1964.

8	♔f2!	

A wonderful move, after which Black's pieces seem to be on silly squares. Of course the knight is taboo:

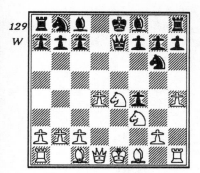

129
W

8 ... ♕xe4 9 ♗b5+ and 10
♖e1.

8	...	♗g4
9	h5	♘h4
10	♗xf4	

So White has regained
the pawn and his well-cen-
tralised position gives him
a clear advantage.

| 10 | ... | ♘c6 |
| 11 | ♗b5! | |

This ensures that Black's
king will find no sanctuary.

11	...	0-0-0
12	♗xc6	bc
13	♕d3	

Unpinning and also
threatening ♕a6+.

| 13 | ... | ♘xf3 |

13 ... ♗xf3 is out of the
question as Black must retain this bishop to try to
plug the holes around his
king.

14	gf	♗f5
15	♕a6+	♔b8
16	♘c5	♗c8
17	♕xc6	♖xd4

If Black doesn't take the
pawn he is totally lost.

| 18 | ♖ae1! | |

The queen has no square
as c7 must remain de-
fended.

18	...	♖xf4
19	♕b5+	♔a8
20	♕c6+	♔b8
21	♖xe7	♗xe7
22	♖d1	♖f6

22 ... ♗xc5 23 ♕xc5 ♗b7
24 ♖d3! is very strong.

| 23 | ♘d7+ | ♗xd7 |
| 24 | ♕xd7 | ♖d8 |

24 ... ♗c5+ would put up
a little more resistance,
but the ending is techni-
cally lost.

25	♕b5+	♔c8
26	♖xd8+	♗xd8
27	♕a4	

If Black's queenside
pawns were united he
might have some slight
drawing chances.

| 27 | ... | g5 |
| 28 | ♕xa7 | ♖f4 |

28 ... g4 fails to 29 ♕a8+
and 30 ♕a4+.

29	♕a6+	♔b8
30	♕d3	♗e7
31	♕xh7	g4
32	♔g3	1-0

Game 40
Schlechter – Teichmann
Vienna 1903

1	e4	e5
2	f4	ef
3	♘f3	f5 *(130)*

This only serves to wea-
ken Black's kingside and
even in 1903 it wasn't

thought of very highly.

130
W

4 e5!

4 ef d5 would justify Black's third move.

4 ... g5

Other moves also lead to a bad game:

a) 4 ... d5 5 h4!? followed by d4 and ♗xf4.

b) 4 ... d6 5 ♕e2 ♗e7 6 d4 ♘c6 7 ♗xf4 de 8 de ♘d4 9 ♕c4 ♘e6 (9 ... ♘xf3+ 10 gf ♗h4+ 11 ♔e2 is good for White) 10 ♗d3 with the better game for White.

5 d4 g4

5 ... d5 6 c4 ♗e6 7 ♘c3 ♗b4 8 h4 was good for White in Glaskov - Yaroshevsky, Moscow 1971.

6 ♗xf4!

This traditional piece sacrifice is given added venom by the fact that Black has played ... f5.

6 ... gf
7 ♕xf3 ♕h4+

This is the only sensible way to stop ♕h5+.

8 g3 ♕g4
9 ♕e3

Black has gained a moment's breathing space, but is unable to do anything with it.

9 ... ♘c6
10 ♗e2 ♕g6
11 ♘c3 ♗b4
12 d5!

Forcing one of Black's few developed pieces to retreat.

12 ... ♘d8
13 0-0-0 h6
14 g4!

White opens lines on the kingside, which provide added fuel for the attack.

14 ... ♘e7
15 d6 ♘e6

If the knight had moved, White could have won easily by 16 gf or 16 ♘d5.

16 de ♗c5
17 ♕g3 ♗xe7

Material equality has been restored, but Black hasn't solved any of his problems.

18 gf ♕xf5
19 ♗e3 ♗g5
20 ♘d5 ♗xe3+
21 ♕xe3 ♔d8

21 ... ♕g5+ is a little better. After 22 ♕xg5 hg 23 ♗g4! ♖b8 24 ♗xe6 de 25 ♘xc7+ White is a pawn up with a good position.

22 ♖hg1 ♕f8
23 ♖df1 ♕c5
24 ♕f3 ♖f8 *(131)*

Black is playing without his queenside and so it is

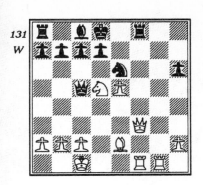

131
W

not surprising that White now has a decisive blow.

25 ♖g8! 1-0

An elegant finish. 25 ... ♖xg8 26 ♕f6+ ♔e8 27 ♕f7+.

9) Falkbeer Counter-Gambit

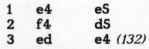

1	e4	e5
2	f4	d5
3	ed	e4 *(132)*

132
W

Instead of accepting the pawn on offer, Black decides to sacrifice one himself. In return, he hopes to be able to develop swiftly and easily, whilst also demonstrating how out of place the advance f2-f4 now is. At one stage this counter-gambit was scoring so well that it prompted Rudolf Spielmann to write his tragic article "From the deathbed of the King's Gambit". As we shall see, this was certainly a trifle premature.

On his fourth move White has tried several continuations, but in this book we shall only be examining 4 d3!. Modern practice has shown that to free his position White has to exchange Black's strong e-pawn as quickly as possible.

Game 41
Murey – Nikitin
USSR 1970

1	e4	e5
2	f4	d5
3	ed	

I should just mention in passing that declining the Falkbeer with 3 ♘f3 has a number of supporters. However, this idea sprang to prominence when Black was scoring well, and now that White seems able to prove an advantage in practically every variation, there is no need to decline the gambit.

3 ... e4

3 ... c6 is the Nimzowitsch Counter-Gambit (see chapter ten).

4 d3! ed?!

This is feeble and simply contributes towards White's development. There are two serious alternatives, one of which, 4 ... ♘f6, will be the subject of subsequent games.

4 ... ♕xd5 is also insufficient for equality, but White must play carefully. For example, 5 ♕e2 ♘f6 6 ♘d2! (6 ♘c3 ♗b4 is not so clear) and now:

a) 6 ... ♗f5 7 de ♗xe4 (7 ... ♘xe4 8 g4) 8 g4 gives White a clear advantage e.g. 8 ... ♗e7 9 ♘xe4 ♕xe4 (According to Keres 9 ... ♘xe4 10 ♗g2 ♕a5+ 11 ♔f1 ♘d6 12 ♗d2 is very good for White) 10 ♗g2! ♕xe2+ 11 ♘xe2 c6 12 g5 and White has a considerable advantage due to his bishop pair and active development.

b) 6 ... ♗g4 7 ♘gf3 ♗xf3 (If 7 ... ♘c6, analysis by Glaskov shows how White can retain the advantage: 8 de ♕h5 9 ♕b5 0-0-0 10 ♕xh5 ♘xh5 11 ♘c4 ♘b4 {11 ... ♗xf3 12 gf ♘d4 13 ♗d3 ♘xf3+ 14 ♔f2 is good for White} 12 ♗d3! {Previously only 12 ♘a3? had been considered, which allows Black a strong attack in return for the pawn} 12 ... ♘xd3+ 13 cd. Black cannot win back his pawn, as the following variation shows: 13 ... ♗xf3 14 gf ♖xd3 15 ♘e5!

♖d4 16 ♗e3 ♖b4 17 ♘xf7 ♖g8 18 0-0-0 with a clear advantage for White) 8 gf e3 9 ♘e4 ♗e7 10 ♗xe3 ♘h5 (Keres considers that after 10 ... 0-0 White can gain the advantage with 11 ♗g2 and 12 0-0) 11 ♘c3 ♕f5 12 0-0-0 ♘xf4 13 ♕d2 *(133)*

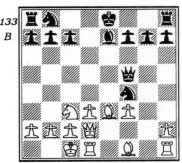

133 B

Black has fallen seriously behind in development. 13 ... ♗g5 (13 ... ♘e6 14 f4; or 13 ... ♘d5 14 ♗h3! are both good for White) 14 h4 ♗h6 15 ♗h3! ♘xh3 16 ♗xh6 gh 17 ♕e3+ and Black is unable to defend, e.g. 17 ... ♔d8 18 ♕d4+; or 17 ... ♕e6 18 ♕d4 0-0 19 ♖xh3! wins quickly; 17 ... ♔f8 18 ♖xh3! (18 ♕xh6+ is also good) 18 ... ♕xh3 19 ♕c5+. If Black goes to the g-file he gets mated and if he goes to the e-file he loses his rook.

5 ♗xd3

5 ♕xd3 is equally good, after which Black has very little play for the pawn, e.g 5 ... ♘f6 6 ♘c3 (6 c4) 6 ... ♗e7 (or 6 ... ♗c5 7 ♗d2 0-0

8 0-0-0 ♘bd7 9 g3! with a good game for White in Stoltz - Marshall, Folkestone 1933) 7 ♗e3 followed by 8 0-0-0.

5 ...   ♛xd5

Black grabs his chance to restore material equality, realising that if he doesn't do so now he probably never will. But there is a price to be paid for bringing out the queen so early. When you look at the alternative, though, it is hard to criticise Black's choice: 5 ... ♘f6 6 ♘c3 ♗e7 (6 ... ♘xd5 7 ♗b5+ is strong) 7 ♘f3 0-0 8 0-0 ♘bd7 9 ♗c4 ♘b6 10 ♗b3. The only way for Black to get his pieces out is by 10 ... ♗b4 but after 11 ♘e5 ♗xc3 12 bc ♘bxd5 13 ♗a3 ♖e8 14 ♛d4 White stood clearly better in Keres - Lilienthal, Moscow 1941.

6 ♘c3   ♛e6+

Of course, 6 ... ♛xg2 7 ♗e4 ♛g4 8 ♛xg4 ♗xg4 9 ♗xb7 wins for White.

7 ♘ge2   ♘h6 *(134)*

Black also got into great difficulties after 7 ... ♘f6 8 0-0 ♛b6+ 9 ♔h1 ♗e7 10 ♛e1, Keres - Vidmar, Corr. 1936.

8 f5!

This simple pawn sacrifice opens up further lines and diagonals as well as gaining even more tempi for the attack.

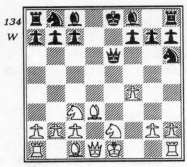

134 W

8	...	♘xf5
9	0-0	♘e3
10	♗xe3	♛xe3+
11	♔h1	♗d6
12	♘f4!	

Combinations flow naturally when you are far ahead in development and the opponent's king is still in the middle.

12	...	0-0
13	♛h5	g6

After 13 ... h6 14 ♖ae1 gives White a massive position.

14 ♘xg6!

The attack crashes through whilst the black pieces stand and watch.

14	...	hg
15	♗xg6	fg
16	♛xg6+	♔h8
17	♘d5	♖xf1+
18	♖xf1	♛e2
19	♛h6+	♔g8
20	♘f6+	*(135)*

Mate follows shortly: 20 ... ♔f7 21 ♛h7+ ♔e6 (21 ... ♔f8 22 ♛g8+ ♔e7 23 ♛e8) 22 ♛g8+ and mate follows.

1-0

Game 42
Spassky – Matanovic
Belgrade 1964

1	e4	e5
2	f4	d5
3	ed	e4
4	d3	♘f6 (136)

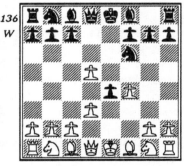

5   de!
Experience has shown this capture to be the strongest in this position.

5   ...   ♘xe4
6   ♗e3!?
White takes immediate control of the sensitive a7-g1 diagonal, not even worrying about ... ♕h4+. 6 ♘f3 can be seen in games

43 and 44.

6   ...   ♕h4+
Black has to take up the challenge or he will end up in an inferior position, e.g. 6 ... ♗d6 7 ♘f3 0-0 8 ♗d3 ♖e8 9 0-0 ♘f6 10 ♘e5!? ♘bd7 11 ♘c4 ♘f8 12 ♔h1 with the better game for White (Glaskov).

7   g3   ♘xg3
8   ♘f3!
Of course, when Mikhail Tal had this position he was unable to resist the exchange sacrifice, but even he couldn't generate enough compensation: 8 hg?! ♕xh1 9 ♕e2 ♗b4+ 10 c3 ♗d6 11 ♗g2 ♕h6 12 ♗d4+ ♔d8 13 ♘f3 ♗g4 and Black's play along the e-file and extra exchange clearly outweigh any random attacking chances White might have (Tal - Trifunovic, Havana 1963).

8   ...   ♕e7
Of course, now that White has an extra tempo, it would be quite foolhardy to allow him to sacrifice the exchange by playing 8 ... ♕h5.

9   hg   ♕xe3+
10   ♕e2   ♕xe2+
10 ... ♗c5 11 ♘c3 doesn't change the assessment.

11   ♘xe2 (137)
So Black has managed to exchange queens and obtain the bishop pair. One

would think he is over the worst - but this is by no means the case for a number of reasons:

a) White has a useful lead in development which means that he should get first use of the open e-file. Note that the rook on h1 is already well developed.

b) His dynamic pawn structure gives him a firm grip on the centre.

c) White's knights have some fine squares in the centre to occupy, which means that they are in no way inferior to the bishops.

11 ... ♗g4

11 ... ♗f5 12 ♘bd2 c6 13 ♘d4 ♗d7 14 ♗f3! gave White the better game in Vilner - Shukmann, Moscow 1977.

11 ... ♗c5! would have kept Black's disadvantage to a minimum.

12	♘c3	♗b4
13	♘g5!	♗xe2
14	♔xe2	♗xc3
15	bc	h6

16 ♔d3! (138)

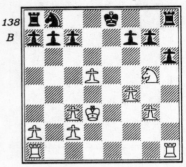

Now Black has the difficult decision of whether to leave his king in the centre or castle.

16 ... ♖f8

This move was strongly criticised after the game, when it was suggested that by 16 ... 0-0 17 ♘e4 ♖d8 Black could achieve an equal game. This does not seem to be the case, however: 18 c4 c6 19 ♖h5! (It is always enjoyable to develop a rook in this fashion) 19 ... ♘a6 20 d6 b6 21 ♖d1 ♘c5+ 22 ♖xc5! bc 23 ♔c3 with a very good endgame for White in Listengarten - Kozlov, Baku 1977.

17 ♘f3

With the black king in the centre, this is much stronger than ♘e4. From f3, the knight has the choice of several good squares and in fact the major part of White's advantage can be attributed to his superior minor piece.

17	...	♞a6
18	♖ae1+	♚d7
19	c4	f6

Black was, of course, worried about the e5-square, but now he has seriously weakened e6. He is relying on his knight to cover this square from c5.

| 20 | ♚d4 | |

With the threat of 21 c5.

20	...	b6
21	f5!	♞c5
22	♞h4	

Black's position is full of holes.

| 22 | ... | ♖fe8 *(139)* |

| 23 | ♖e6! | |

The culmination of White's strategy. Taking the rook would leave Black in a near hopeless position: 23 ... ♞xe6 24 fe+ ♚e7 25 ♞f5+ ♚f8 26 c5!

| 23 | ... | g5! |

The best chance.

| 24 | ♞g6? | |

This is careless, throwing away most of the advantage. Instead, 24 ♞g2! leaves Black in a sorry state, e.g. 24 ... ♞xe6 25 fe+ ♚e7 26 ♞e3 ♖h8 27 g4 and White's knight is the strongest piece on the board.

24	...	♞xe6
25	fe+	♖xe6!
26	de+	♚xe6
27	♖xh6	♚f7 *(140)*

And now the point of Black's little trick is revealed: the knight is trapped and ... ♚g7 is going to win back the piece.

| 28 | ♞e5+ | fe+ |
| 29 | ♚xe5 | c5 |

White still has slightly the better of it, but the weakness of his queenside eases Black's defensive task.

30	♚f5	♚e7
31	♚xg5	♖f8
32	♖h2	

This is passive, but 32 ♖h7+ ♚d6 33 ♖xa7 doesn't really offer any chances, e.g. 33 ... ♖f3 34 g4 ♖c3 35 ♚f5 ♖xc4 36 g5 ♖xc2 37 g6 c4 and Black has a dangerous passed pawn of his own.

32	...	♔d6
33	g4	♖g8+
34	♔f4	♖f8+
35	♔g3	♔e5!
36	♖e2+	♔d4
37	g5	♔xc4
38	♔g4	♔c3

Black has enough counterplay on the queenside.

39	g6	c4
40	♔g5	b5
41	g7	

And at this point the players agreed to a draw, as after 41 ... ♖g8 42 ♔g6 a5 43 ♔f7 ♖xg7+ 44 ♔xg7 b4 45 ♔f6 a4 the outcome is apparent.

½-½

Game 43
Bronstein - Tal
Riga 1968

1	e4	e5
2	f4	d5
3	ed	e4
4	d3	♘f6
5	de	♘xe4
6	♘f3	*(141)*

White's most popular and probably strongest move in this position. 6 ... ♕h4+ is stopped and White judges that the play on the a7-g1 diagonal is not too dangerous.

6 ... ♗c5

Other moves don't really meet the demands of the position:

a) 6 ... c6 7 ♘bd2! ♘xd2 8 ♗xd2 ♕xd5 9 ♗d3 with a strong initiative for White.

b) 6 ... ♗f5 7 ♗e3 c6 8 ♗c4 b5 9 ♗b3 c5 10 d6! c4 11 ♕d5 ♘d7 12 ♕xf5 ♘xd6 13 ♕d5 and White stands clearly better, Alekhine - Tarrasch, St Petersburg 1914.

7 ♕e2 *(142)*

7 ♗d3 was recommended long ago by Tartakower and although it seems good for White, nobody appears to have heard him. After 7 ... ♘f2 8 ♕e2+ ♕e7 9 ♖f1 ♘xd3+ 10 cd ♕xe2+ 11 ♔xe2 White has the better game.

7 ... ♗f5

Black's position is much too loose to try to exploit the weak dark squares:

a) 7 ... ♗f2+ 8 ♔d1 ♕xd5+ 9 ♘fd2 f5 10 ♘c3 ♕d4 11 ♘xe4 fe 12 c3 ♕e3. White has a pawn if he wants it, but 13 ♕h5+ promises much more.

b) 7 ... ♕xd5 8 ♘fd2! is similar to 'a', and also very good for White.

c) 7 ... 0-0 should be answered by 8 ♕xe4 ♖e8 9 ♘e5 f6 10 ♗d3 g6 11 ♕c4! and White's position is clearly preferable.

d) 7 ... f5 has also been seen, but after 8 ♗e3 ♕xd5 9 ♗xc5 ♕xc5 10 ♘c3 White had obtained the better position (Spielmann - Wolf, Dusseldorf 1908).

e) 7 ... ♕e7 is also well met by 8 ♗e3!. White achieved a clear advantage in the game Arnason - D' Amore, Groningen 1980/81, after 8 ... ♗xe3 9 ♕xe3 ♘d7 10 ♘bd2 ♘df6 11 ♘xe4 ♘xe4 12 0-0-0 0-0 13 ♗d3.

8 ♘c3

In the game that so depressed Spielmann, he played 8 g4? against Tarrasch in Ostrau 1923. After 8 ... 0-0 9 gf ♖e8 Black had an enormous attack.

8 ... ♕e7 *(143)*

8 ... 0-0 is unsound: 9 ♘xe4 ♖e8 10 ♘e5 ♗xe4 11 ♕xe4 f6 12 d6! ♕xd6 13 ♗e3!

(to block the e-file) 13 ... ♗xe3 14 ♕c4+ (Blackburne - Marco, Berlin 1897).

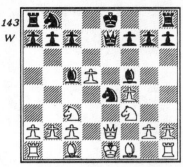

143 W

9 ♗e3! ♘xc3

9 ... ♗xe3 is the subject of the next game.

The attempt to avoid simplification with 9 ... ♗b4 isn't very good for Black, e.g. 10 ♗d4 (10 ♗d2 also gives White some advantage) 10 ... 0-0 11 0-0-0 ♖e8 (11 ... ♗xc3 12 ♗xc3 ♕c5 meets an elegant refutation: 13 ♗xg7! ♔xg7 14 ♘h4) 12 ♘xe4 (12 ♕b5 also looks good) 12 ... ♗xe4 13 ♗e5 ♗g6 14 ♕c4 and White is a pawn up (Sembukhov - Brichkov, USSR Corr. 1985/86).

10 ♗xc5 ♘xe2
11 ♗xe7 ♘xf4
12 ♗a3! ♘d7

After 12 ... ♘xd5 13 0-0-0 c6 14 ♘g5!, the threat of ♖e1+ is very hard to meet.

13 0-0-0 ♗e4

Unfortunately for Black, 13 ... 0-0-0 comes up against a strange refutation: 14 ♖d4! ♘g6 15 g4!

14	♘g5	♗xd5 *(144)*

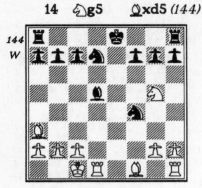

15 **g3!?**

15 ♖e1+ looks simple and strong (15 ... ♘e6 16 c4), but Bronstein was dreaming of the brilliancy prize.

| 15 | ... | ♗xh1 |
| 16 | gf | c5 |

To stave off immediate disaster, Black has to close the a3-f8 diagonal.

17	♗c4	♗c6
18	♘xf7	b5
19	♘d6+	

Of course, White should not be side-tracked by 19 ♘xh8.

| 19 | ... | ♔e7 |
| 20 | ♘xb5 | ♖hf8?! |

Black's best choice was probably 20 ... ♗xb5 21 ♗xb5 ♖hd8. White doesn't have to cash in with ♗xd7 and ♗xc5+ which gives Black decent drawing chances; instead he can keep up the pressure, perhaps with 22 b3!?. The text allows White to improve the position of his knight, with devastating effect.

21	♘d4!	♗g2
22	♘e6	♖f5
23	♖g1	♗e4 *(145)*

24 **♘c7?**

Incredibly, Bronstein fails to play 24 ♖e1 which wins on the spot (24 ... ♘f6 25 ♘xc5).

24	...	♖d8
25	♖xg7+	♔f6
26	♖f7+	♔g6
27	♖e7	♘f6
28	♘e6	♖c8
29	b3!	

Of course, with two pawns for the exchange and a strong attack, White still has an extremely good position.

29	...	♖h5
30	♘g5	♗d5
31	♗d3+	♔h6
32	♗b2	

White's pair of bishops are truly dominant. Tal could have resigned here.

32	...	c4
33	♗f5	c3
34	♗xc8	cb+
35	♔xb2	♖xh2
36	♖xa7	♖f2

37	♖a4	♔g6
38	♖d4	h5
39	a4	h4
40	a5	♗g2
41	a6	♘h5
42	♗b7	♘xf4
43	♖xf4	1-0

Game 44
Bangiev – Gutgarch
USSR Corr. 1985/87

1	e4	e5
2	f4	d5
3	ed	e4
4	d3	♘f6
5	de	♘xe4
6	♘f3	♗c5
7	♕e2	♗f5
8	♘c3	♕e7
9	♗e3	♗xe3
10	♕xe3	♘xc3
11	♕xe7+	♔xe7
12	bc	*(146)*

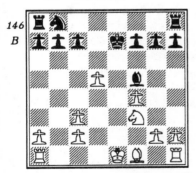

146
B

This is a critical position for the assessment of the Falkbeer. Although Black is sure to get his pawn back, he will waste time in doing so and when you add this to the weak position of his king, White's advantage begins to look serious.

12 ... ♗e4

Or 12 ... ♗xc2 13 ♔d2 ♗g6 (or 13 ... ♗f5 14 ♖e1+ ♔f6 15 ♘d4 ♗d7 16 h3 with kingside expansion to follow) 14 ♖e1+ ♔d6 15 ♘d4 (15 ♘g5!? looks interesting). Black's position is most unsatisfactory. The only two pieces he has succeeded in getting off the back rank are both in serious trouble: 15 ... ♔xd5 fails to 16 f5 ♗h5 17 g4, 18 ♗g2+ and 19 ♗xb7; 15 ... ♘d7 allows 16 ♘b5+, so Black has to try something like 15 ... h5, but then 16 f5 ♗h7 17 ♖b1! forces ... b6 which makes it extremely difficult for Black to develop.

13 ♘g5!

13 c4? ♗xf3 14 gf ♘d7 only leads to equality.

13 ... ♗xc2!?

Black is willing to waste a tempo in order to play lines similar to those in the twelfth move note but with White's knight on the inferior g5-square.

The alternative is 13 ... ♗xd5, after which 14 0-0-0! gives White the better game, e.g.

a) 14 ... ♗xa2 15 c4 b5 16 cb a6 17 ♗d3!? (Glaskov recommends 17 ♔b2) 17 ... ab?! 18 ♖he1+ ♗e6 (There is no square for the king) 19 f5 ♗f6 20 fe ♔xg5 21 ef ♖f8 22 ♖e8 and White soon won in Foune – Mathieu, Corr. 1985.

b) 14 ... ♗e6 15 ♘xe6 (15 ♗d3 also looks tempting, but the text does guarantee a clear advantage) 15 ... fe 16 ♗c4 ♖f8 (16 ... ♘d7 17 ♗xe6) 17 ♖he1 ♖f6 18 f5! with a good game for White.

c) 14 ... c6 15 c4 ♗e6 16 ♗d3 with threats of ♖he1 and f5.

d) 14 ... ♖d8 15 c4 ♗e6 16 ♖xd8 ♔xd8 17 ♘xe6+ fe 18 ♗d3 h6 19 ♖e1! ♔d7 20 ♖e3 ♘c6 21 ♖g3 and White wins (Korchnoi and Zak).

14   ♔d2   ♗g6
15   ♖e1+ *(147)*

147
B

15   ...   ♔f8

Other moves seem to be even worse:

a) 15 ... ♔d6 16 f5!

b) 15 ... ♔f6 16 g4! ♖d8 17 c4 c6 18 ♘h3 and Black is in serious danger of being mated.

c) 15 ... ♔d7 16 ♗d3 f6 17 ♘e6 with a clear advantage.

16   ♘b5!?

White finds an interesting way to create attacking chances. 16 g4 also looks good.

16   ...   c6
17   f5!

This is the point behind White's previous move. The black bishop is forced to h5, as after 17 ... ♗xf5 18 ♖hf1 g6 19 g4 White should win.

17   ...   ♗h5
18   dc   ♘xc6
19   ♗xc6   bc
20   c4

White creates a safe square for his king. His advantage springs from Black's total lack of co-ordination.

20   ...   g6

Black's bishop will now return to the game, but his kingside remains in a tangle. If instead 20 ... h6, White gains a clear advantage by 21 ♘e4 f6 22 ♔c3 ♗f7 23 ♘c5.

21   f6   h6
22   ♘e4   ♗g4
23   ♔c3   ♔g8
24   ♘c5   g5

Bangiev recommends 24 ... ♔h7 25 ♖e7 ♖hf8 26 h3 ♗c8 as being only slightly better for White. This seems very generous towards Black: 27 h4!?, pre-

venting any ideas of g5 and
♔g6; or 27 ♖he1, with the
idea of ♖e8, both look
strong.

25   ♖e7 *(148)*

25   ...   ♔h7!?

25 ... ♗h5 26 h4 is very
bad so Black preferred to
connect his rooks and hope
to survive the coming
onslaught.

26   ♖xf7+   ♔g6
27   ♖g7+!

White forces Black to
take the f-pawn with his
king, in order to improve

his attacking chances.

27	...	♔xf6
28	♖c7	♖hc8
29	♖f1+	♔e5

29 ... ♔g6 30 ♖cf7! leaves
Black in a mating net.

30	♘d3+	♔d6
31	♖h7	♖f8
32	c5+	♔d5
33	♖e7!	♖ae8
34	♖fe1	♖xe7
35	♖xe7	♗e6

Black has just managed
to avoid getting mated, but
now he is going to lose all
his pawns.

36	♘b4+	♔e5
37	♘xc6+	♔f6
38	♖xa7	♗d5
39	♖a6	♗xg2
40	♘d4+	♔e7
41	♖xh6	♖a8
42	♖g6	♖xa2
43	♖xg5	♗h3
44	♘c2	♔f6
45	♖h5	♗f5
46	♘b4	1-0

10) Nimzowitsch Counter-Gambit

1	e4	e5
2	f4	d5
3	ed	c6 *(149)*

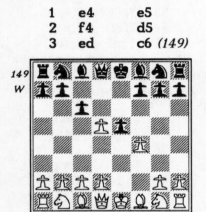

149
W

In recent times, this defence has risen from obscurity to virtual poll position amongst the defences to the King's Gambit. This is not so surprising as the Nimzowitsch is very modern in outlook: Black is not interested in a pawn but prefers active piece play. After the moves 4 ♘c3 ef 5 ♘f3 ♗d6 6 d4 ♘e7 7 dc ♘bxc6 we arrive in the main line of this variation. If you have already studied the chapter on the Modern Defence you will notice certain similarities including, sometimes, an identical pawn structure. This pawn structure is, of course, what compensates for Black's active pieces. White's 4-2 majority on the queenside should guarantee him a large advantage in any endgame.

I should mention that the sudden rise in popularity of this variation coincided with the publication of a couple of good wins for Black in the trend-setting *Informator* (so you know what you have to study if you spot wins for Black in there). Let's have a look at some games.

Game 45
Gallagher – Milovanovic
Liechtenstein 1990

1	e4	e5
2	f4	d5
3	ed	c6
4	♘c3!	

4 dc falls in with Black's plans. The game Ree - Short, Wijk aan Zee 1986, continued 4 ... ♘xc6 5 ♗b5 ef 6 ♘f3 ♗d6 7 d4 ♘e7 8

0-0 0-0 9 ♞a3 ♝g4 10 ♞c4 ♝c7 with an unclear position, very similar to game 31.

4 ♛e2 leads to a roughly level game after 4 ... cd! 5 fe (5 ♛xe5+ ♝e7 6 ♛xg7 ♝f6 wins the queen; 6 ♞f3 is better when Black has some compensation for the pawn) 5 ... ♞c6 6 ♞f3 ♝g4 7 ♛f2!? ♝xf3 8 gf ♝e7 (8 ... ♞xe5 9 d4 ♞c6 10 ♞c3 ♝e7 11 ♝f4 with good play for White) 9 ♛e2 ♝h4+ 10 ♚d1 ♞h6 and, according to Bangiev, the position is level.

4 ... cd

More common is 4 ... ef, which will be the subject of subsequent games.

5 fe ♞c6!?

More usual is 5 ... d4 6 ♞e4 ♛d5 (6 ... ♞c6 7 ♞f3 ♛d5 8 ♞f2 ♝f5 9 ♝d3 ♝g6 10 0-0 and Black had nothing to show for the pawn in Teichmann - Marshall, Baden-Baden 1914) 7 ♝d3 (7 d3 is interesting. The game Boudre - Flear, Pau 1988, continued: 7 ... ♞c6 8 ♞f3 ♞xe5 9 ♝e2 f5?! 10 ♞ed2 ♞g4 11 ♞c4 b5 12 h3 bc 13 hg fg 14 dc ♛d6 15 0-0! with good attacking chances for White; 7 ♛e2 has also been suggested but after 7 ... ♞c6 8 ♞f3 ♝g4 9 c4 ♛a5 Black has a good game) 7 ... ♞c6 8 ♛e2 ♞h6 (maybe Black should try to get

away with 8 ... ♞xe5) 9 ♝c4 ♛a5 10 ♞f3 ♝g4 11 ♞d6+ and White had the advantage, Opocensky - Johner, Baden-Baden 1914.

6 d4

6 ♞f3 is sensible after which 6 ... d4 7 ♞e4 transposes to the above note.

6	...	♛h4+
7	g3	♛xd4
8	♝f4!	♝b4!

Black, correctly, doesn't try to keep his weak d-pawn but instead makes sure that White's pawn structure is not too healthy.

9 ♛xd4

9 ♞e2 is dubious, e.g. 9 ... ♛e4! 10 ♜g1 ♞xe5 11 ♝g2 ♞f3+ 12 ♝xf3 (12 ♚f2 ♝c5+) 12 ... ♛xf3 13 ♛d2 ♞e7 with at least equality for Black.

9	...	♞xd4
10	0-0-0	♝xc3
11	bc	♞c6!

For some reason, I had expected 11 ... ♞e6, but the text is much better. From c6 the knight attacks the e-pawn, prevents an annoying check on b5 and doesn't get in the way of the bishop.

12	♜xd5	♞ge7
13	♜d6	♝e6
14	♞f3	

The extra pawn isn't so important, but Black does have some weak squares in his camp for White to occupy. Nevertheless, with accurate play Black should be able to hold the balance.

14 ... h6?

This gives White the time he requires to launch a strong attack.

15 ♘d4! ♘xd4
16 cd ♘f5

Black had little choice but to accept the offer.

17 ♗b5+ ♔f8 *(150)*

If 17 ... ♔e7 then 18 d5! ♗c8 19 ♖e1 with very good play for White.

150
W

18 ♖xe6

White could also leave the rook on d6 and get a strong passed pawn in return for the exchange, but the attack along the f-file looked even better.

18 ... fe
19 ♖f1!

Indirectly defending the d-pawn and threatening g4.

19 ... a6

Black makes e8 available for his king.

20 ♗d3 ♔e7
21 ♗d2! ♔d7

Taking on d4 was out of the question: 21 ... ♘xd4 22 ♗b4+ ♔d7 23 ♖f7+ ♔c6 24 ♗e4+.

22 d5 ♖hf8
23 ♗b4?

I missed a very simple win here. After 23 ♗xf5 ♖xf5 24 ♖xf5 ef 25 ♗b4! the pawns are unstoppable.

23 ... ♘e7
24 de+ ♔xe6
25 ♗c4+ ♔d7
26 ♖d1+ ♔e8
27 ♖d6

White still has fine compensation for the exchange, but Black can now at least play actively with his rooks.

27 ... ♖c8
28 ♗e6 ♖f1+
29 ♔b2 ♖d8
30 ♗c4!

If 30 ♖b6 ♘d5.

30 ... ♖f2
31 ♖b6 ♖d7

31 ... ♘d5 would have lost now to 32 ♖e6+ ♔f7 33 ♖d6!

32 ♗b3 ♘c6
33 ♗a4

White threatens 34 ♖xb7 ♖xb7 35 ♗xc6+ ♖d7 36 e6.

33 ... ♖e2!
34 ♗d6 ♖f7
35 ♗b3 ♖d7
36 ♗a4

I was in extreme time trouble here, which explains my opponent's attempt to play for a win with ...

36	...	♔d8??
37	♗xc6	

... and Black can't recapture.

37	...	♖xd6
38	ed	bc
39	♖xc6	♖xh2
40	♖xa6	g5
41	♖a7	h5
42	♖g7	g4
43	a4	♖h3
44	a5	♖xg3
45	a6	♖e3
46	a7	1-0

Game 46
Ermenko - Kurguz
Corr. 1982/83

1	e4	e5
2	f4	d5
3	ed	c6
4	♘c3	ef
5	♘f3 (151)	

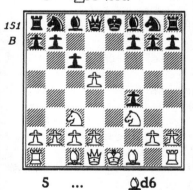

5	...	♗d6

5 ... ♘f6 6 d4 ♗d6 transposes; 5 ... cd 6 d4 leaves Black unable to defend his f-pawn in a satisfactory manner (6 ... g5 7 h4). Gallagher - Barczay, Kecskemet 1990 continued: 6 ... ♗d6 7 ♘xd5 ♕a5+ 8 ♘c3 ♘f6? (8 ... ♘e7 is better) 9 ♗b5+ ♗d7 10 ♕e2+ ♔d8 (10 ... ♔f8 is more solid) 11 0-0 ♖e8 12 ♘e5! ♗xe5 (Black can try 12 ... ♘c6, but after 13 ♘xf7+ ♔c7 14 ♕c4 ♗e6 White has a dashing queen sacrifice: 15 ♘xd6! ♗xc4 16 ♘xc4 ♕b4 17 ♗xf4+ ♔d8 18 ♗d6!) 13 de ♘c6 14 ♗xf4. My opponent glanced at his watch and decided to call it a day.

6	d4	♘f6

6 ... ♘e7 is the subject of games 47-50.

7	♕e2+	

This check comes at an awkward moment for Black. As in other variations of the King's Gambit, Black has to choose between a slightly unpleasant endgame, or losing the right to castle.

7	...	♕e7

After 7 ... ♔f8, White should play 8 ♘e5! and now:

a) 8 ... cd 9 ♗xf4 ♘c6 10 ♕f2 (10 0-0-0 ♗xe5 11 de ♗g4 12 ♕d2 ♗xd1 13 ef ♗h5 14 fg+ ♔xg7 15 ♗h6+ ♔g8 16 ♕xd5 ♗g6 17 ♗c4 with advantage to White, according to Glaskov) 10 ... ♘g4?! (10 ... ♕e7 11 0-0-0 ♘xe5 12 de ♗xe5 13 ♗xe5 ♕xe5 14 ♘xd5 ♘xd5 15 ♕c5+ ♕e7 is only a little better for White) 11 ♘xg4 ♗xg4 12 ♗d3 (The simple 12 ♗e2 would have emphasised the frailty of Black's position, e.g. 12 ... ♗xf4 13 ♕xf4 ♗xe2 14 ♘xe2 ♕e7 15 0-0! and Black has a weak d-pawn and a misplaced king) 12 ... ♗xf4 13 ♕xf4 h5 14 0-0 and White has the better game, Gallagher - Nemet, Suhr 1990.

b) 8 ... ♘xd5 occurred in Gallagher - Fedorov, Saverne 1990. After 9 ♘xd5 cd 10 ♗xf4 ♕c7 11 ♕f2 ♘c6 12 ♘d3 ♗xf4 13 ♘xf4 ♗g4 14 ♗e2! ♖e8 15 0-0 ♗xe2 16 ♘xe2 an almost identical position to the twelfth move note in 'a' had arisen. White has a clear advantage.

8   ♕xe7+   ♔xe7 *(152)*

152
W

9   ♘e5

9 ♗c4, with the idea of preventing Black from obtaining a pawn in the centre and to create some threats against f7, is an interesting alternative.

Black now has:

a) 9 ... ♗f5 10 0-0 (10 ♘e5 is interesting and led to an extremely quick win in Gallagher - Schmutz, Bern 1990, after 10 ... ♖e8?! 11 0-0 ♗xc2 12 ♘xf7! b5 13 ♘xd6 ♔xd6 14 ♗xf4+ ♔d7 15 dc+ 1-0) 10 ... ♗xc2 (10 ... cd 11 ♘xd5+ ♘xd5 12 ♗xd5 ♘c6 13 c3 left Black with a very weak f-pawn in Cheremisin - Abelman, Moscow 1956) 11 ♖e1+ ♔f8 12 dc! ♘xc6 and now either 13 ♘b5 ♗b8 14 ♘e5 or 13 ♘e5 ♘xe5 14 de ♗c5+ 15 ♔f1 lead to a White advantage (Glaskov).

b) 9 ... b5! (Black immediately attacks those pieces which exert control over d5) 10 ♗b3 b4 11 ♘e2 ♘xd5 12 ♗xd5 cd 13 ♗xf4 ♗a6 14 ♗xd6+ ♔xd6 15 ♘g3 (15 ♘f4 would have offered better chances of an edge) 15 ... ♖e8+ 16 ♔d2 ♘c6 17 ♖ae1 g6 18 ♖xe8 ♖xe8 19 ♖e1 ♖xe1 20 ♔xe1 f6 with an equal endgame in J. Polgar - Breim, Reykjavik 1988.

9   ...   ♘xd5

9 ... ♗f5 can be met by 10 ♗c4 transposing to 'a' in the previous note, or by 10 ♗xf4 ♗xc2 11 ♔d2! ♗e4 12 dc ♘xc6 13 ♖e1 ♗b4 14 ♗g5 and Black loses material (Korchnoi). The text is more logical.

10   ♘xd5+   cd
11   ♗xf4 *(153)*

The respective pawn structures offer White slightly the better chances, but he has to take care not to exchange off the wrong pieces. For example, in a rook endgame, Black's pawn would be hardly weak at all and he would have a ready-made minority attack. White should try to ensure that the light-squared bishops remain on the board as his is clearly the superior piece.

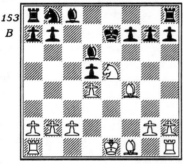

153
B

11 ... ♘c6

11 ... f6 is also known to tournament practice. After 12 ♘d3 ♘c6 13 0-0-0 ♗xf4+ 14 ♘xf4 ♔d6, White can obtain the better chances with 15 ♗e2 ♗f5 (otherwise this bishop will remain passive) 16 ♗f3 ♗e4 17 c4! ♗xf3 18 c5+.

12 0-0-0 ♗e6

The game Skrobek - Sydor, Polish Ch 1978 led to a slight edge for White after 12 ... f6 13 ♘xc6+ bc 14 ♖e1+ ♗e6 15 ♗xd6+ ♔xd6 16

♗d3. White has the superior bishop.

13 c3

White defends d4 in order to develop his bishop to d3.

13 ... ♖ac8

13 ... ♘xe5 14 de ♗c5 15 ♗g5+ causes Black problems, as after 15 ... f6 16 ef+ gf 17 ♗f4, White has two pawn islands against four for Black.

14 ♘xc6+

White decides that it is time to clarify the situation.

14 ... bc

14 ... ♖xc6 15 ♗xd6+ ♔xd6 16 ♗d3 is another possibility.

15 ♗xd6+ ♔xd6
16 ♘d3 c5?!

Black was obviously worried about White fixing his pawns on light squares, but after 16 ... c5 White's advantage becomes even more marked.

17 dc+ ♔xc5
18 ♗c2

The d4-square is very suitable for a white rook, from where it will be able to keep an eye on all parts of the board. The bishop is also well placed on c2 where it has the option of switching diagonals to b3, increasing the pressure on d5.

18 ... a5

19 ♖d4 ♗d7

Black manoeuvres his bishop around to c6 in order to create some counterplay on the e-file.

20 ♖hd1 ♗c6
21 b4+?!

Of course, if Black takes on b4, the connected passed pawns will decide the outcome. However, 21 b4+ does rather rush things and a more measured approach, involving softening up the black kingside, would probably have been better.

21 ... ♔b6
22 ba+ ♔xa5
23 ♗b3

Black has now lost his d-pawn, so it's time to activate.

23 ... ♖he8
24 ♖1d2

Not 24 ♗xd5 ♗a4!, but 24 ♔b2 looks best as it should save a tempo on the text.

24 ... ♖e3

Black keeps in the game by counter-attacking against the white pawns.

25 ♔b2 ♔b6
26 c4!?

White gives up trying to win the d-pawn and instead hopes to take advantage of the exposed position of the black king. 26 ♖b4+ was less committal.

26 ... dc
27 ♖xc4 ♖e7

28 ♖dc2 ♖ec7 (154)

154
W

29 ♔a3!

White creates mating chances by covering the b4-square, and if 29 ... ♖a8+ then 30 ♔b4 and White hopes that the pin on the c-file combined with the outside passed pawn will give him some winning chances.

29 ... f5

This blunders away a pawn. Black should have played 29 ... f6.

30 ♖b4+ ♔a7

30 ... ♔a6 31 ♖c5 threatens ♗c4.

31 ♖c5 ♗b7
32 ♖a5+ ♗a6
33 ♖xf5

With an extra pawn and the more active rooks, the win is assured. The remaining moves were: 33 ... ♖c5 34 ♖f7+ ♖8c7 35 ♖bf4 ♗b7 36 g3 ♖xf7?! 37 ♖xf7 ♖g5 38 ♗c2 ♔b6 39 ♗xh7 ♖a5+ 40 ♔b4 ♖xa2 41 h4 g5 42 h5 ♗c6 43 ♗f5 ♖a4+ 44 ♔b3 ♔c5 45 h6 ♖a8 46 ♖c7

♖b8+ 47 ♔c3 ♔d6 48 ♖c8
1-0.

Game 47
Spassky – Zsu. Polgar
Wellington 1988

1	e4	e5
2	f4	d5
3	ed	c6
4	♘c3	ef
5	♘f3	♗d6
6	d4	♘e7 *(155)*

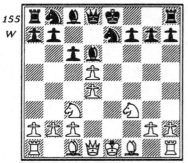

155
W

In this way Black rules
out the annoying check on
e2 - his advantage is on the
kingside, so it is natural to
avoid the queen exchange
that normally occurs after
this check.

    7   dc

7 ♗c4 will be seen later.
7 ♗d3 is interesting and
after 7 ... 0-0 8 0-0 ♘xd5 9
♘xd5 cd 10 ♘e5 ♘c6 11
♘xc6 bc 12 ♗xf4 White had
the upper hand in J. Polgar
– S. Jackson, Thessaloniki
1988. It is quite possible
that Black's play can be
improved; 7 ... cd looks

more critical.

    7   ...   ♘bxc6
    8   d5?!

Although this advance is
extremely tempting, if
Black plays accurately she
should be able to exploit
the weakness of the dark
squares.

8 ♗c4 will be seen later
and 8 ♘e4 should trans-
pose (to 8 ♗c4). 8 ♗d3 is a
speciality of the Canadian
master Lawrence Day. In
his game against Schulte,
Toronto 1988, Black found
an interesting queen man-
oeuvre: 8 ... ♗g4 9 ♘e2
♗xf3 10 gf ♕a5+ 11 c3 ♕g5.
Now White decided to eva-
cuate his king to the
queenside with 12 ♔d2!?.
The position is very complicated but Black's chances shouldn't be worse.

    8   ...   ♘b4
    9   ♗c4 *(156)*

9 ♗b5+ looks logical, but
after 9 ... ♗d7 10 ♗xd7+
♕xd7 11 0-0 ♖d8! Black has
a good game.

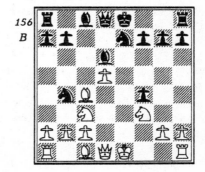

156
B

9 ... ♗f5

9 ... 0-0 is also very sensible and after 10 a3 Black has the fascinating possibilty 10 ... b5!. This has been extensively analysed by the American master Mike Valvo and he employed this move to beat Deep Thought (maybe computers aren't so terrible if they play the King's Gambit!): 11 ♗b3 (Gone are the days when a computer used to grab everything that was offered. The game Hoyes - Gild. Garcia, New York 1987, saw the human take the bait with 11 ♗xb5 {11 ♘xb5 ♘bxd5 is very dangerous for White} 11 ... ♘bxd5 12 ♘xd5 ♘xd5 13 ♗c6 ♗a6 14 ♕xd5 ♖e8+ 15 ♔d1 ♗e2+ 16 ♔d2 ♗c4 17 ♗xa8 ♗xd5 18 ♗xd5 ♗b4+ 0-1. However, this game is not as smooth as it appears. In fact 17 ♗xa8 is a dreadful blunder as 17 ♕d4! ♗e5 18 ♖e1!! wins for White. Therefore Black should have played 14 ... ♕e7+ 15 ♕e4 ♕xe4+ 16 ♗xe4 ♖ae8 with the better game) 11 ... ♘a6 12 ♘xb5 ♕a5+ 13 ♘c3 ♘c5 14 ♗a2 ♗a6! 15 b4 ♕c7 16 bc ♖fe8 17 ♘e2 ♕xc5. Black has sufficient compensation for the piece and he eventually won on move 48.

10 ♗b3 *(157)*

10 ♘d4 looks natural but

is well met by 10 ... ♗c5!, e.g.

a) 11 a3 ♗xd4 12 ab ♕b6 13 ♗xf4 0-0 and White's king won't be able to find a safe haven.

b) 11 ♘xf5 ♘xf5 12 ♗xf4 (12 ♕e2+ ♘e3!) 12 ... ♕e7+ with good attacking chances.

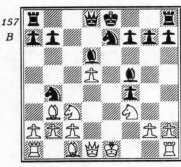

10 ... 0-0?

Black misses her chance; unfortunately "the doc" did not do so against me: 10 ... ♕b6! 11 a3 ♘a6 12 ♕d4 ♘c5! 13 0-0 0-0 14 ♔h1 ♗d3! with the better game for Black in Gallagher - Nunn, Bayswater 1987.

11 0-0

White is now ready to play moves such as ♘d4, and then to try to pick up the f4-pawn.

11	...	♗g4
12	♘e4	♘f5
13	c3	♘a6
14	♗c2	

Now that White's bishop has been re-routed to a more pleasant diagonal, he has the better game.

| 14 | ... | ♗c7 |

14 ... ♘h4 15 ♕d3!

| 15 | ♘f2! |

This forces some favourable exchanges.

15	...	♗xf3
16	♕xf3	♘e3
17	♗xe3	fe
18	♘g4	♕g5
19	♖ae1

Of course 19 ♘xe3 is bad because of 19 ... ♗b6.

| 19 | ... | ♖ae8 |
| 20 | ♔h1 |

If Black defends her pawn with 20 ... ♗b6 then 21 ♗a4! is annoying, e.g. 21 ... ♖e7 22 d6 ♖e6 23 ♗b3 ♖xd6 *(158)*.

158
W

Now 24 ♘xe3 gives White a slight advantage; 24 ♕xf7+!? is dangerous, but Black appears to have adequate defensive resources, e.g. 24 ... ♖xf7 25 ♖xf7 ♕d5 26 ♖ef1 h5! (the only way to avoid mate) 27 ♖f8+ (27 ♖7f5 ♕xg4 28 ♗xd5+ ♔h7 29 h3 ♕e2 gets nowhere) 27 ... ♔h7 28 ♗c2+

♕g6!. It turns out that after the queen is captured White's knight is trapped and that 29 ♖h8+ ♔xh8 30 ♗xg6 ♖d8 31 ♘e5 e2 wins for Black.

20	...	e2!?
21	♖xe2	♖xe2
22	♕xe2	♕xd5
23	♗b3

White's pieces are better co-ordinated and he has attacking chances against f7.

23	...	♕d7
24	♘e5	♗xe5
25	♕xe5	♘c7
26	h3?!

26 ♖d1 was more accurate.

| 26 | ... | ♕c8? |

This move is quite inexplicable. 26 ... ♘e6 had to be played with good drawing chances.

| 27 | ♕e7! | ♔h8 |

Now it's too late for 27 ... ♘e6 as 28 ♖xf7 wins.

| 28 | ♖xf7 | ♖xf7 |
| 29 | ♗xf7 |

Often queen and knight work better than queen and bishop in the ending, but this is certainly not the case here. Apart from Black's chronically weak back row, her knight is totally dominated by the bishop.

29	...	b6
30	b4	a5
31	b5!	h6

Not 31 ... ♘xb5 32 ♗e8!

32	a4	♘a8
33	♗e6	♕b8

Black has almost been pushed off the edge of the board.

34	♗d5	♘c7
35	♗c6	♕c8
36	c4	♘a8
37	♕b7	♕xb7
38	♗xb7	♘c7
39	c5	bc
40	b6	♘e6
41	♗d5	♘f8
42	♗c6	1-0

Game 48
Illescas – Nunn
Dubai 1986

1	e4	e5
2	f4	d5
3	ed	c6
4	♘c3	ef
5	♘f3	♗d6
6	d4	♘e7
7	dc	♘bxc6
8	♗c4	0-0
9	0-0	(159)

9	...	♗g4

This slightly annoying

pin is the only way for Black to put any real pressure on the white position. Other moves lead to a better game for White:

a) 9 ... ♗f5 10 ♘h4! (This emphasises the weakness of f4) 10 ... ♖c8 (10 ... ♕b6 can be met by 11 ♘d5! as after 11 ... ♕xd4+ 12 ♕xd4 ♘xd4 13 ♘xe7+ ♗xe7 14 ♘xf5 ♘xf5 15 ♗xf4, the two bishops and queenside pawn majority give White the better game, or 11 ... ♘xd5 12 ♘xf5!) 11 ♔h1 (Sidestepping any ♘xd4 tricks) 11 ... ♗b8 12 ♗xf4 ♘xd4 13 ♘xf5 ♘exf5 14 ♗d3 (Black's knights are suspended unhappily in the middle of the board) 14 ... ♘e7 15 ♗xb8 ♖xb8 16 ♕h5 f5 17 ♖ad1 with advantage to White in Hellers – Valkesalmi, Thessaloniki 1988. Black only lasted another few moves: 17 ... ♕b6 18 ♗c4+ ♔h8 19 ♘a4 ♕f6 20 ♘c5 ♕c6 21 b4 ♘xc2 22 ♕e2 ♕e4 23 ♘xe4 1-0.

b) 9 ... ♘g6 occurred in the game Popovych – Shahade, Philadelphia 1989, but after 10 ♘e4 ♗f5 11 ♘xd6 ♕xd6 12 c3 a6?! 13 ♗d3 ♗xd3 14 ♕xd3 ♖fe8 15 ♗d2 White had a clear advantage.

10 ♘e4

This is the most natural, threatening to take the two bishops and preparing to solidify d4 by playing c3. However, 10 ♘e2 also deserves attention, e.g. 10 ... ♘g6 11 c3 ♘ce7?! (11 ... ♛c7 looks better) 12 ♘g5! ♛c7 13 ♛b3 ♘c6 14 ♗xf7+! ♖xf7 15 ♛xf7+ ♛xf7 16 ♘xf7 ♔xf7 17 ♘xf4 with advantage to White, Podgorny - Sevecek, Corr. 1986.

10 ... ♗c7

10 ... ♖c8 is a possible alternative when 11 ♘xd6 ♛xd6 leaves White facing problems with his d-pawn and on the c-file. Better is 11 c3 and after 11 ... ♗b8 12 ♗b3 looks best. This position has not yet occurred in practice, but experience would suggest that White has good chances.

11 c3

White bolsters his centre, considering that an advance of his d-pawn would be premature.

11 ... ♘d5?!

This natural-looking move leads Black into serious difficulties. 11 ... ♘g6 is similar to games 49 and 50.

12 ♘c5! ♖b8

12 ... b6 13 ♘a6 is good for White.

13 ♛e1!

This shows very good understanding of the position. White aims for a queen exchange after which Black's chances on the

kingside will be reduced and eventually White's queenside pawn majority will come into its own.

13 ... ♖e8

Illescas considered this to be a serious error, offering instead 13 ... g5 as unclear. However, Mikhalchishin pointed out in his article in *New in Chess* that White has two interesting ways to continue:

a) 14 ♘xg5 ♛xg5 15 ♘e4 ♛f5 16 ♗xd5 ♖be8 17 ♛f2 ♖xe4 18 ♗xe4 ♛xe4 19 ♗xf4 ♗xf4 20 ♛xf4 ♛xf4 21 ♖xf4 ♗e6 22 b3 b5 23 ♖d1 with a clear advantage to White.

b) 14 ♗xd5 ♛xd5 15 ♘e4 ♗d8 16 ♘fxg5!? ♗xg5 17 ♗xf4 (17 ♖xf4!? ♗h5 18 ♛g3!) 17 ... ♖be8 18 ♛g3 ♖xe4 19 ♛xg4 h6 20 h4 with a mess.

14 ♛h4 ♛xh4

14 ... ♗xf3 15 ♛xd8 ♖bxd8 16 ♖xf3 leaves White clearly on top.

15 ♘xh4 ♘e3
16 ♗xe3 ♖xe3
17 ♖ae1 ♖xe1
18 ♖xe1 *(160)*

After a series of exchanges the position has clarified and we can now see that Black is in trouble. It is apparent that White has a mobile pawn majority, but hard to imagine that Black has a similar four against two on the kingside. White's rook is also proudly patrolling the only open file, whilst Black's has the miserable task of defending a pawn.

18 ... g5

It's only here that the game Gallagher – Davidovic, Haringey 1988 went its separate way with 18 ... ♔f8 19 ♘f3 ♗b6? (19 ... h6 was better) 20 ♘g5 h6 21 ♘xf7 ♗c7 (Black had assumed that the knight would be in trouble, but forgot about one critical square) 22 ♘h8! g5 (The only move) 23 ♘e6+ ♗xe6 24 ♖xe6. With an extra pawn and a strong attack, White is not far from victory. The remaining moves were 24 ... ♘a5 25 ♘g6+ ♔f7 26 ♗d5 ♖d8 27 c4 ♗b6 28 ♖xb6+! ♖xd5 29 cd ab 30 ♘e5+! ♔e7 31 b4! 1-0.

19 h3! ♗h5?!

19 ... ♗c8 was better.

20 ♘f5?

White could have won with 20 ♘d7! gh 21 ♘xb8 ♘xb8 22 ♖e7 ♗d6 23 ♖xb7. Black's pawns are useless.

20	...	♗g6
21	♘e7+	♔g7
22	♘xc6	bc
23	♘a6	♖c8
24	♘xc7	♖xc7
25	♖e5	*(161)*

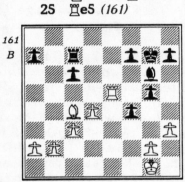

Another group of exchanges and a very favourable ending for White has arisen.

25 ... f6

26 ♖c5 ♗e4

26 ... ♖b7 was better.

27 d5! ♖d7

Black gives up a pawn and pins his hopes on blockading the queenside, as he realises that 27 ... ♔f8 28 b4 ♔e7 29 b5 is hopeless.

28 dc ♖c7

Of course, after 28 ... ♖d1+ 29 ♔f2 Black's checks will run out.

29 ♗b5?

This falls in with Black's plan. It would have been stronger to play 29 b4! as after 29 ... ♖xc6? 30 ♖xc6

♗xc6 31 ♗d3 White's queen-side pawns will decide the issue.

29	...	♔f7
30	b4	♔e6
31	a4	♔d6
32	a5	h5?

Time trouble has arrived and Black seriously weakens his kingside. The h-pawn has to stay back in order to be able to meet h4 with h6. Better was 32 ... ♗xc6 as the king and pawn ending should be a draw.

33	h4!	♗xc6
34	♗xc6	♖xc6
35	hg	fg
36	♖xg5	♖xc3
37	♖xh5	

Black might have some drawing chances if his f-pawn wasn't so far advanced, but on f4 it is too exposed.

37	...	♖c4
38	b5	♖c5

38 ... ♖a4 39 b6 takes a little longer, but still wins.

39	♖xc5	♔xc5
40	b6	1-0

After 40 ... ab 41 ab ♔xb6 42 ♔f2 ♔c6 43 ♔f3 ♔d6 44 ♔xf4 ♔e6 45 ♔g5 White wins.

Game 49
Westerinen - Motwani
London 1988

1	e4	e5
2	f4	d5
3	ed	c6
4	♘c3	ef
5	♘f3	♗d6
6	d4	♘e7
7	♗c4	*(162)*

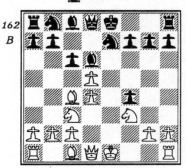

162 B

This is probably the most accurate move order as it makes Black think about whether he should take on d5 or not.

7	...	cd

It could well be that Black should not make this capture. After 7 ... 0-0 8 0-0 ♗g4 White has nothing better than 9 dc transposing to Illescas - Nunn, whilst after 7 ... cd we arrive at the same position, but with White's bishop arguably better placed on b3.

8	♗xd5	

Of course 8 ♘xd5?? loses a piece.

8	...	0-0

The attempt to justify his seventh move with 8 ... ♘xd5 9 ♘xd5 ♕a5+ 10 ♘c3 is not attractive for Black. The weakness of his f-pawn is felt more than ever. For example, 10 ... 0-0 11 0-0 ♗g4 12 ♘e4 (12 ♘e2 looks strong) 12 ... ♗c7 13 ♘f2 ♗h5 14 ♘h3!? ♕f5 15 ♕d2! and White has the better game, Gallagher - Brito, Las Palmas 1990. 15 ... ♗xf3 16 ♖xf3 g5 fails to 17 ♘xg5 ♕xg5 19 ♖g3.

9	**0-0**	**♘bc6**
10	**♗b3**	**♗g4**
11	**♘e4**	**♗c7**

11 ... ♖c8 makes less sense with the bishop already at b3.

12 c3

White could consider trying to blow Black away with 12 d5, but after 12 ... ♗b6+ 13 ♔h1 ♘d4 14 d6 ♘g6 he seems overextended.

12 ... ♘g6

The knight is more securely placed here than on d5.

13 h3!?

For 13 ♘f2, see game 50.

I should just note here that if the bishop had been on c4, rather than b3 (i.e. if Black had not played 7 ... cd), then this continuation would not be possible: 13 h3 ♗xf3 14 ♕xf3 (14 ♖xf3 ♘(either)e5) 14 ... ♘xd4! 15 ♕h5 ♘e5 16 ♘g5 h6 17 ♘xf7 ♘xf7 18 ♗xf4 ♗xf4 19 ♖xf4 ♘e6! and Black defends.

13 ... ♗f5

13 ... ♗h5!? should be met by 14 ♕d3, unpinning and introducing the possibility of ♕b5 at an appropriate moment.

14 ♘fg5! (163)

From nowhere, White whips up a nasty attack.

163
B

14 ... h6

This is obviously the critical move, but in the game Gallagher - Almada, Chiasso 1991, Black avoided the complications and chose instead 14 ... ♗xe4 15 ♘xe4 ♖e8. Black's idea is that if he can force White to move his knight from e4, he may be able to get a dangerous attack with ... f3 followed by ... ♕d6. However, he was unable to carry out his plan: 16 ♕f3! (Luring Black's knight to a dubious square) 16 ... ♘h4 17 ♕d3 ♘e5 (17 ... ♕e7 is met by 18 ♗xf4) 18 ♕b5! a6 (18 ... ♘g6 19 ♘g5!) 19 ♕d5 ♕xd5 20 ♗xd5 ♘d3 21 ♖d1! ♘xc1 22 ♖axc1 (White just has to avoid some tricks to gain the full point) 22 ... ♖e7 23 ♖e1 ♖ae8 24 ♔f2! ♔f8 (24 ... b6?

25 ♗c6! f5 26 ♘f6+!) 25 ♘c5! f3 26 ♖xe7 ♖xe7 27 ♗xf3 ♘f5 28 g4 and White soon converted his material advantage.

15 ♕h5!

Taking on f7 would not have offered sufficient play.

15 ... hg

Black has one other very interesting try, 15 ... ♘xd4. Now 16 cd ♕xd4+ is good for Black, and if 16 ♖d1 hg 17 ♖xd4 (Or 17 ♘xg5 ♘e2+! and wins) 17 ... ♗b6, e.g. 18 ♘xg5 ♗xd4+ 19 cd ♕xd4+ 20 ♔h1 ♘e5 21 ♘xf7 ♘xf7 22 ♕xf5 ♕f6 and White doesn't have quite enough for the exchange; so White has to play 16 ♘xf7 ♖xf7 17 ♗xf7+ ♔xf7 *(164)*.

164
W

A fascinating position has arisen where White has several possibilities:

a) 18 ♗xf4. Opening the f-file should normally be decisive, but Black has a tactical defence: 18 ... ♗xf4 19 ♖xf4 ♘e2+! 20 ♔h1 ♘xf4

21 ♕xf5+ ♔g8 22 g3 ♕d5! and Black has a winning position.

b) 18 cd ♕xd4+ 19 ♘f2 ♗d3 20 ♖d1 ♗b6 21 ♕f3 ♖e8! and Black has a strong attack.

c) 18 ♘g3!!. This incredible move seems to give White the advantage:

c1) 18 ... ♗d3 19 ♗xf4! ♗xf1 20 ♖xf1 and White will eventually emerge with an extra pawn.

c2) 18 ... fg 19 cd ♕xd4+ 20 ♔h1 ♔g8 21 ♕xf5 ♖f8 22 ♗e3! with a good game for White, e.g. 22 ... ♕d6 23 ♕c2 ♖f2?! 24 ♗xf2 gf 25 ♕b3+ ♔h7 26 g3 and White defends.

c3) 18 ... ♕h4 19 cd!

16 ♘xg5 ♘h8 *(165)*

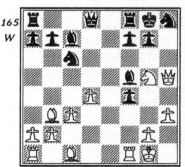

165
W

17 ♘xf7! ♘xf7
18 ♕xf5 ♕f6
19 ♕xf6!?

19 ♕g4 leaves White with a strong attack, but Westerinen judged that the pawns and the continuing problems of the black king-

side, even after the queen
exchange, were more than
enough for the piece.

| 19 | ... | gf |
| 20 | ♗xf4 | ♖xf4 |

20 ... ♕d8 21 ♖f3 looks
good for White.

21	♖xf4	♔g7
22	♖g4+!	♔h6
23	♖f1	

There is no respite for
Black.

23	...	♘g5
24	h4	♘h7
25	♗c2!	♘e7
26	♖e1	

There is no defence.

26	...	♖f7
27	♗b3	♖af8
28	♗xf7	♖xf7

With rook and three
pawns against two knights,
the rest is just a matter of
technique: 29 ♖ge4 ♘g6 30
g3 f5 31 ♖e6 ♘f6 32 c4 ♔h5
33 ♖f1 ♘g4 34 d5 f4 35 d6
f3 36 c5 ♘6e5 37 ♖e7 ♖f8 38
d7 f2+ 39 ♖xf2 ♘xf2 40
♖xe5+ ♔g4 41 ♖g5+ ♔h3 42
d8=♕ 1-0.

Game 50
Hebden – Nunn
London 1987

1	e4	e5
2	f4	d5
3	ed	c6
4	♘c3	ef
5	♘f3	♗d6
6	d4	♘e7
7	♗c4	cd

8	♗xd5	0-0
9	0-0	♘bc6
10	♗b3	♗g4
11	♘e4	♗c7
12	c3	♘g6 *(166)*

| 13 | ♘f2 | |

White adopts a different
strategy to the previous
game. With this knight
manoeuvre he plans to lay
siege to f4 with every
means at his disposal.

| 13 | ... | ♗f5 |
| 14 | ♘d3 | ♘a5 |

Black is hard-pressed to
find any counterplay so he
gives himself the option of
removing White's potent-
ially dangerous bishop. 15
♗c2 would allow 15 ... ♘c4.

| 15 | ♘fe1 | |

White's play is not particularly subtle, but the f-
pawn is certainly beginning
to feel the pressure.

| 15 | ... | ♘xb3 |

Nunn criticised this move
and gave 15 ... ♕g5 16 ♕f3
♗g4 17 ♕f2 ♘xb3 18 ab ♕b5
as unclear. However, Mik-
halchishin, who seems to

have been placing all King's
Gambit theory under the
microscope, considers that
White has the better chances after 19 ♘xf4 ♗xf4 (19
... ♕xb3 20 ♘ed3 is a little
better for White) 20 ♗xf4
♗e2 21 c4 ♕e8 22 ♗d6 ♗xf1
23 ♔xf1 ♘e7 24 ♕e2 ♘f5 25
♗xf8 ♕xf8 26 ♘c2 ♕d6 27
♔g1 ♘xd4 28 ♕d3.

16 ab   ♕h4 *(167)*

167
W

Nunn gives some var-
iations in *Informator* to
show that 16 ... ♕g5 is insufficient: 17 ♕f3! ♖ae8 18
♘xf4 ♗g4 19 ♕g3! ♖xe1 20
♖xe1 ♘xf4 21 ♖e4 ♘e2+ 22
♖xe2 ♕xc1+ 23 ♖xc1 ♗xg3
24 ♖e7 with a clear advantage to White.

17 ♕f3

The f-pawn is lost and
it's just a question of
whether Black can drum up
enough counterplay or not.

17 ...   ♖ae8
18 ♗xf4

Obviously it would be
very risky for White to help
himself to a queenside

pawn.

18 ...   ♘xf4
19 ♘xf4

Black's bishops offer
partial compensation for
the pawn.

19 ...   ♗e4
20 ♕h5   ♕d8
21 g3

21 ♖xa7 would have met
with a sad end: 21 ... ♕b8!
Now White is threatening
to take the pawn.

21 ...   a6?!

Even so, Nunn considers
it necessary to have played
21 ... f5, after which he
assesses the position as
slightly better for White.

22 b4?!

It would have been more
accurate to have completed
his development with ♘eg2
and ♖ae1 at once.

22 ...   f5
23 ♘eg2   ♖f6
24 ♖ae1   ♖h6
25 ♕e2   g5
26 ♘d3   ♗c6 *(168)*

168
W

27 ♕f2?

This throws away all of

White's advantage. Better was 27 ♕d2 as 27 ... ♖xe1 28 ♖xe1 f4 can be met by 29 ♘e5 f3 30 ♘xc6 bc 31 ♘e3 with a winning position.

27 ... ♖f8!

Now it is clear that the white queen is on a potentially embarrassing square.

28 c4

And now 28 ♘e5 would allow 28 ... ♗b5.

28 ... f4
29 gf?

And after this White is losing. He could still have held the balance with accurate play. Nunn gives the following variation: 29 d5! ♖xh2! 30 dc ♕xd3 31 ♘xf4!

♖xf2 32 ♘xd3 ♖xf1+ 33 ♖xf1 bc 34 ♖xf8+ ♔xf8 35 g4 with a drawn endgame.

29 ... gf
30 ♘dxf4 ♗xg2!
31 ♕xg2+ ♔h8

White can't deal with all the threats to his kingside, e.g. 32 ♕e4 ♕h4.

32 ♘e6 ♗xh2+
33 ♔h1

33 ♕xh2 ♖g8+ 34 ♕g2 ♖xg2+ 35 ♔xg2 ♖xe6! 36 ♖xe6 ♕g8+ is rather elegant.

33 ... ♗e5+
34 ♔g1 ♗xd4+
35 ♖f2 ♗xf2+
36 ♕xf2 ♖xe6
0-1

11) Classical Defence

1	e4	e5
2	f4	♗c5 *(169)*

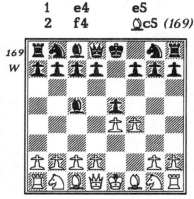

169
W

Black is not interested in the complications arising from the King's Gambit Accepted and declines in classical form, immediately bringing his king's bishop to its best square.

There are now two main schemes of development at White's disposal. The first involves a quick c3 and d4, so as to build a strong pawn centre as quickly as possible. This can be rather doubled-edged as White may well fall behind in development and have his centre subjected to strong pressure. The second, quieter, method involves bringing out the minor pieces quickly, and maybe playing ♘a4, to remove Black's strong bishop.

In my opinion, both systems offer White reasonable chances of obtaining the advantage.

Game 51
Larsen – Joyner
Birmingham 1951

1	e4	e5
2	f4	♗c5
3	♘f3	d6

There are also a couple of rarely played alternatives:

a) 3 ... ♘c6 4 fe (4 ♘xe5 is recommended by Zaitsev, as after 4 ... ♘xe5 5 d4 ♗xd4 6 ♕xd4 ♕h4+ 7 ♕f2 White's two bishops give him the better game. Black should try 4 ... ♘f6 and after 5 ♘c3 0-0 6 ♗e2 ♖e8 he has some compensation for the pawn. 4 ♘c3 looks good as after 4 ... d6 5 ♗b5 White has transposed into a favourable line {see game 54}) 4 ... d6 (4 ... ♘xe5 doesn't work: 5 ♘xe5 ♕h4+ 6 g3 ♕xe4+ 7 ♕e2 ♕xh1 8 d4 {Korchnoi and Zak give 8 ♘g6+} 8 ... ♗e7 9 ♘f3 Black is in serious trouble, e.g. 9 ... d6 10 ♗e3 ♗f5 11 ♘bd2 ♗xc2 12 ♖c1 ♗f5 13 ♖xc7) 5 ed ♕xd6 6 c3!. This enables White to take shelter behind a big pawn centre until he has completed his development. Khavsky - Ivanov, Leningrad 1971 continued: 6 ... ♗g4 7 d4 0-0-0 8 ♗e3 f5 9 ♕c2 ♗xf3 10 gf ♗b6 11 ♘d2 with a clear advantage to White.

b) 3 ... d5. This position can also arise from the Falkbeer Counter-Gambit Declined: 4 ♘xe5 ♘f6 (4 ... de? 5 ♕h5 ♕e7 6 ♗c4 is very good for White) 5 d4 ♗b6 6 ed ♕xd5 7 ♗e3 ♘c6 8 ♘c3 ♗a5. Black hopes that his control of the central white squares will offer sufficient compensation for the pawn. However, White's next move dashes these hopes: 9 ♗e2! *(170)*.

170
B

Now Black has no time for 9 ... ♘e4 10 0-0 ♗xc3 because of 11 ♗c4! and after 9 ... ♗xc3 10 bc ♕e4 11 ♕d3 ♘xe5 12 fe ♕xg2 13 0-0-0 White has a considerable advantage.

4   c3

4 ♗c4 will be the subject of subsequent games.

4   ...   ♗g4

With this pin, Black joins in the struggle for d4. However, as we shall see, White is able to gain the advantage. There are a number of alteratives, of which 4 ... f5 and 4 ... ♘f6 can be seen in games 52 and 53 respectively. The others are examined below.

a) 4 ... ♘c6 5 ♗b5 ♗d7 6 d4 ed 7 cd ♗b6 8 0-0 ♘f6 9 ♘c3 0-0 10 ♔h1. It is clear that White's centre is very strong and Black always has to be on the look out against a possible e5.

b) 4 ... ♗b6. This prophylactic move is not without some danger for White, especially if he naïvely continues with 5 d4. After 5 ... ed 6 cd either 6 ... ♗g4 or 6 ... ♘f6 gives Black good play. White has to play more slowly. 5 ♗d3 merits attention, but my preference is for 5 ♘a3. The knight is bound for c4, from where it will exert pressure on e5, and have the option of removing the annoying bishop. The game Arnason - I. Sokolov, Haninge 1989 continued: 5 ... ♘f6 6 d3 ♘g4 7 d4 f5 with a complex struggle in which Black managed to hold the balance. Instead of 6 d3, White can try 6 fe. Now Black has two possibilities (of course 6 ... ♘xe4 loses to 7 ♕a4+):

a) 6 ... ♘g4 7 d4 de 8 h3 ♘f6 9 ♘xe5 ♘xe4 10 ♕h5! g6 (After 10 ... ♕f6, White has the strong reply 11 ♗b5+. Now 11 ... c6 12 ♖f1 is good and after 11 ... ♗d7 White must be careful to avoid 12 ♗xd7+ ♘xd7 13 ♖f1 because of 13 ... ♕xf1+. 12 ♖f1 immediately is again strong) 11 ♕h6 and White stands clearly better.

b) 6 ... de 7 ♘c4 ♘xe4 (7 ... ♘c6 can be met by 8 d3 0-0 9 ♘xb6 ab 10 ♗e2 with an edge) 8 ♘xb6 ab 9 ♕e2 ♘f6 10 ♕xe5+ (How is Black to escape the check?) 10 ... ♕e7 11 ♕xe7+ ♔xe7 12 ♗c4!? (White relinquishes the bishop pair in order to alleviate the pressure on a2) 12 ... ♗e6 13 ♗xe6 ♔xe6 14 d4 (White has the better pawn structure and the black king might find itself a little exposed).

The more active 10 ... ♗e6 is met by 11 ♘g5. Now 11 ... ♘bd7 12 ♘xe6 ♘xe5 13 ♘xd8 ♖xd8 14 d4 is good for White, as is 11 ... ♕e7 12 ♘xe6. After 11 ... 0-0 12 ♘xe6 fe White does not take the pawn, but plays 13 ♗c4! with a good game.

c) 4 ... ♕e7. White can now follow the recommendation of Greco's: 5 d4 ed 6 cd ♗b4+ (6 ... ♕xe4+ 7 ♔f2 wins for White, e.g. 7 ... ♗b6 8 ♗b5+ followed by ♖e1) 7 ♘c3! (If 7 ♔f2 ♘f6! is rather unclear) 7 ... ♗xc3+ 8 bc ♕xe4+ 9 ♔f2 with good attacking chances in return for the pawn.

5 fe

5 h3 should be good enough for an edge.

5 ... de

6 ♕a4+!

This idea was discovered by Frank Marshall and guarantees a pleasant middlegame.

6 ... ♗d7

This is the only move as 6 ... ♕d7 7 ♗b5 c6 8 ♘xe5 and 6 ... ♘c6 7 ♘xe5 ♕h4+ 8 g3 ♗f2+ 9 ♔xf2 ♕f6+ 10 ♔g1 ♕xe5 11 ♗g2 are very good for White.

7 ♕c2 ♘c6

After 7 ... ♕e7 White can play 8 d4. Reti - Barasz, Timisoara 1912, continued: 8 ... ♗d6 8 ♘bd2 ♘c6 10 ♗c4 0-0-0 11 0-0 with advantage to White.

8 b4! ♗d6 (171)

9 ♗e2

171
W

9 ♗c4 is a decent alternative, e.g. 9 ... ♘f6 10 d3 ♕e7 11 0-0 0-0-0 12 a4 with good attacking chances, Bronstein – Panov, Moscow 1947.

Larsen prefers to keep the c4-square for his knight.

    9   ...   ♕e7
    10   ♘a3   a5
    11   b5   ♘d8

Larsen gives the following variation: 11 ... ♗xa3 12 ♗xa3 ♕xa3 13 bc ♗xc6 14 ♘xe5 ♕a4 15 ♕xa4 ♗xa4 16 ♗c4 ♘h6 17 0-0 with advantage to White. He also points out that if White wants to avoid the queen exchange he can play 9 ♘a3 and 10 ♘c4.

    12   ♘c4   f6

Black has to try and hold the e5-point at all costs.

    13   0-0   ♘h6
    14   d4   ♘hf7
    15   a4   0-0
    16   ♘xd6!

At first sight a strange move but White wants to turn his attention towards the a3-f8 diagonal.

    16   ...   ♘xd6?

Black should have played 16 ... cd although 17 ♗a3 and 18 ♖ad1 will still cause him some problems.

    17   ♗a3   ♘8f7 (172)

Black is not very alert. 17 ... b6 was necessary in order to take the sting out of the coming advance.

172
W

    18   c4!   ed
    19   c5   ♕xe4
    20   ♗d3   ♕e3+
    21   ♔h1   ♘xb5

"Desperation. The point of the white combination is that the knight can only retreat to c8 or e8, in both cases disconnecting the black rooks. 22 c6 would then threaten ♗xh7+ followed by ♗xf8. After, for instance, 21 ... ♘c8 22 c6 ♖d8 23 cd the situation is not less hopeless for Black than in the game" (Larsen).

    22   ab   c6
    23   ♗xh7+   ♔h8
    24   ♘h4   ♘e5

25   ♖ae1   ♕h6

25 ... ♕xa3 26 ♖xe5 fe 27 ♘g6+ ♔xh7 28 ♘xf8++ wins.

26   ♘g6+   ♘xg6
27   ♗xg6   ♗e8
28   ♗f5   cb
29   c6   b4
30   ♗c1   g5
32   c7   ♗c6
33   ♖e7   1-0

Game 52
Gallagher – Costa
Biel 1990

1   e4   e5
2   f4   ♗c5
3   ♘f3   d6
4   c3   f5!? *(173)*

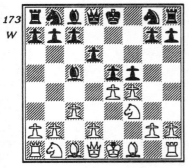

This is obviously the sharpest choice at Black's disposal and from now on the game will be balanced on the edge of a precipice.

5   fe

5 ef ♕e7! is difficult for White; 5 d4 is also dubious. Keres gives 5 ... ed 6 ♗c4 fe 7 ♘g5 d5! (5 fe prevents this defence) 8 ♘xe4 dc 9 ♕h5+ ♔f8 10 ♕xc5+ ♕e7

with a better ending for Black.

5   ...   de

5 ... fe allows 6 ♕a4+ ♘c6 7 ♕xe4 de 8 ♗b5 with a good game.

6   d4   ed
7   ♗c4! *(174)*

White hurries to occupy this crucial diagonal. There is certainly no time for 7 cd, but Glaskov has suggested 7 e5!? as an alternative.

7   ...   fe!

This is the only way for Black to justify his previous play. If it is not sound he must accept his fate. Other moves have been tried though:

a) 7 ... d3 8 ♗g5! ♘f6 9 e5 h6 10 ♗h4 g5 11 ef gh 12 ♘e5 and White had a very good game in Spielmann – Rubinstein, Trieberg 1921.

b) 7 ... ♘c6 8 b4! ♗b6 9 ♕b3 ♘h6 (Black has to defend f7. If 9 ... ♘f6 10 b5 ♘a5 11 ♗f7+ ♔f8 12 ♗a3+; or 9 ... ♘ge7 10 ♗f7+ ♔f8 11

0-0!) 10 ♗g5 (10 0-0 fe 11 ♗g5! also gives good attacking chances) 10 ... ♛d6 11 ♘bd2. Black is going to come under heavy fire from White's raging bishops which keep his king locked in the centre, e.g. 11 ... dc 12 ♛xc3 ♗d4 13 ♘xd4 ♛xd4 14 ♛xd4 ♘xd4 15 0-0-0 and the exchange of queens has hardly diminished White's attack.

c) 7 ... ♘f6. This has been Black's most popular choice here, but White can obtain a clear advantage without any great difficulty: 8 e5 ♘e4 9 cd ♗b4+ (9 ... ♗b6 10 ♘c3 ♘c6 11 ♗e3 is good for White) 10 ♗d2 (10 ♚e2 has also seen the light of day for some strange reason) 10 ... ♘xd2 11 ♘bxd2 and White is clearly better.

8 ♘g5

I played this automatically as I knew that White was supposed to take the rook and after a few nervous moments beat off the attack. As we shall see, the game didn't go exactly according to plan. Afterwards, I felt quite downhearted (and not only because it cost a big prize). It somehow didn't feel right to be grabbing pieces and then fending off a massive attack. That's not why you play the King's Gambit! A new idea was necessary; so my attention turned to 8 ♘xd4! (175).

175
B

White removes Black's potentially dangerous d-pawn and, in return for the slight material deficit, has great attacking chances. Black is especially weak on the a2-g8 diagonal as well as having difficulties on the f-file. The immediate threat is ♛h5+ and Black has two ways to avoiding this:

a) 8 ... ♗xd4 9 cd ♘c6 10 ♗e3 (10 d5 ♘e5 11 ♛h5+ can also be considered but 10 ♗e3 is more flexible) 10 ... ♘f6 11 0-0 Black has problems completing his development, e.g.

a1) 11 ... ♗g4 is well met by 12 ♛b3. Now 12 ... ♘a5 is bad because of 13 ♛b5+ c6 14 ♛e5+; 12 ... ♘xd4 13 ♛xb7 ♘c2? loses to 14 ♖xf6! e.g. 14 ... gf 15 ♛xe4+ or 14 ... ♛d1+ 15 ♖f1 or 14 ... ♘xe3 15 ♛c6+ ♗d7 16 ♛xe4+. Instead of 13 ... ♘c2, Black can try 13 ... ♖b8, but then 14 ♕xa7 and Black still can't play 14 ... ♘c2 (15 ♕a4+) whilst his king remains stuck in the centre.

a2) 11 ... ♘a5 12 ♖xf6! (12 ♘c3!?) 12 ... ♘xc4 13 ♕h5+ (13 ♖f2?! is not met by 13 ... ♘xe3? 14 ♕h5+ winning but by 13 ... ♗e6!) 13 ... g6 14 ♖xg6 hg 15 ♕xg6+!. White undoubtedly has a very dangerous attack, for example:

a21) 15 ... ♔f8 16 ♗h6+ ♖xh6 17 ♕xh6+ ♔e7 18 ♕g7+ and after 18 ... ♔e8 or 18 ... ♔d6 19 ♘c3! brings the remaining white pieces into the attack.

a22) 15 ... ♔d7 16 ♕f7+ ♕e7 17 ♕xc4. White has very good play for the exchange with his queenside pieces about to enter the game. 17 ... ♕h4 is bad because of 18 ♕d5+ ♔e8 19 ♕e5+ followed by 20 ♘c3.

a3) Maybe Black should try 11 ... ♕e7, but after 12 ♘c3 ♗g4 13 ♕a4 we can see that Black's king will not be very safe on the queenside and 13 ... ♗d7 14 ♘b5! looks strong.

b) 8 ... ♘f6 9 ♗g5 (This threatens to take on f6, followed by ♕h5+ and is more precise than 9 0-0, which after 9 ... ♘c6 10 ♗e3 ♘e5! seems good for Black)

9 ... ♗xd4 10 cd ♘c6. The drawback of White's ninth move is that he can't defend his d-pawn (Obviously we're not going to retreat the bishop) and 11 d5 ♘e5 is not very attractive.

b1) 11 ♗xf6 comes into consideration and is quite likely to end in a draw after 11 ... ♕xf6 12 ♕h5+ g6 13 ♕d5! ♘b4 (13 ... ♘xd4 14 ♖f1!) 14 ♕b5+ (14 ♕xe4+ ♕e7 is about equal) 14 ... ♘c6 15 ♕d5.

b2) 11 ♘c3!. From the above variations, it has become apparent that White has to invest further material to fuel the attack. It is very dangerous for Black to take the pawn.

b21) 11 ... ♕xd4 12 ♕xd4! ♘xd4 13 0-0-0 ♘e6 (other moves are no better, e.g. 13 ... ♘f5 allows 14 ♘xe4 and 13 ... c5 14 ♗xf6 gf 15 ♘xe4 is very good for White) 14 ♗xf6 gf 15 ♘xe4 and White is close to winning.

b22) 11 ... ♘xd4 is well met by 12 0-0 with nasty threats of 12 ♗xf6 and 12 ♘xe4.

It is also difficult to find a good move for Black if he doesn't take on d4. 11 ... ♘a5 and 11 ... ♗g4, for example, both lose at once to 12 ♗xf6.

I think that we can conclude that 8 ♘xd4 offers

White good chances for the advantage, whilst eagerly awaiting some practical tests.

    8   **...**   ♘**f6**

8 ... e3 is refuted by 9 ♗f7+ ♚f8 10 ♗xg8 ♕xg5 11 0-0+ ♗f5 12 cd!

    9   ♘**f7**   ♕**e7**
    10 ♘**xh8** *(176)*

So White has won his rook, but Black's pieces are very active and his central pawns menacing. Nevertheless, theory considers the position as very good for White, but I think this game will change that assessment.

It is worth noting that if White plays 10 cd, Black can achieve a good game by 10 ... ♗b4+ 11 ♘c3 ♖f8 12 ♘e5 ♘g4!

    10   **...**   ♘**c6**

Other moves seem to lead to a good game for White:

a) 10 ... d3 11 ♗g5 ♗f2+ 12 ♚xf2 ♕c5+ 13 ♗e3 ♕xc4 14 h3 ♗e6 15 ♘d2 ♕d5 16 g4 ♘c6 17 c4 ♕d7 18 g5 ♗g4 19 ♕f1! and White is winning, Stoltz – Spielmann, Stockholm 1932.

b) 10 ... ♗g4 11 ♕b3 ♘bd7 12 ♕xb7 ♖b8 13 ♕c6 d3 14 b4! (Korchnoi).

    11 ♗**g5**

This looks very natural, preventing 11 ... ♗g4, but after Black's next move White is in some trouble. Probably the best move is 11 ♘f7. This was pointed out to me by my wife! As I sat huddled over the chessboard, desperately trying to repair the variation, she strolled by, baby on one arm, and remarked "Why don't you take that knight out of the corner?" And indeed, the move does have its points: firstly, and most importantly, it covers the e5-square; secondly, it prevents Black from castling; and thirdly, the knight may be able to hop out one day, leaving White a whole rook up.

On the minus side however, time is being spent which could have gone towards development, and the knight is also much more vulnerable to immediate capture on f7. Let's have a look at some concrete variations.

a) 11 ... d3 12 b4! *(177)*

This crucial move takes

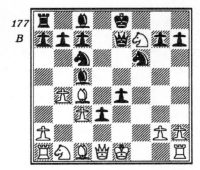

away the c5-square from Black. The importance of this can be seen from the following variation: 12 ♗g5?! ♗f2+! 13 ♔xf2 ♕c5+ 14 ♗e3 (14 ♔g3) 14 ... ♕xc4 with a dangerous attack for Black. After 12 b4! Black has:

a1) 12 ... ♘xb4. This fails to 13 cb ♗xb4+ 14 ♗d2 e3 15 ♕a4+ ♗d7 16 ♗xb4!. White is now so many pieces up that he will hardly notice returning a few to defuse the attack.

a2) 12 ... ♗g4 13 ♕b3 ♗b6 14 a4!. After studying this position for some time, I came to the conclusion that White can't really develop very effectively and is better off creating a few threats of his own on the queenside. White has taken over the initiative which ensures that Black doesn't have enough play for the rook. 14 ... a6 15 a5 ♗a7 16 b5 confirms this assessment.

b) 11 ... ♗g4! 12 ♕b3 ♗b6!. Black calmly takes a time out in order to protect b7. In doing so, he has also created the annoying threat of ... ♘a5. If Black can win the knight on f7, he will clearly have very good play for a mere exchange. Moves such as 13 0-0 and 13 ♗g5 can be discarded because of ... ♘a5, e.g. 13 0-0 d3+ 14 ♔h1 ♘a5 15 ♕a4+ ♗d7 16 ♗b5 c6 with advantage to Black. 13 ♘g5 can also be met by 13 ... ♘a5!. This leaves White with:

b1) 13 ♕b5!?. Black should now play 13 ... d3! (178) (13 ... a6 14 ♕g5 ♘a5 15 ♘e5!).

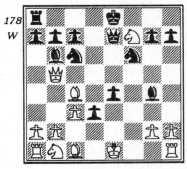

How is White to continue? One of the main worries is that Black is now threatening to play e3, as ♗xd3 loses the knight on f7. 14 ♗e3 is an interesting attempt to blockade the pawns, but after 14 ... ♗xe3 15 ♕xb7 ♖b8 16 ♕xc6+ ♗d7 17 ♕xc7 ♖xb2 Black's attack is worth at least a draw, e.g. 18 ♗b3 ♖e2+ 19 ♔d1 (19 ♔f1) 19 ... ♗g4! with a murderous attack; 14 ♘g5 allows Black to castle with a good game; 14 ♕g5 e3 15 ♗xd3 (15 ♕xg7 d2+ 16 ♘xd2 ed++ 17 ♔xd2 ♗e3+ 18 ♔c2 ♗f5+ 19 ♔b3 ♘a5+ and Black is winning) 15 ... ♔xf7 and the attack will continue; another idea is 14 ♗f4 e3 15 ♘e5 but 15 ... d2+ 16 ♘xd2 ed+ 17 ♔xd2 0-0-0+ is strong. So 13 ♕b5 doesn't seem to solve White's problems.

b2) 13 ♕a3! appears to be White's strongest, with the idea of 13 ... ♗c5 14 ♕b3 and a draw by repetition (Not 14 b4? ♘xb4). Black can play for a win with 14 ... ♕d7 but this would be risky because White's position has clearly been improved by the two little queen moves.

11	...	♘e5
12	cd	

I certainly underestimated Black's reply when I played this, but the Keres recommendation (12 ♗xf6) doesn't look so hot either: 12 ♗xf6 and now:

a) 12 ... gf? 13 ♕h5+ ♔f8 14 ♘g6+ ♘xg6 15 ♕d5! with a good game for White.

b) 12 ... ♕xf6 (Keres didn't consider this natural move) *(179)*.

13 ♕h5+ (13 ♖f1 ♕h4+ 14 g3 ♕xh2 looks terrible for

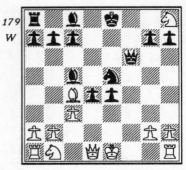

179 W

White) 13 ... g6 14 ♕xh7 (14 ♗f7+ doesn't work; 14 ... ♔e7 15 ♗xg6 and now not 15 ... hg 16 ♕xe5+ but 15 ... dc!) 14 ... dc! 15 ♖f1 (15 ♘xc3 ♕f2+ 16 ♔d1 ♗g4+ 17 ♔c1 0-0-0 is crushing) 15 ... ♘f3+ (Even 15 ... cb 16 ♖xf6 ba=♕ probably gives White no more than perpetual check) 16 gf (16 ♖xf3 ef isn't better) 16 ... cb. White has no mate, e.g. 17 ♗f7+ ♔d8 18 ♕g8+ ♔d7 19 ♕e8+ ♔d6 20 ♕f8+ ♕e7 and Black wins.

12	...	♗g4!

12 ... ♗b4+ 13 ♘c3 ♘xc4 14 0-0! clearly favours White.

13	♕a4+	♗d7
14	♕b3	♗xd4!

There is now no way to prevent ... ♘d3+ and 15 ♕xb7 ♗c6 16 ♗b5 ♕b4+ wins for Black.

15	♘c3	♘d3+
16	♗xd3?!	

After this capture the white king is left stranded in the centre surrounded by open files. But even after 16 ♔d2 ♘c5 17 ♕d1 0-0-0 Black has a tremendous attack.

| 16 | ... | ed+ |
| 17 | ♔f1 | |

Forced, as 17 ♔d2 ♗xc3+ 18 bc ♘e4+ wins.

| 17 | ... | 0-0-0 |
| 18 | ♘f7 *(180)* | |

Only now I realised that my intended 18 ♖e1 lost to 18 ... ♕c5!

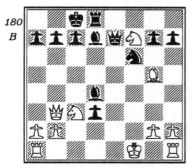

180
B

| 18 | ... | ♖f8! |

Very logical, but there were a couple of ways to go wrong, e.g. 18 ... ♕c5 19 ♘xd8! ♕f5+ 20 ♔e1 ♕f2+ 21 ♔d1 ♗g4+ 22 ♔c1 and White is in the game; 18 ... ♗e6 19 ♖e1! was the other trick.

| 19 | ♕c4 | |

Unfortunately, exchanging queens by 19 ♖e1 ♕xf7 20 ♕xf7 ♖xf7 only accelerates the end.

| 19 | ... | ♗b6! |

The final nail in the coffin. 19 ... ♕xf7 would be a serious mistake on account of 20 ♕xd4 and 19 ... ♗xc3

20 ♕xc3 ♕e2+ 21 ♔g1 is another false trail: after 21 ... ♘e4 White can defend with 22 ♕e1 and after 21 ... ♗c6 with 22 ♕d2.

| 20 | ♘e4 | ♖xf7 |

Even if Black had fallen into my trap, he would probably still win: 20 ... ♕xe4 21 ♘d6+ ♔b8 22 ♘xe4 ♘xe4+ 23 ♔e1 ♘f2.

| 21 | ♘d6+ | |

A quicker exit would have been 21 ♗xf6 ♖xf6+ 22 ♘xf6 ♕e2 mate.

| 21 | ... | ♕xd6 |
| 22 | ♕xf7 | ♕c5! |

The rest is a massacre.

23	♗h4	♕f5+
24	♔e1	♕e4+
25	♔d2	♗a5+
	0-1	

Game 53
Gallagher - Dzevlan
Royan 1989

1	e4	e5
2	f4	♗c5
3	♘f3	d6
4	c3	♘f6 *(181)*

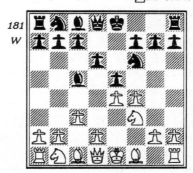

181
W

The most popular way of combatting the c3-system. The e-pawn is pressurised, but without the risk involved with 4 ... f5.

5 d4

White has a major alternative here; 5 fe de and now:

a) 6 d4 ed 7 cd ♗b4+ (7 ... ♘xe4 8 dc ♕xd1+ 9 ♔xd1 ♘f2+ 10 ♔c2! ♘xh1 11 ♗e3 is good for White) 8 ♗d2 ♕e7 9 ♗d3! (An improvement on 9 e5 ♘d5 10 ♘c3 ♗e6 when Black has a firm grip on the centre) 9 ... ♘xe4 10 ♗xe4 ♕xe4+ 11 ♔f2 ♗xd2 12 ♘bxd2 ♕d3? (This is a serious error: 12 ... ♕d5 would have left an unclear situation on the board) 13 ♖e1+ ♗e6 14 ♕a4+ c6 15 ♕b4! ♘d7 16 ♕xb7 0-0 17 ♕xc6 and Black didn't have enough for the pawn in S. Polgar - Flear, Brussels 1987.

b) 6 ♘xe5 0-0 (6 ... ♕e7 7 d4 ♗d6 8 ♘f3 ♘xe4 9 ♗e2 0-0 10 0-0 c5 and now Glaskov's suggestion of 11 ♗d3 was tried out in the game Thinat - Garie, Corr. 1990. After 11 ... cd 12 ♖e1 f5 13 cd ♘d7 14 ♘c3 ♘df6 15 ♗g5 ♕f7 16 ♗xf6 ♘xc3 17 bc ♕xf6 18 ♕b3+ ♔h8 19 ♘e5 b6, White could have gained a clear advantage with 20 ♕d5! e.g. 20 ... ♖b8 21 ♗c4 ♗b7 22 ♘f7+ ♔g8 23 ♕xd6 winning) 7 d4 ♗d6

8 ♘f3 ♘xe4 9 ♗d3 ♖e8 10 0-0 h6 11 ♘bd2 ♘f6 12 ♘c4 (Tartakower - Schlechter, St. Petersburg 1909) and now 12 ... ♘c6 would have given Black an equal game.

5 ... ed

5 ... ♗b6?! 6 fe de 7 ♘xe5 0-0 is a dubious sacrifice, as the continuation of the game J. Polgar - Sharif, Brussels 1987, showed: 8 ♗g5! c5 9 dc ♕xd1+ 10 ♔xd1 ♗xc5 11 ♗xf6 gf 12 ♘f3 and Black's bishops do not fully compensate for the pawn.

6 cd ♗b4+

Also possible is 6 ... ♗b6, maintaining pressure on d4 and offering some tactical possibilities against the white centre. Play can continue 7 ♘c3 0-0 8 e5! (White has to play this advance now, as otherwise every one of Black's natural developing moves, ... ♘c6, ... ♗g4 and ... ♖e8, will bring further pressure against the centre, forcing him forward under less favourable circumstances) 8 ... de 9 fe ♘d5 10 ♗g5 ♘xc3 (10 ... f6 11 ♗c4! c6 12 ef gf 13 ♗h6 ♖e8+ 14 ♔f2 was clearly better for White in Suttles - Addison, USA Ch 1965) 11 bc *(182)*.

11 ... ♕e8 (This move has been awarded an exclamation mark in a number of previous books, but in fact

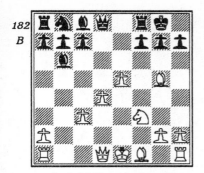

182
B

it probably loses by force. Better is 11 ... ♕d5 but White still has a good game, e.g. 12 ♗d3 h6 13 c4! and White's centre is very strong or 12 ... ♗g4 13 ♕c2!) 12 ♗d3 f6 *(183)*.

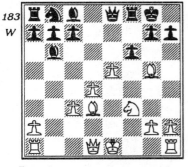

183
W

Previous commentators have only given 13 ♗f4 ♗g4 with a good game for Black, but after 13 0-0! White's attack is decisive, e.g. 13 ... fg 14 ♘xg5. White has strong threats on the a2-g8 diagonal, along the f-file and against h7. Black has several defensive tries:

a) 14 ... ♗e6 15 ♗xh7+ ♔h8 16 ♕h5!! and Black can resign.

b) 14 ... h6 15 ♕b3+ ♔h8 16 ♖xf8+ ♕xf8 17 ♘f7+ ♔g8 18 ♘xh6++ ♔h8 19 ♖f1 ♕e8 20 ♗g6! ♗e6 21 ♕xe6! winning.

c) 14 ... g6 15 ♕b3+ ♔g7 (15 ... ♔h8 16 ♖xf8+ ♕xf8 17 ♖f1 ♗f5 {17 ... ♕e8 18 ♖f7} 18 ♗xf5 gf 19 ♕e6 is crushing) 16 ♖xf8 ♕xf8 17 ♖f1 winning.

d) 14 ... ♖xf1+ 15 ♕xf1 h6 (or 15 ... g6 16 ♗c4+ and 17 ♕f6+ wins; 15 ... ♗e6 of course allows 16 ♘xe6 and 17 ♗c4; 15 ... ♕e7 can be met by 16 ♗c4+ {16 ♗xh7+!? ♔h8 17 ♗g6 also looks strong} 16 ... ♔h8 17 ♕f7 ♕xf7 {17 ... ♕d8 18 ♕h5 wins} 18 ♘xf7+ ♔g8 19 ♘d6+ and White is winning) 16 ♗c4+ ♔h8 17 ♘f7+ ♔h7 18 ♕d3+ g6 19 ♕e3! ♕f8 (If 19 ... g5 20 ♖f1 with the idea of ♖f6 wins) 20 ♖f1 ♔g7 21 ♘xh6! and White wins.

Black doesn't fare much better if he declines to take on g5, e.g. 13 ... fe 14 ♘xe5! ♕xe5 15 ♖xf8+ ♔xf8 16 ♕f1+! ♔g8 17 ♖e1! and White wins. Maybe Black can try 13 ... h6 but his kingside is in tatters, e.g. 14 ♗f4 fe 15 ♘xe5 ♖xf4 loses to 16 ♖xf4 ♕xe5 17 ♖e4! with the idea of ♖e8+.

	7	♗d2	♗xd2+
	8	♘bxd2 *(184)*	
	8	...	♕e7

In the game J. Polgar - Djuric, Adelaide 1986/87,

184 B

Black played 8 ... 0-0 and after 9 ♗d3 ♘c6 10 0-0 ♘b4 11 ♗b1 c5 12 a3 ♘c6 13 d5 ♘e7 14 a4 the players have arrived in a strange sort of Benoni. The position favours White as Black will find it difficult to achieve any queenside counterplay.

9 ♗d3

9 ♕c2 is an interesting alternative, e.g. 9 ... ♗f5 10 ♗d3 ♗xe4 11 ♗xe4 d5 12 0-0-0 ♘xe4 13 ♘xe4 de 14 ♖he1 f5 (Hay – Shaw, Australia 1970). Estrin now gives 15 g4! g6 16 gf gf 17 d5! with a dangerous initiative for White.

9 ... 0-0

9 ... ♘d5 leads nowhere after 10 g3; 9 ... ♘xe4 10 ♘xe4 d5 11 0-0 de 12 ♗xe4 0-0 13 ♕c2 is pleasant for White, but this might be Black's best course of action.

10 0-0?! *(185)*

This careless move allows Black to complicate the issue. Instead, 10 ♕e2 would give White a clear advantage.

185 B

10 ... ♘d5!

This move, which I'd completely overlooked, was played instantly by my opponent.

11 ed

Owing to the threats of ... ♘e3 and ... ♘xf4, this is forced.

11 ... ♕e3+
12 ♔h1 ♕xd3
13 ♖c1 ♘d7!

Now 14 ♖xc7 ♘f6 leaves White in bad shape. Suddenly, I had to look for a way to hold my position together.

14 ♘c4! ♕e4?

Black's sense of danger had deserted him. After 14 ... ♕xd1 15 ♖fxd1 ♘f6 16 ♘e3 ♖e8 17 ♖d3 ♖e7 the chances are about equal. White's pressure on the queenside compensates for his bad pawn structure.

15 ♘g5! ♕xd5
16 ♕d3 ♘f6?

It is understandable that

Black was not enamoured
with 16 ... g6, but nevertheless this was the only way
to stay in the game (16 ... f5
17 ♘e3 ♕a5 18 b4 is very
strong). 17 f5 looks like a
good way to develop the
attack, whilst 17 ♘e3 should
also come into consideration.

    17 ♘e3   ♕xa2

17 ... ♕a5 18 b4! will come
to the same thing.

    18 ♖a1!

The queen is forced from
control of d5.

    18 ...   ♕xb2
    19 ♘d5!   g6

A very sad move to have
to play.

    20 ♘xf6+ ♔g7
    21 ♖ab1

Now driving the queen
off the long diagonal.

    21 ...   ♕a2
    22 d5   1-0

After 22 .... ♔xf6 23 ♕c3+
♔e7 (23 ... ♔f5 24 g4+ ♔xg4
25 ♕h3 mate) 24 ♖fe1+ ♔d7
25 ♕f6.

Game 54
Hebden – Lane
London 1987

    1 e4   e5
    2 f4   ♗c5
    3 ♘f3   d6
    4 ♘c3 *(186)*

This is the most accurate
move order if White plans
to avoid playing 4 c3, re-
serving the right to develop
the king's bishop to a
square other than c4.

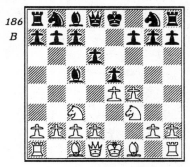

186
B

    4 ...   ♘c6

4 ... ♘f6 is the subject of
games 55 and 56; and 4 ...
♗g4 has also been tried,
but 5 ♘a4 looks promising
for White. In this variation
it is very common for
White to exchange off
Black's bishop in this fashion. Hebden – Schaerer,
Lugano 1984 now contin-
ued: 5 ... ef 6 d4 ♗xf3 7 gf
♕h4+ 8 ♔e2 ♗b6 8 ♘xb6 ab
10 ♕d2 g5 11 ♔d1 and
White's two bishops and
strong centre compensate
for the pawn. If White
doesn't wish to play in such
a way, then 5 h3 is to be recommended.

    5 ♗b5!

This shows up Black's
fourth move as inaccurate.

    5 ...   ♗d7

If Black allows his pawn
structure to be ruined then
White would have a com-
fortable advantage, e.g. 5 ...

♗g4 6 ♗xc6+ bc 7 fe de 8 h3 ♗xf3 9 ♕xf3 with a clear advantage for White in Schlechter - Tietz, Carlsbad 1906.

6	♘a4	♗b6
7	♘xb6	ab
8	d3	*(187)*

187
B

White has a small advantage, but also a simple position to play. The advance f2-f4 is responsible for the larger part of this advantage, giving White more space and pressurising Black's centre.

8	...	♕e7?!

Black starts to think about castling long, but his king will never be safe on the queenside. It was better to play 8 ... ♘ge7 9 0-0 0-0 10 f5 f6 11 ♗c4+ ♔h8 12 c3 with an edge for White in Capablanca - Molina, New York 1906.

9	0-0	♘f6
10	♔h1	h6

White is playing useful moves, whilst Black is dithering over what to do with his king.

11	♕e1	0-0-0?!

Wherever he goes he will be followed, but there were more chances of withstanding a kingside onslaught.

12	a4	ef
13	♗xf4	♘b8

Black wasn't very keen on 13 ... ♘e5 14 ♗xe5 de 15 ♕c3.

14	♘d4	c6
15	♕c3	♘e8
16	a5	ba
17	♖xa5	♘c7
18	♗c4	

Although Black has managed to surround his king with his pieces, White is better on every part of the board. However, Black's next move is responsible for hastening the end.

18	...	b5?
19	♗xb5!	cb
20	♖a7	1-0

If 20 ... ♘e8 21 ♘f5 or 20 ... ♗e6 21 ♘xb5 ♖d7 22 ♗xd6.

Game 55
Balashov - Matanovic
Skopje 1970

1	e4	e5
2	f4	♗c5
3	♘f3	d6
4	♘c3	♘f6
5	♗c4	*(188)*
5	...	♘c6

In the second game of

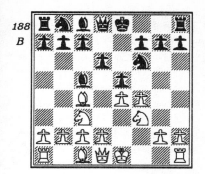

the recent Candidates' match between Short and Speelman, London 1991, Black preferred 5 ... c6 here. After 6 d3 b5!? 7 ♗b3 ♕e7 8 ♕e2 ♘bd7 9 ♖f1 ♗b4 10 fe (10 ♕f2!?) 10 ... de 11 g4?! ♘c5 12 g5 ♘fd7 13 ♗d2 a5 14 ♘h4 ♘xb3 the players agreed to a draw in an unclear position. The game Chigorin - Mieses, Ostend 1905, is also noteworthy: 5 ... c6 6 fe de 7 ♕e2 ♘bd7 8 d3 b5 9 ♗b3 a5 10 a4! b4 11 ♘d1 ♗a6 12 ♘e3 with the better game for White.

5 ... ♗e6 6 ♗xe6 fe 7 d3 transposes to the fourth game of the same Short – Speelman match. Play continued: 7 ... ef (7 ... 0-0 8 ♘a4 is good for White) 8 ♗xf4 0-0 9 ♘a4! ♗b4+!? (Black makes sure that if White is to get the bishop he'll have to weaken his queenside in the process. Of course, 9 ... ♘xe4 10 de ♖xf4 11 ♘xc5 wins for White) 10 c3 ♗a5 11 b4 ♗b6

12 ♘xb6 ab 13 0-0 ♘c6 (13 ... ♘xe4 doesn't work this time because of 14 ♘d4!; maybe 13 ... ♘bd7 is best) 14 b5 ♘e7 15 ♕b3 ♕d7 16 ♘d4 d5 and now according to Kavalek 17 ♗g5! would have given White a clear advantage (comments based on notes by Speelman in *Informator*).

6 d3 ♗g4

There are a large nunber of alternatives, but the text, along with 6 ... a6 (game 56), is the most common:

a) 6 ... 0-0 7 f5! (White seals off the centre in order to concentrate on the kingside) 7 ... h6 8 ♘d5! ♘d4 (Or 8 ... ♘a5 9 ♘xf6+ ♕xf6 10 g4!) 9 ♘xd4 ♗xd4 10 ♘xf6+ ♕xf6 11 c3 ♗b6 12 ♕h5 with a clear advantage for White in Hebden - Martinovsky, London 1986.

b) 6 ... ♘g4 is bad because of 7 ♘g5!. For example, 7 ... 0-0 (7 ... h6 8 f5!) 8 f5 ♗f2+ 9 ♔f1 ♘e3+ 10 ♗xe3 ♗xe3 11 h4 with a dangerous attack.

c) 6 ... ♘a5 7 ♕e2!? (7 ♗b3) 7 ... ♘xc4 8 dc (White's pawn structure has quite a cramping effect on the black position) 8 ... ♕e7 (maybe 8 ... ef is best) 9 f5 ♗b4 10 ♗d2 ♗d7 11 0-0-0 with advantage to White in Alekhine - Grinberg, Odessa 1916.

d) 6 ... ♗e6 7 ♗b5!. This is not really a waste of time as Black's bishop is poorly placed on e6. One possible variation is 7 ... 0-0 8 f5 ♗d7 9 ♗g5 ♘d4 10 ♗xd7 ♕xd7 11 ♗xf6 with a good game for White (*ECO*).

7   ♘a4! *(189)*

7 h3 has also been seen, but it's much better to relieve the pressure on the a7-g1 diagonal immediately.

189
B

7   ...   ♗xf3?!

Again, there are a whole host of alternatives:

a) 7 ... ♘d4 8 ♘xc5 dc 9 c3! ♘xf3+ 10 gf ♗h5. Analysis by Bogoljubov now shows White's best course: 11 ♕e2 ♕d6 12 fe! ♕xe5 13 f4! ♕e7 14 ♕g2 with a good game for White.

b) 7 ... ef 8 ♘xc5 dc 9 ♗xf4 ♘h5 10 ♗e3 ♘e5? (Better is 10 ... 0-0 11 0-0 ♘e5 and Glaskov now points out that White can obtain the advantage by 12 ♗xc5 ♗xf3 13 gf ♕g5+ 14 ♔h1 ♘xc4 15 ♗xf8 ♘e3 16 ♖g1 ♕f4 17 ♗xg7! ♘xg7 18 ♕e2) 11 ♘xe5! ♕xd1 12 ♗xf7+ ♔e7 13 ♗xc5+ ♔f6 14 0-0+ ♔xe5 15 ♖f5 mate, Alekhine – Tenner, Cologne 1907.

c) 7 ... ♗b6 (The most solid) 8 ♘xb6 ab 9 c3 0-0 (9 ... d5 10 ed ♘xd5 11 h3! gives White an edge; 9 ... ef also fails to equalise, e.g. 10 ♗xf4 ♘h5 11 ♗e3 ♘e5 12 ♗b3! ♗xf3 13 gf ♕h4+ 14 ♔d2 with the advantage) 10 0-0 (10 h3 ♗xf3 11 ♕xf3 ♘a5 12 ♗b5 is met by 12 ... ♘b3!) 10 ... ♘a5 11 ♗b5 with an edge.

8   ♕xf3   ♘d4
9   ♕d1!?

9 ♕g3 is probably stronger, for example:

a) 9 ... ♘xc2+ 10 ♔d1 ♘xa1 11 ♕xg7 ♖f8 12 ♘xc5 dc 13 fe ♘xe4 14 ♖f1 ♕e7 (if 14 ... ♕d7 15 ♗xf7+!) 15 ♗h6 with the better game for White (Keres).

b) 9 ... ef 10 ♕xg7 ♖f8 11 ♘xc5 dc 12 ♗xf4 b5 13 ♗xb5+ ♘xb5 14 ♗g5 ♖g8 15 ♕xf6 ♖xg5 16 ♕c6+ ♔f8 17 ♕xb5 with advantage to White in Honfi – Salm, Corr. 1958.

9   ...   b5 *(190)*
10   ♗xf7+!

This is the only way to fight for the advantage.

10   ...   ♔xf7
11   ♘xc5   dc

In the game Lane – S. Jackson, British Ch 1989,

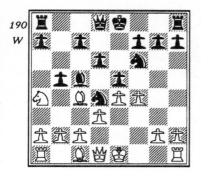

Black decided not to test the validity of the sacrifice and played 11 ... ef. After 12 ♘b3 ♘e6 13 0-0 g5 14 g3! fg? 15 ♗xg5! White had a crushing attack.

12	fe	♘d7
13	c3	♘e6
14	0-0+	

White has very good play for the piece, as his central pawn phalanx takes away nearly all the useful squares from the knights.

| 14 | ... | ♔e8 |

14 ... ♔g8 15 d4 cd 16 cd h6 17 ♕b3 looks dangerous as well.

| 15 | d4 | cd |
| 16 | cd | ♕e7? |

Black misses his chance to escape into an ending. After 16 ... ♘xe5 17 de ♕xd1 18 ♖xd1 ♔e7 White has only a slight advantage.

| 17 | ♗e3 | |

Now Black can do little against the coming pawn mass.

| 17 | ... | ♖f8 |
| 18 | d5 | ♖xf1+ |

| 19 | ♕xf1 | ♘d8 |
| 20 | e6 | ♘f6 |

It is too late to contemplate giving back the piece with 20 ... ♘xe6 as the black king will be stuck in the middle.

| 21 | ♖c1 | |

Threatening 22 ♗c5.

| 21 | ... | ♘xe4 |
| 22 | ♕xb5+ | c6 |

22 ... ♔f8 looks better.

| 23 | ♖xc6! | ♔f8 |
| 24 | ♖c1 | ♔g8? |

This loses at once. 24 ... ♘d6 would put up a little more resistance.

25	♖c7!	♕d6
26	♕e8+	♕f8
27	♖xg7+	1-0

Game 56
Bangiev – Malaniuk
Tallinn 1986

1	e4	e5
2	f4	♗c5
3	♘f3	d6
4	♘c3	♘f6
5	♗c4	♘c6
6	d3	a6 *(191)*

Black is willing to waste a tempo, in order to give a retreat square to his bishop.

7 ♖f1!?

There is something very unaesthetic about this move, but nevertheless it is an interesting novelty. White accepts the fact that after 6 ... a6 he has little hope of castling kingside, but he still wants early play on the f-file. There are several alternatives:

a) 7 f5!? h6 (7 ... ♘d4 8 ♗g5 {8 ♘d5!?} 8 ... c6 9 ♘xd4 ♗xd4 10 ♕f3 with a pleasant game for White) 8 ♘d5 ♘a5 9 ♕e2 b5 10 ♗b3 ♘xb3 11 ♘xf6+ ♕xf6 12 ab ♗b7 13 ♗e3 ♗xe3 14 ♕xe3 0-0-0 15 c4! with an edge for White in Gallagher – Davidovic, Szolnok 1987.

b) 7 ♘g5!? (The start of a rather crude attack) 7 ... 0-0 8 f5 b5 9 ♗xf7+ (Consistent) 9 ... ♖xf7 10 ♘xf7 ♔xf7 11 ♗g5 (11 g4!) 11 ... ♘e7 12 ♕f3 ♗b7 13 0-0-0 c6 14 g4 ♕g8 15 ♔b1 ♗b6 16 ♗c1 ♖f8 with an unclear position, Hergott – Reyes, Dubai 1986.

c) 7 fe de 8 ♗g5 h6 9 ♗xf6 (Glaskov points out that 9 ♗h4 is met by 9 ... ♗e6 and after 10 ♘d5 g5!) 9 ... ♕xf6 10 ♘d5 ♕d6 11 ♕d2 ♗e6 with a roughly equal game.

7 ... ef

7 ... ♗g4 has also been tried, but after 8 h3 ♗xf3 9 ♕xf3 ♕e7 10 ♕g3 ♘d4 11 fe de (Bangiev – Weigend, Corr. 1985/86) 12 ♕xg7! White could have gained a clear advantage.

8	♗xf4	♘a5
9	♗g5	♘xc4
10	dc	h6
11	♗h4	♗e6

After 11 ... c6, Bangiev intended 12 ♘d4 with a good game.

12 ♕d3

Once again we can see that the pawn structure is favourable for White.

12 ... ♖g8

Black is desperate to break the pin and the immediate 12 ... g5 allows 13 ♘xg5!

13	0-0-0	g5
14	♗f2	

Bangiev criticises this move, preferring 14 ♗g3 with the idea of e5.

14	...	♗xf2
15	♖xf2	g4!
16	♘d4	♘d7
17	♘d5	♕g5+
18	♕d2!?	♗xd5?

This leaves Black too weak on the kingside. Bangiev gives 18 ... 0-0-0 19 ♘f5 ♖h8 20 ♘fe3 ♖de8 as unclear.

19	cd	♘e5
20	♘f5	♖h8
21	♖df1	♕xd2+
22	♔xd2	h5

23 ♘e3

Both sides have very strong knights, but White has the edge due to his superior king position.

23 ...   ♔e7
24 ♔c3   b5
25 ♔d4   ♖ac8

Black doesn't want to sit and wait, so he seeks some counterplay on the queen-side.

26 c4   c5+
27 dc

If White doesn't make this capture, he will be unable to penetrate the black position.

27 ...   ♘xc6+
28 ♔c3   ♘e5
29 b3   bc
30 bc

30 ♘xc4 looks better as an exchange of minor pieces would leave Black struggling to defend all his weaknesses. The position is now about equal. As Black winning a long ending is not really what this book is about, the remaining moves are given in brief: 30 ... ♖c5?! 31 ♖d2 ♔e6 32 ♖d5 ♖hc8 33 ♖xc5 ♖xc5 34 ♖f5 ♘c6 35 ♘d5 ♘e5 36 ♔b3?! (Better was 36 ♖f6+ ♔d7 37 ♘e3) 36 ... a5 37 a4 h4 38 ♘e3 ♖c8 39 ♔c3 ♖b8 40 ♘c2 ♖b1 41 ♖h5 ♖g1 42 ♖xh4 ♖xg2 43 ♘e3 ♖a2 44 ♘xg4 ♖a3+ 45 ♔c2 ♘xc4 46 ♖h6+ ♔d7 47 ♖f6 ♔e7 48 ♖f5 ♖h3 49 ♖g5 ♔e6 50 ♖g8 ♘e5 51 ♘xe5 ♔xe5 52 ♖g5+ ♔xe4 53 ♖xa5 f5 54 ♖a8 f4 55 a5 ♖xh2+ 56 ♔d1? ♔d3 57 ♔e1 ♔e3 58 ♖e8+ ♔f3 59 a6 ♖a2 60 ♖a8 d5 61 a7 ♖e2+ 62 ♔d1 ♖e7 63 ♔d2 ♔e4 64 ♔e2 d4 0-1.

12) Second Move Alternatives

Game 57
Bronstein – Yusupov
USSR 1981

1	e4	e5
2	f4	♘f6 (192)

This counter-attacking move has never attracted a great following, as the best that Black can hope for is transposition to the Schallop Defence.

2 ... ♕h4+ is the subject of game 58.

2 ... d6 is extremely passive and is only likely to be played by devotees of the Philidor Defence. White has no particular difficulty in achieving a pleasant position with a space advantage. Here are a couple of examples after 3 ♘f3:

a) 3 ... ♘d7 4 d4 ♘gf6 5 fe ♘xe4 6 ♗d3 d5 7 ♘c3!? ♘xc3 8 bc ♗e7 9 0-0 0-0 10 ♕e1 ♖e8 11 ♕g3 ♘f8 12 ♘g5 f6 13 ef ♗xf6 14 ♗d2 c5 15 ♖xf6! ♕xf6 16 ♖f1 ♕e7 17 ♖xf8+ ♗xf8 18 ♕f3+ ♗g8 19 ♗xh7+ ♔h8 20 ♕h5 ♗g4 21 ♕h4 ♕f6 22 ♗g6+ ♔g8 23 ♗f7+ ♔f8 24 ♕xg4 ♖e4 25 ♘h7+ ♔xf7 26 ♘xf6 ♖xg4 27 ♘xg4 with a winning endgame for White in Vritsky – Lepman, Simferopol 1986.

b) 3 ... ♘c6 4 d4 ed 5 ♘xd4 ♘f6 6 ♘c3 ♗d7 7 ♗e3 ♗e7 8 ♕d2 0-0 9 0-0-0 a6 10 ♗e2 ♕c8 11 h3 ♘xd4 12 ♗xd4 ♗c6 13 ♗f3 ♖d8 14 g4 with a clearly better position for White, Shikova – Honfi, Plovdiv 1980.

3 ♘f3

3 fe is also playable. The game Fischer – Wade, Vinkovci 1968, continued: 3 ... ♘xe4 4 ♘f3 ♘g5 5 d4 ♘xf3+ 6 ♕xf3 ♕h4+ 7 ♕f2 ♕xf2+ 8 ♔xf2 ♘c6 9 c3 d6 10 ed ♗xd6 11 ♘d2 ♗e6 12 ♘e4 ♗e7 13 ♘g5 ♗xg5 14

♗xg5 with a better endgame for White.

3 ... ♘xe4

Black can play 3 ... d5 and after 4 fe ♘xe4 (4 ... de 5 ef ef 6 ♕xf3 ♘c6 7 ♗b5 ♕xf6 8 ♕xf6 gf 9 d4! gives White a good game) 5 d3 ♘c5 we transpose back to the game.

3 ... ef is the Schallop Defence.

4 fe

After 4 ♕e2, Black should avoid 4 ... ♘c5 5 d4 ♘e6 6 f5! winning. Better is 4 ... d5.

4 ... d5
5 d3 ♘c5
6 d4 ♘e6 *(193)*

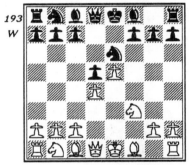

193
W

6 ... ♘e4 is dubious as Black would soon be forced to exchange it off, at the same time assisting White's development, e.g. Rohde – Martz, Lone Pine 1977, continued: 7 ♗d3 (7 c4) 7 ... ♗e7 8 0-0 0-0 (8 ... c5 9 c4 is good for White) 9 ♘bd2! ♘xd2 10 ♗xd2 c5?! 11 dc ♗xc5+ 12 ♔h1 ♗g4 13 ♕e1

♘c6 14 ♗xh7+! winning.

7 c4!

It's important to gain some space on the queen-side and to place d5 under some pressure.

7 ... ♗b4+

7 ... c6 8 ♘c3 ♗e7 9 ♗e3 0-0 10 ♕d2 b6 11 ♗d3 ♘a6 12 cd cd 13 ♖d1 led to a good game for White in Bronstein – Holmov, Vilnius 1975.

8 ♗d2 ♗xd2+
9 ♕xd2 c6
10 ♘c3 0-0
11 ♖c1 ♘c7?

Black has spent five moves wandering around with this knight only to end up on c7. 11 ... b6 followed by ... ♗a6 would have been a better try.

12 cd cd

12 ... ♘xd5 seems more logical, but after 13 ♘xd5 ♕xd5 14 ♗c4 ♕e4+ 15 ♕e2 ♕xe2+ 16 ♔xe2 White has a very active position.

13 ♗d3

Black's kingside is beginning to look decidedly shaky.

13 ... ♗g4
14 ♘g5! f5

This is forced as 14 ... h6 loses to 15 ♘h7! ♖e8 16 0-0 intending ♘f6+.

15 h3

15 0-0 would have been even stronger, for example: 15 ... h6 16 ♘xd5! ♘xd5 17 ♘e6 ♕e7 18 ♘xf8 ♔xf8 19

h3 ♗h5 20 ♖xf5+, winning.

| 15 | ... | ♗h5 |
| 16 | 0-0 | ♗g6 |

16 ... h6 17 ♘xd5! is similar to the previous note.

| 17 | ♘b5! | |

White's knight forces his way into the fine outpost on d6, as 17 ... ♘xb5 18 ♘e6! wins, e.g. 18 ... ♕b6 19 ♘xf8 ♕xd4+ 20 ♔h1 ♔xf8 21 ♕g5! ♕xd3 22 ♕d8+ ♔f7 23 e6+ ♔xe6 24 ♖fe1+.

17	...	♘ba6
18	♘d6	h6
19	♘f3	♘e6
20	♔h1!	♖b8
21	♘g1!	

White threatens to win the f-pawn and gives himself the possibility of re-routing the knight to a more effective square (c3 or f4).

| 21 | ... | ♕g5 |
| 22 | ♕f2 | ♘b4 |

More solid would have been 22 ... ♘ac7 and 23 ... ♘e8.

| 23 | ♗b5! | f4 |

23 ... ♘xa2 24 ♖a1.

| 24 | ♘f3! | |

Times have changed, so the knight returns.

24	...	♕e7
25	♕d2	♘a6
26	♗d3	♗h5 (194)

An exchange of bishops would have enabled White to penetrate on the king-side white squares.

| 27 | ♗c2! | |

With the idea of ♕d3.

27	...	♘ac7
28	♕d3	g6
29	♗b3	♔h8
30	♗a4	

Over the next ten moves or so, White slowly improves his position, not wishing to undertake anything drastic until the time control has been negotiated.

30	...	♖g8
31	♕d2	♖g7
32	♕f2	♖f8
33	♖c3	g5
34	♖fc1	♗g6
35	♗c2	♘e8
36	♗xg6	♖xg6
37	♕c2	♖gg8
38	♘c8	♕f7
39	♕b3	♘6g7
40	♘d6!	♘xd6
41	ed	

With a strong passed pawn, control of the c-file and a beautiful outpost on e5, White has a decisive advantage.

| 41 | ... | ♕e6 |
| 42 | ♕xb7 | g4 |

The d-pawn is taboo. 42
... ♛xd6 43 ♜c6.

43	hg	♛xg4
44	♞e5!	♛g5
45	♛e7!	

White avoids the last
trap: 45 ♞f7+ ♜xf7 46 ♛xf7
♞f5.

45	...	♜f6
46	♜c7	♜e8
47	♞f7+	♜xf7
48	♛xg5	1-0

Game 58
N. McDonald – Bachmayr
Zug 1991

1	e4	e5
2	f4	♛h4+

About an hour before the
game McDonald decided to
play the first King's Gambit
of his life. I hurriedly gave
him a few tips in some of
the critical lines, but when
he enquired about 2 ...♛h4+
I replied "Oh don't worry
Neil, nobody ever plays
that!".

3	g3	♛e7 (195)

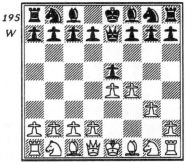

195
W

4   fe

This leads to an endgame
with only a small advan-
tage. If White feels like
punishing Black for his
cheeky check, then 4 ♞c3!
is the move. Black now has
a choice of taking on f4 or
playing the solid ... d6:

a) 4 ... ef 5 d4 fg 6 ♗f4!.
White has a very dangerous
initiative and the black
queen is looking rather silly.
Relatively best for Black
is 6 ... d5 (6 ... ♞f6 7 e5 d6 8
♛e2!) and now 7 hg! looks
best (Glaskov recommends
7 ♞xd5, but I believe that
Black has sufficient defensive resources after the
exchange of queens). White
is only a pawn down with a
big lead in development
(Note that the rook on h1 is
already developed). I'm
looking forward to a practical testing.

b) 4 ... d6 5 ♞f3 (5 d4 is
interesting and 5 ♞d5 ♛d8
6 d4 c6 7 ♞c3 deserves
attention. If you count the
useful moves White is
about one and a half up) 5
... ♗g4 6 h3 ♗xf3 7 ♛xf3
♞f6 8 d3. After this calm
move, White's superiority
becomes apparent: the bishop pair and a kingside
space advantage can be
added to the awkward
placing of the black queen.

4	...	d6!

5	ed	♛xe4+
6	♛e2	♛xe2+
7	♘xe2	♗xd6
8	♘bc3	c6

Black is worried about 9 ♘b5 and 8 ... ♗d7 can be met by 9 ♗d4!, but the text does hinder Black's development. A better equalising try would have been 8 ... a6 and after 9 ♗g2, simply 9 ... ♘c6.

9 d3

This is the most natural but White has an interesting alternative: 9 b3 ♘f6 10 ♗b2 ♗g4 11 ♗g2 ♘bd7 12 h3 ♗f5 13 0-0-0 0-0-0 14 ♖hf1 ♗g6 15 ♘f4 with an edge for White, Murey - Eng, Beersheeva 1985.

9	...	♘f6
10	♗g5	♘bd7
11	♗g2	h6
12	♗f4	

White is happy to exchange these bishops as 8 ... c6 also weakened the dark squares.

12	...	♗xf4
13	♘xf4	0-0 *(196)*

It was more accurate to have played 13 ... ♘c5. After 14 b4 ♘e6 15 ♘xe6 ♗xe6 16 b5 ♘d5 17 ♘xd5 ♗xd5 18 ♗xd5 cd 19 ♔d2 White has a slightly better endgame, but with careful defence Black should be assured of a draw.

14 b4!

White finds a very good plan ... ♘c5 is prevented and the b-pawn can be advanced further in order to soften up the long diagonal.

14	...	♖e8+
15	♔d2	♘e5
16	b5	♗g4
17	bc	bc

Black has a temporary initiative, but his weak queenside is not going to go away.

18	h3	♗f3
19	♖hf1	♗xg2
20	♘xg2	♖ad8
21	♖ae1	c5
22	♖f5!	

The only move but a good one.

22	...	♘c4+
23	♔d1	♖xe1+
24	♔xe1	♖e8+
25	♔f2	♘e5
26	♘e3	♖e6
27	♖f4!	

Because of the threat of ♖a4, Black has little choice but to allow an exchange of rooks. After this, the white knights will be able to occupy menacing squares, harassing the queenside pawns, whilst the more active position of his king will add to his advantage.

27	...	♖a6
28	♖a4	♖xa4
29	♘xa4	♘ed7
30	♘c4	♘d5
31	a3	♘c7

This knight manoeuvre was Black's best way to try to hold the queenside.

32	♘d6	♔f8
33	♔e3	a6
34	♘b7	♘b5

The alternative 34 ... ♘e6 35 ♔e4 ♔e7 36 ♔d5 is unattractive for Black. The attempt to complicate with

36 ... f5 fails to 37 ♘axc5 ♘dxc5 38 ♘xc5 f4 39 ♘xe6! f3 40 ♘d4 f2 41 ♘f5+ and the pawn is stopped just in time.

35	♘axc5	♘xc5
36	♘xc5	♘xa3
37	c4	♘c2+
38	♔d2	♘b4
39	♔c3	a5
40	d4	♘c6
41	d5	♘e5
42	♔d4	f6
43	d6	h5
44	♔d5	♔e8
45	♔e6	1-0

McDonald certainly hadn't expected his first - King's Gambit to provide one of his best positional games!

Index of Variations